Intellectual Freedom and Social Responsibility
in American Librarianship, 1967–1974

Intellectual Freedom and Social Responsibility in American Librarianship, 1967–1974

by

TONI SAMEK

WITH A FOREWORD BY
SANFORD BERMAN

McFarland & Company, Inc., Publishers
Jefferson, North Carolina, and London

Library of Congress Cataloguing-in-Publication Data

Samek, Toni, 1964–
    Intellectual freedom and social responsibility in American
librarianship, 1967–1974 / by Toni Samek; with a foreword by
Sanford Berman.
       p.   cm.
    Includes bibliographical references (p.) and index.
    ISBN 0-7864-0916-9 (softcover : 50# alkaline paper) ∞
    1. Libraries and society — United States — History — 20th
century.   2. Library science — Social aspects — United States —
History — 20th century.   3. Library science — Political aspects —
United States — History — 20th century.   4. Librarians —
Professional ethics — United States — History — 20th century.
5. Freedom of information — United States.   6. American
Library Association — History — 20th century.   I. Title.
Z716.4.S26   2001
021— dc21   00-55391

British Library cataloguing data are available

Cover image: ©2000 Artville

Manufactured in the United States of America

McFarland & Company, Inc., Publishers
  Box 611, Jefferson, North Carolina 28640
    www.mcfarlandpub.com

To the memory of
Jackie Eubanks

Acknowledgments

I extend a warm and heartfelt thank you to the many wonderful people who supported me in the making of this book and who influenced my education.

Thank you to the following friends and colleagues: Michele Besant, Sanford Berman, Bob and Gretchen Brundin, James V. Carmichael, Tove Ghent, Peter Heyworth, Norman Horrocks, Christine Jenkins, John and Diane Misick, Christine Pawley, Alvin M. Schrader, Joy Stieglitz, Cheri Stewart, Chris Wiesenthal, and Charles Willett.

Thank you to the faculty and staff of the School of Library and Information Studies, University of Wisconsin–Madison; to the faculty, staff, and students of the School of Library and Information Studies, University of Alberta; to the staff of the State Historical Society of Wisconsin (especially James P. Danky); to the staff of the State Historical Society of Wisconsin, Archives; to the staff of the University of Illinois at Urbana-Champaign, University Archives; and to research assistants Taralee Alcock, Kate MacInnes, Lori Van Rooijen, and Donna Sikorsky. A special thank you to teachers Michael W. Apple, James L. Baughman, Charles A. Bunge, and Louise S. Robbins.

Finally, without the warm and wise counsel of the following people, there simply would be no book: my mentor and friend Wayne A. Wiegand, my editor and friend Tarun Ghose, my loving parents Robert (in memory) and Krystyna Samek, and my cherished husband Burton Howell.

Contents

Foreword

by Sanford Berman

The controversies within librarianship over social responsibility and intellectual freedom that Toni Samek so painstakingly (and fascinatingly) chronicles for the period 1967–1974 persist into the new millennium. Her thoughtful, detailed study can well provide a basis for better understanding where — as a profession — we have been, and where we're going.

Two recurring themes in Samek's analysis are the concept of *neutrality*, as propounded most notably by David K. Berninghausen, and the question of what *intellectual freedom*— enshrined in the Library Bill of Rights and subsequent "interpretations"— really means in practice, and who it applies to.

Perhaps surprising to some, I don't think neutrality, as an ideal, is necessarily a Bad Thing — provided it's undertaken within a context of real social and economic justice, of actual equality and empowerment. But that wasn't the reality in the sixties. Nor is it today. In fact — although with striking and laudable exceptions — most libraries now, just as before, are not "neutral" at all. Instead, they are distinctly biased toward property, wealth, bigness, mainstream "culture," and established authority. And so, overwhelmingly, are professional institutions like the American Library Association. In April 1997, I made these points during a talk at the University of Illinois at Urbana-Champaign:

> Despite the frequent rhetoric about free-and-public, libraries seem increasingly to identify with the middle and upper classes, with wealth and property. Fines — of any kind — are arguably classist, discriminatory — yet there's no discernible trend or movement to abandon them. And the same for fees for basic services — like Internet use or online database searches or getting a book that's at another branch. If anything, these are multi-

plying. Baltimore County's Charlie Robinson declared candidly
in a *Library Journal* interview last year what I suspect is widespread but seldom admitted: that his library was firmly and
unapologetically a middle-class institution serving the middle
class. No one needs to be a savant to appreciate that resources
expended on investment and business tools and services astro-
nomically exceed what is devoted to similar materials and outreach to workers, labor union members, and poor folks. There's
literally no comparison. Where I work, as simply an indication
of mind-set and orientation, senior mangers regularly get informational routings from the director's office. Much in these pack-
ets is directly library-related: newsletters and reports from other
library systems and groups — but invariably there are also bul-
letins and announcements from local chambers of commerce,
along with *everything* issued by a Twin Cities right-wing think
tank called the Center for the American Experiment. The slant
of these routings I've challenged at least twice, not urging that
the business and conservative stuff be dropped, but rather that
material from labor, antipoverty, women's, and ethnic sources
be included. The routings continue as always, the assumption
being that to emphasize business and property and wealth is
right and normal and somehow *not* political.

Finally, anyone who's attended an ALA conference or read
about public-private tie-ins in the library press realizes that
libraries are increasingly and overtly being commercialized.
Indeed, we last week created a new heading at Hennepin County
Library (HCL): Libraries — United States — Commercialization.
The heading reflects a discussion on precisely that development
in Herbert Schiller's 1996 book, *Information Inequality: The
Deepening Social Crisis in America.* The first program at this
year's San Francisco conference will doubtless — as in past
years — be billed, not as the ALA Opening Session, but as the
Ameritech Opening Session. At this year's midwinter meeting
in Washington, D.C., a major panel problem sponsored by
ALCTS featured 12 speakers talking about outsourcing. Every
one of them was vendor. Not one represented consumers or
expressed an anti-outsourcing viewpoint. That was about selection. The day before, a two-hour session on outsourcing cataloging did include two librarians, who essentially reported how
they did it good (i.e., abdicated their cataloging responsibilities), but their presentations were dwarfed by a twice-as-long
performance by someone from OCLC who, in effect, conducted
an unabashed infomercial. When, at the very end, I questioned
out loud the quality and value of outsourced catalog records, I
was greeted by an almost totally hostile response from both
speakers and audience. And then there's San Francisco Public
Library, as an example, naming whole areas or rooms to com-

memorate corporate donations — like the Exxon or Amoco Room (I forget which). That's akin to providing daily, nonstop advertising to the beneficent donor. And it *is* political. It affects — undoes — the feeling of a neutral, nonthreatening, nonhuckstering turf that a public library ought to have.

In June 1990, at its annual conference in Chicago, ALA (first the membership, then the council) approved a "Policy on Library Services to Poor People," originated in Minnesota by MLA's Social Responsibilities Round Table (MSRRT). Grounded in the elemental recognition that poor people do not enjoy the same access to library resources and information that people with adequate incomes do, the policy sought to promote the elimination of barriers to library use by low-income people, provision of relevant services determined by underserved populations themselves, raising public awareness of poverty-related issues and resources, and acting to directly reduce if not eliminate poverty itself through support of such legislative initiatives as living wage laws and universal health care. One decade later, the policy has yet to be seriously and systematically implemented. (For details on how it was officially derailed, see my Foreword to Karen Venturella's *Poor People and Library Services* [Jefferson, NC: McFarland, 1998]). To Berninghausen & Co. that very non-implementation would probably be hailed as an exercise in "neutrality."

"Intellectual freedom," as promulgated by the Library Establishment (particularly ALA's Office for Intellectual Freedom and Intellectual Freedom Committee), has always been much too narrowly conceived. It has largely marbleized into a fixation on challenges to specific library materials — like the *Harry Potter* series and R. L. Stine's *Goosebumps* books — and frantic opposition to Dr. Laura's crusade for Internet filtering. Of course, challenges happen. Frequently. Often, but not always, the motive *is* censorious. And in such cases, the effort should be resisted, invoking the First Amendment and Library Bill of Rights. However, two things need to be observed about challenges or "requests for reconsideration."

First it *should* be the staff and public's right to question materials selection — unless we believe that selectors are always infallible, that they just can't make mistakes. (A library user some years ago at HCL complained about a kid's book dealing with Down's syndrome that consistently employed the obsolete and demeaning terms "mongoloid" and "mongolism." Obviously, this was something that staff had overlooked in weeding. So it was rightly, if belatedly, withdrawn. About a year and a half ago, I asked for reconsideration of a French picture book that had been secured through a jobber without any reviews or other evaluation. The selection was outsourced, done sight unseen. In fact, the book peddled every imaginable stereotype concerning Native Americans, clearly violating most guidelines for bias-free writing and illustrating. Well, they retained the title, but I think it was proper to question the choice.)

Second while individual challenges usually garner headlines (and ALA attention), they don't represent the true extent or depth of library censorship. This "outside" censorship is almost certainly less pervasive and less damaging to intellectual freedom than what I call "inside" censorship. When, for instance, *Of Mice and Men* is dropped from a school reading list in Peru, Illinois, that's definitely not good; but neither is it a national calamity or a truly meaningful case of book banning — because the chance is that the Steinbeck novel is still available in the school library, in the public library, and in the local or electronic bookstore. The prototypical Dr. Laura–style filtering — the ostensible object of which is to protect minors from violence and especially sex on the Web — should concern librarians and patrons, too. After all, filters are notoriously unable to differentiate between "legitimate" and "obscene" sexual matter and, if universally applied within a library, would limit access by adults to Constitutionally protected speech. Well, ALA has adopted guidelines opposing filtering as an abridgment of the First Amendment, and librarians have instead developed online kid-guides that promote "safe" sites. But the irony here is that the profession seems to be suddenly defending the presence in libraries of often graphic, explicit sexual images and texts in electronic form that it just as diligently excludes from libraries in print or video formats. (To be candid, there are real, on-the-floor problems in many libraries involving patrons who not only access visual erotica on the Internet, but then deliberately attempt to impose those images on other library users, for instance by printing copies and laying them out publicly — or leaving a terminal with possibly offensive graphics still appearing on the screen. However, these are behavioral problems best addressed by rules and protocols and particularly by remote printers and privacy screens.)

These, then, are the fare more widespread and serious kinds of censorship — that is, limiting access to ideas and opinions and cultural expression, as well as throttling speech itself — that are practiced *within* and *by* libraries:

- the failure to select whole categories or genres of material, despite public interest and demand on the one hand or the need to reflect a broad spectrum of human belief and activity on the other
- irresponsible, circulation-based weeding, consigning sometimes valuable and unique works to the dumpster
- economic censorship in the form of fines collected solely for rev-

enue and the imposition of fees for services like video and bestseller
borrowing that make them unavailable to poor or fixed-income
people
- inadequate if not outright erroneous cataloging, as well as restrictive shelving practices, rendering much material inaccessible even
though it *is* in the collection
- repression in the workplace, denying staff the opportunity to express
themselves without fear on professional and policy issues, and —
especially by means of electronic monitoring — creating an atmosphere of intimidation and submissiveness

To slightly amplify the selection category: Self-censorship is librarianship's "dirty little secret." Put another way, it's the fact of seldom-
acknowledged and hard-to-justify boundaries or exclusions. As examples,
most libraries don't collect comics or many graphic novels. Few get any
zines whatever, although that's arguably the hottest contemporary publishing scene. Recent surveys show that small press fiction and poetry, as
well as many other well-reviewed freethought, labor, and alternative press
titles, are woefully underrepresented in both public and academic libraries.
And then there's sex, particularly if it's in the form of photos or film or
deals with beyond-the-pale topics like anal intercourse or S&M. Ordinar-
ily, libraries would have bought multiple copies of anything by Madonna.
But her graphic *Sex* book, which featured a number of S&M pics, was
barely bought at all — or treated (as at Minneapolis Public Library) like a
communicable disease: one copy sequestered behind the reference desk,
only to be glimpsed in-house after giving up your driver's license as col-
lateral. (As an ironic contrast, libraries like Hennepin County that didn't
get Madonna's tome at all, *did* buy *Madonnarama* [San Francisco: Cleis
Press, 1993], a collection of essays and criticism *about* her book. So there's
abundant commentary available regarding a work that purposely *isn't* available!) In "Really Banned Books" (April 1998 *Counterpoise*), Earl Lee writes,
"Few, if any books are banned outright in this country. But many *are* overlooked, ignored, sidelined and squeezed out of the market place." "Many
small press books," he concluded, "are unable to find a place in bookstores
or libraries." Books with sexual content — like the excellent products from
Down There Press (San Francisco) and Factor Press (Mobile, Alabama)—
top his list of virtually banned material.

Becoming increasingly dominant within librarianship — albeit never
recognized or described by the Intellectual Freedom junta — is what might
be termed the Techno-Blockbuster philosophy, which views digital technology as the overriding fact of the future, making traditional formats like

books, magazines, CDs, and videos ultimately superfluous, yet which emphasizes — for the time being — conglomerate-published, Madison Avenue–hyped bestsellers, which may be bought in massive quantities to satisfy artificially created demand. And they aren't just acquired. They're prominently displayed and publicized by libraries as though there were some special, intrinsic, compelling worth to them. They are consciously pushed in ways that most midlist or small and alternative press materials are not, reflecting a bias in favor or bigness and big money. This is what I said about the whole issue in that 1997 speech:

> The shibboleth is that libraries are supposed to oppose censorship and provide the widest possible spectrum of perspectives and information — cultural, social, economic, political, religious, sexual. At the national and state policy levels, something curious has happened. The ALA and state associations rightly battle legislation like the Communications Decency Act, and support school and public libraries facing challenges to particular books or films or magazines. However, the time and energy spent on these matters is so overwhelming that as a profession we don't seem to have noticed, much less done anything about, the growing actuality that the very channels and producers of intellectual and cultural goods are shrinking in breadth and vitality and diversity. It's what Schiller, Ben Bagdikian, Michael Parenti, Noam Chomsky, Norman Solomon, and Robert McChesney have tried to warn us about for years. And what *The Nation* has stunningly documented with respect to publishing alone in two recent issues. It's the rapid concentration of media ownership; the expansion of conglomerate publishing; the death of independent bookstores (and the variety they promoted) under the onslaught of Borders and Barnes & Noble superstores, as well as K-Mart discount operations; the giveaway of public airwaves to the Big Boys; and the not-surprising dictation by superstores like K-Mart, Blockbuster Video, Baker & Taylor (through its "best" lists) of what gets published, what gets pushed, and even what gets expurgated (e.g., sanitized rap). The bottom line militates against producing or distributing novel, experimental, or critical material that may have limited markets.
>
> To be a little melodramatic, while we're agonizing over *Of Mice and Men*'s being dropped from that school reading list in Peru, Illinois, Ted Turner, Disney, Viacom, and Bertelsmann are walking away with the whole damn store. These giants decide what's okay, what's fit to be read, or seen, or heard. And like well-bred sheep, we buy right into it. Our library orders hundreds of copies of books that in some instances haven't been published yet — and in others haven't even been *written*. Why?

Because Random House announced it will spend $50,000 on hyping the new Grisham or Mary Higgins Clark novel or Marcia Clark memoir. Quality, relevance, accuracy, style — none of that's as important as sales and hypes. We become willing accomplices in the homogenization and commodification of culture and thought.

Finally, related to that last category of inside censorship, the vaunted Library Bill of Rights and ALA's Professional Code of Ethics do *not* firmly and explicitly support or encourage free speech on the job, the right to openly state opinions on professional and policy matters without fear of reprisal. Samek documents the abject failure of these declarations and their keepers to assist such colleagues as Joan Bodger, Ellis Hodgin, and Zoia Horn in their struggles against internal muzzling and governmental repression. It is no different now, 30 years later. Managerial prerogatives still trump librarians' rights to unfettered expression. And appeals to the profession's intellectual freedom guardians by beleaguered colleagues are reflexively and sometimes angrily rejected as "micromanagement." Or simply not acknowledged at all.

My saddening conclusion about workplace speech in libraries is that it's generally not free or legally protected. And that the only staff who *may* enjoy some measure of personal liberty are either those covered by academic freedom guarantees in university settings or represented by a union. Despite my directly and swiftly informing ALA's Office for Intellectual Freedom, Intellectual Freedom Committee, and Intellectual Freedom Round Table (to which I belonged) about my early–1999 denial of free speech at Hennepin County Library (fully documented in the December 1999 *Librarians at Liberty*) and asking for their help, none of them ever assisted me. Indeed, they never even responded. No did ALA leaders. And precisely the same non-response greeted my plea for help in January 2000, when I discovered that six books by and about me had been expunged from the HCL online catalog and possibly also from the shelves. So the somber fact remains that ALA *still* fails the individual librarian, instead favoring bureaucratic and managerial interests. (In part, this is an almost inevitable outcome of its membership criteria: *anyone* willing to pay dues can join, so while ALA may, indeed, be composed largely of librarians, there are also significant numbers of trustees, vendors, and publishers, among other "outsiders." And such decision making bodies as the ALA Council and Executives Board are notoriously freighted with administrators and administrator-wannabes.)

Yes, the situation remains bleak. Yet many colleagues retain the vision of a profession that truly and permanently weds the principles of social responsibility and intellectual freedom, resulting in libraries that are

- equally accessible to everyone
- dynamic sources of all kinds of information and ideas, available in a huckster-free setting; and
- open places, where rules and policies emerge from unshackled, transparent discussion among users and staff.

Samek's work demonstrates how hard it has been to realize that vision. It's up to the rest of us to keep trying.

Edina, Minnesota
April 2000

Introduction

Information is not simply collected.
— Allan Rachlin

Between 1967 and 1974, several librarians formed a group to push for change in the American Library Association (ALA). Within a span of six years, they prompted other librarians to examine their role in the dissemination of culture and to ask basic questions concerning the terrain that the profession covers and the limitations to intellectual freedom (if any) that it may entail. The questions raised by this advocate group were based on a concept of social responsibility that was the product of contemporary social, political, and cultural agitation. The dissent and resulting turmoil exposed the basic tension between an ideal vision of democracy and the day-to-day workings of American institutions during the 1960s.[1] In librarianship, the social responsibility movement revealed an inherent discrepancy between the rhetoric of ideals associated with the library profession and the reality of what was being practiced in the library. At the heart of the debate was the issue of professional "neutrality."

Working alongside educators, journalists, religious workers, and others involved in shaping the nation's culture, librarians of the 1960s were trained to create "balanced" library collections representing many points of view and to provide access to these materials. Both goals required that librarians take a "neutral" stance and disregard personal moral persuasions. But Celeste West, a key voice in the social responsibility movement, argued that it was not possible for librarians to take apolitical, nonaligned positions in their professional work. The chances of encountering an "unbiased" librarian, she said, were about as great as meeting an "objective" journalist. The notion of an unbiased individual was, to her, an impossible construct. An examination of library collections in the 1960s led her to speak out about the imbalances and deficiencies in acquisitions.

1

In particular, she advocated a place on library shelves for the alternative press.[2]

During the 1960s, the alternative press flourished as the voice of the American "counterculture" and documented the experience of alienated sectors of society such as disenchanted youth, women, ethnic minorities, trade union workers, and political radicals. Many of the viewpoints and experiences of these otherwise marginalized groups had never been recorded elsewhere. The alternative publishers who chronicled non-mainstream opinions were commonly subjected to actions against them by both individuals and groups that often culminated in legal and/or illegal harassment and boycotts.

By drawing attention to librarians' neglect of the alternative press, West and other advocates for social responsibility also drew attention to the discrepancy between professional rhetoric and the realities of library practice. Although as early as 1939, the profession had carefully crafted a Library's Bill of Rights which directed librarians to "fairly represent" materials on "all sides of questions on which differences of opinion exist" and to oppose censorship of "books and other reading matter" because of "the race or nationality or the political or religious views of the writers," in practice, in the 1960s West and her cohorts repeatedly found the alternative press to be inadequately represented in library collections.[3] Implications of this neglect were threefold.

First, because library users did not have adequate access to the products of the alternative press, they did not have access to the viewpoints expressed therein. Thus, libraries failed to provide access and exposure to the wide spectrum of viewpoints necessary for a valid conclusion. Second, because the alternative press was not being adequately preserved as part of the cultural record, many voices from the 1960s would be lost to future generations. Third, because of the absence of alternative perspectives, the mainstream media was over-represented in library collections. These three negligences helped maintain the status quo.

West was especially irritated by the third point. She argued that to be silent and support the status quo, as most librarians did, was in itself a political stance. The social responsibility movement not only encouraged librarians to be fair in their work, but it also educated librarians to recognize the political context of their work. This threatened a profession that prided itself on its "neutral" stance. Furthermore, in their attempt to preserve the traditional role of librarians and maintain the status quo, some in the professional establishment sought to discredit the social responsibility movement. As a result, the ensuing debate over "neutrality" introduced a professional identity crisis that characterized the mood of American librarianship in the 1960s.

In ALA history, 1967 was a watershed year, in large part because librarians, who introduced the concept of social responsibility in behind-the-scenes discussions, turned their talk into action. Two notable events occurred. First, at the annual ALA conference in San Francisco, a group of librarians publicly protested during a pro-Vietnam speech by General Maxwell D. Taylor. Although protesting librarians represented only a tiny fraction of peace activists, the fact that some took a stand on a so-called non-library issue was significant. Second, in October, 1967, the former Sarah Lawrence College president (1945–1959) Harold Taylor spoke to the Middle Atlantic Regional Library Conference about socially responsible professionalism. Taylor noted librarianship's practice of disseminating white middle-class cultural values and, with regard to social attitudes, urged librarians to reassess their role as educators.[4]

Less than a year later, a group of activist librarians proposed that ALA schedule a new round table program discussion on the social responsibility of librarians and libraries at its next annual conference in Kansas City. They called themselves the Organizing Committee for ALA Round Table on Social Responsibilities of Libraries. Very quickly, the group became the consortium in ALA that drew under its fold other groups who lacked power within the organization — black militants, political radicals, members of women's liberation groups, and individuals interested in library unions.[5]

In 1969, a second group began advocating change. A number of library school students and young practicing librarians lobbied for more social relevancy in their education and careers. In June, a group of 100 people met in Washington, D.C., for a meeting labeled "Congress for Change" (CFC). These people shared a common dissatisfaction with the way ALA was run and used CFC to pull together and plan a program for the upcoming annual conference in Atlantic City. At the conference, CFC joined forces with the Organizing Committee for ALA Round Table on Social Responsibilities of Libraries. Together, the two groups lobbied the Association to recognize the politics and culture of the 1960s. By submitting, for ALA's approval, resolutions on such issues as intellectual freedom, anti-war sentiment, anti-ballistic missile systems, and poverty, they launched the social responsibility movement in American librarianship.

Up to that time, ALA's leadership had focused on the advancement of libraries in the nation. Following the conference in Atlantic City, library activists pressed ALA's leadership to address issues such as library unions, working conditions, wages, recruitment, the place of minorities and women in the profession, and the professional concept of intellectual freedom. To maintain pressure, the Organizing Committee for ALA Round Table on Social Responsibilities of Libraries created task forces to advocate for

minorities, women, gays and lesbians, American Indians, migrant workers, political prisoners, and the peace movement. Perhaps most importantly,
the group created a task force on intellectual freedom. In conjunction with
two other ALA bodies, the Office for Intellectual Freedom and the Intellectual Freedom Committee, the Task Force on Intellectual Freedom was
established for the purpose of creating a fund for the support of librarians whose intellectual freedom efforts were being challenged.

For a brief time it appeared as though the reformers' vision of a more
democratic and proactive ALA would be realized. The situation appeared
particularly hopeful when ALA President William S. Dix informed the
membership in 1970 that an Activities Committee for New Directions for
ALA (ACONDA) would be created to evaluate the association's structure
and goals. But as it became apparent that the idea of reforming ALA was
no longer just a murmur, some became uneasy about where the movement
would lead. In particular, in a November 15, 1972, *Library Journal* article
entitled "Antithesis in Librarianship: Social Responsibility vs. the Library
Bill of Rights," ALA member David K. Berninghausen attacked the social
responsibility movement.[6]

In Berninghausen's view, the Library Bill of Rights (1948–) served
both to codify and standardize a purist moral stance on intellectual freedom by which impartiality and "neutrality" on non-library issues served
as the central principle of the profession. The concept of "social responsibility" that emerged in the context of librarianship in the late 1960s was,
in Berninghausen's opinion, a New Left tactic that threatened ALA's traditional "neutrality" and purpose.

In 1973, the debate continued to escalate when *Library Journal* published a collection of responses entitled "Social Responsibility and the
Library Bill of Rights: The Berninghausen Debate." Here, authors collec-
tively railed at Berninghausen for proposing that social responsibility
depended on an anti-intellectual freedom rationale, for misinterpreting the
social responsibility movement, for assuming that social responsibility led
to censorship, and for suggesting that intellectual freedom was the only
ethic of the profession. The rebuttal also outlined a critique of Berninghausen's proposition that intellectual freedom and social responsibility
were antithetical. Because Berninghausen idealized "balance" in library
collections, social responsibility advocates framed their critique of his
stance around the issue of the alternative press. They suggested, for example, that because of the profession's ignorance and neglect of the alternative press, it was "guilty of partisanship toward those social groups that
have the largest and most conservatively respectable power base."[7]

Although the discussion on social responsibility had evolved from faint whisperings in 1967 to feature articles in 1973, the movement none-theless failed to gain a secure foothold within the profession. ALA con-tinued to promote "neutrality."

Research on this book opened up a vast historical territory and pro-vided the broad canvas for an analysis of important phenomena in recent American library history. It is against this background that the book depicts and evaluates the interactions between the social responsibility movement and American librarianship's establishment.

The emergence of the social responsibility movement in librarian-ship raises several basic questions. First, in the context of collection devel-opment practices, how did librarianship perform in the production and preservation of culture in the late 1960s and early 1970s? Second, why was the library profession reluctant to abandon a position of "neutrality" in favor of social responsibility? Third, was ALA's acceptance of a round table on social responsibility an example of "repressive tolerance" or was it sim-ply a long-range tactic to keep the power in the hands of a few elites in the profession while espousing a democratic process?[8] And lastly, did the social responsibility movement change ALA's role in the sustenance and shap-ing of culture?

My motives for posing these questions are twofold. First, I want to analyze the cultural role of libraries in our society by drawing upon the theory of hegemony — the imposition of predominant influence (or lead-ership) by one state or group over others.[9] Second, I want to identify and examine those historical events that led a politicized generation of librar-ians to reject the accepted cultural role of the library as propounded by the establishment. This research is intended to extend library and infor-mation studies scholarship further into the realm of socio-political analy-sis and thus to add to our current understanding of the role of libraries and their social context.

According to Mary Lee Bundy and Frederick J. Stielow, their book *Activism in American Librarianship, 1962–1973* is "the first self-consciously academic monograph-length attempt to reprise" the 1960s for librarians. Before this text was published in 1987, Bundy and Stielow noted, analyti-cal coverage of the era could be found in: (1) a 1979 special theme issue of *American Libraries*; (2) two monographs — *Library Issues: The Sixties* (1970) and *Social Responsibilities and Libraries: A Library Journal/School Library Journal Selection* (1976); and (3) a few reprints of 1960s library literature articles. This book is designed to expand Bundy and Stielow's interpreta-tion of how 1960s social movements expressed themselves in American librarianship.[10]

Unpublished manuscripts, archival papers, and published primary and secondary literature constitute my formal research base. Three manuscript collections were particularly important: (1) ALA's Social Responsibility Round Table Papers and (2) the Sanford Berman Papers, both housed at the University Archives, University of Illinois, Urbana-Champaign, and (3) the Radical Research Center Papers housed at the State Historical Society of Wisconsin. The University Archives, University of Illinois, Urbana-Champaign, also houses unpublished ALA conference proceedings. Published primary literature consists of newsletters, journals, monographs, and conference proceedings. The secondary published literature used in this book consists of research studies, dissertations, journal articles, and monographs from a variety of disciplines including mass communications, cultural studies, women's studies, and anticanonical studies. In addition, I also interviewed and corresponded with various individuals who were active participants in the library movements of the 1960s. These interviews helped me further characterize and authenticate the mood and spirit of the times and provided a more personal context for describing the events in question. At times, I used these individuals to examine my presentations of their experiences and views, and my own biases and prejudices.

Once I started to find some answers to my research questions, I also began to analyze the professional discourse — the formal written or spoken discussion of the field. In "Information Work for Social Change," Bundy shows how public institutions — the library included — exert control and power over people, both consciously and unconsciously. Bureaucracies consciously manipulate information in their jurisdictions, and Bundy suggests that more than neglect and ignorance are at play when public officials fall short in the delivery of information to people who require it. She notes that all acts of omissions and commissions — like failing to instruct people of their rights, hiding signs of injustices, and masking institutional inequities — ultimately promote the interests of groups that wish to perpetuate the status quo. In some instances, public institutions consciously collect information that supports a desired perspective, promotes a particular set of interests, and even identifies dissenters who challenge the status quo. Bundy describes another scenario in which information may be withheld without any conscious design. Librarians who do not share the race, class, and community views of their users often unconsciously assume a "controller position" and by their selection decisions limit the type of information they will supply.[11]

Like Bundy, I wanted to contribute critical research to the professional discourse by examining the library in its broad social context. I was interested in finding out whether the problems of librarianship and the turmoil within the profession in the 1960s could be regarded as manifestations of the evolving process of hegemony.

One way to understand how libraries contribute to the dynamics of the evolution and maintenance of hegemony is to consider library collections. Librarians are charged with preserving particular cultural forms (as they define them), mostly the "important" printed records, as well as mediating between these records and the public. Historically, American library collections have mostly represented canons that promote mainstream culture and ideology. Works that have transcended or negated this perspective have often been excluded. A classic example of exclusion is the censorship controversy that resulted from the 1939 publication of John Steinbeck's *The Grapes of Wrath*.

Just months after its publication, Steinbeck's book became the "target of censorship pressures around the country" and was banned by various libraries in Illinois, New Jersey, and California both on account of its so-called "immorality" and because of the "social views advanced by the author."[12] While controversy over the book in part led ALA to adopt the 1939 Library's Bill of Rights, the book nonetheless appeared on banned book lists of several libraries.[13] This incident demonstrated the difficulty of translating rhetoric into practice and suggested that ALA was not an altogether effective opponent of censorship despite its quick adoption of the Library's Bill of Rights.

In the fourth edition of ALA's *Intellectual Freedom Manual*, the Association applauds its so-called quick response to *The Grapes of Wrath* controversy.[14] Unfortunately, the text fails to acknowledge properly the role of library activists of the 1930s who pressured ALA to be more responsive to issues put forth by young members involved with issues such as peace, segregation, library unions, and intellectual freedom. These librarians had been urging ALA to strengthen its position on intellectual freedom for almost a decade before the controversy over *The Grapes of Wrath* and the subsequent adoption of the Library's Bill of Rights had even occurred.

While comparing radical librarians of the 1930s with the rebels of the 1960s, library educator and scholar Jesse Shera noted that "the actors are different, but the script is much the same."[15] In 1931, for example, C. Harvey Brown, director of the Iowa State University Library, Marian Manley of the Business Branch of the Newark Public Library, and Stanley J. Kunitz, poet and editor of the *Wilson Library Bulletin*, formed the Junior Members Round Table (JMRT). While this Round Table's primary purpose was to provide a voice for younger professionals in the Association, much of what the junior members had to say resurfaced in the social responsibility movement discussions years later. Increased ALA responsiveness to its membership was a central issue for activist librarians in the 1930s and again in the 1960s.

The support by ALA for librarians was the central issue on which all the other issues hinged. For example, Philip O. Keeney's dismissal without due process from his position as librarian at the Montana State University in 1937 led to the formation of another library activist group. In 1939, Keeney's appeal was upheld by the Montana Supreme Court. The next year, he took leadership of a new group called the Progressive Librarians' Council in order to provide a united voice for librarians who sought change in the Association and to lobby for federal and state aid for libraries. By the end of its first year, the Progressive Librarians' Council had 235 members. Many were involved with ALA's Staff Organizations Round Table, formed in 1936, and Library Unions Round Table, formed in 1940. In addition, the *Progressive Librarians' Council Bulletin* provided a forum for activities on behalf of freedom of expression. The *Bulletin* printed outspoken opinions "not tolerated" by the traditional communication organs — *Library Journal, Wilson Library Bulletin* and *ALA Bulletin*. Eventually, after ALA's Staff Organizations Round Table and Library Unions Round Table gained momentum and the number of round tables in general increased, the Progressive Librarians' Council disbanded.[16]

The nature of library activism of the 1930s mirrors the 1960s in a number of ways: (1) activists called for ALA to operate democratically; (2) criticized the homogeneity of the professional discourse; and (3) paid attention to the needs of the librarian, not just of the institution. Once I understood the connection between the two historical library movements, I began to suspect that my inquiry into the nature of the crisis in librarianship in the 1960s was too restricted. In particular, I felt that ALA's apparent long-standing lack of support for its members could have been an example of the deliberate but subtle use of force by an entrenched hegemony to maintain its grip.

So I returned to the archives. Rather than search for more evidence of the repression of alternative materials and voices, I looked for incidents of pressures (subtle and legal, or otherwise) exerted on librarians to conform to "neutral" behavior. Because I assumed that those in favor of the "neutral" role of librarians supported the continuation of the existing hegemonic ideology, I looked for and uncovered articles and newspaper accounts of librarians who were either dismissed or were pressured to resign from their positions because they publicly denounced direct or indirect acts of censorship involving their libraries, because they spoke out on so-called "non-library" issues, or because, in some way, they criticized ALA's position on intellectual freedom.

The fifth edition of ALA's *Intellectual Freedom Manual* states that the creation of the Library's Bill of Rights served as the Association's "basic position in opposition to censorship."[17] Yet I discovered that three decades after its adoption, when American librarians Joan Bodger, Ellis Hodgin, Zoia Horn, and others risked their livelihood to oppose violations of intellectual freedom, the professional establishment was slow to respond with financial resources and other support. When I examined the material relating to such cases, three things were clear: (1) Each librarian in question was expected to adhere to the notion of professional "neutrality;" (2) When librarians deviated from this path, they paid a price; and (3) the law supported the idea that a librarian should not mix professionalism with personal politics.

The apparent pressure to conform to a "neutral" code of behavior seemed particularly significant in light of the alternative press movement. On one hand, the Library Bill of Rights instructed librarians to embrace all points of view and to combat censorship. On the other hand, ALA provided little support to those librarians who opposed the suppression of alternative materials. In practice, then, ALA disseminated a subtext that offset the formal message of the Library Bill of Rights. The subtext reinforced the preservation of the status quo. This book addresses the ethos of librarianship, the responsibility of librarians to society, and their struggle to reconcile the inertia of the status quo in the library establishment with social dissent and demands for change.

Despite the pressure to conform, librarians in favor of social responsibility in the 1960s rebelled against the notion of professional "neutrality." As a result, one can regard the social responsibility movement as a tonic that invigorated a static library profession in a time of significant social change. A group of library activists who questioned and rejected ALA's absolutist moral stance on intellectual freedom in favor of a dynamic library that would remain relevant to its community administered this tonic.

This book divides into six chapters that move chronologically from 1967 to 1974. While this approach does not always adequately reflect the dynamic nature of events, at various points in the text I stretch time lines forward or backward in an attempt to construct a smooth-flowing historical narrative. Chapter 1 provides a brief history of the 1960s and makes the connection between the alternative press movement (as an outgrowth of countercultural activity) and the rise of library activism. Chapter 2 foregrounds the study in terms of American library history and traces the development of the profession, especially ALA, through the 1960s; outlines the evolution of the Library Bill of Rights to its 1967 version with respect to its ideological framework; identifies the normal professional activity that librarians developed for the establishment press (or that they did not develop for the alternative press); and, looks into the question of how pre–1960s librarianship dealt with controversies. Chapters 3, 4, and 5 present the story of the social responsibility library movement between 1967 and 1972. Finally, the Epilogue outlines the ideological debate concerning ALA's professional jurisdiction and intellectual freedom that peaked in 1973. The Epilogue also examines the relationship between my research findings and the study's initial theoretical underpinnings and it highlights areas for future inquiry.

Notes

1. Edward P. Morgan, *The Sixties Experience: Hard Lessons About Modern America* (Philadelphia: Temple University Press, 1991), xi.
2. "A Conversation with Celeste West," *Technicalities* 2, no.4 (April 1982): 3–6.
3. *Intellectual Freedom Manual*, 5th ed. (Chicago: American Library Association, Office for Intellectual Freedom, 1996), 7.
4. Harold Taylor, "Society and Revolution," *Library Journal* 93, no. 3 (1 February 1968): 509–512.
5. Boris Raymond, "ACONDA and ANACONDA Revisited: A Retrospective Glance at the Sounds of Fury of the Sixties," *Journal of Library History* 14, no. 3 (Summer 1979): 354.
6. David K. Berninghausen, "Antithesis in Librarianship: Social Responsibility vs. The Library Bill of Rights," *Library Journal* 97, no. 20 (15 November 1972): 3675–3681.
7. Robert F. Wedgeworth et al., "Social Responsibility and the Library Bill of Rights: The Berninghausen Debate," *Library Journal* 98, no. 1 (1 January 1973): 27.
8. Herbert Marcuse, *One Dimensional Man* (London: ABACUS, Sphere Books, 1972).
9. For the concept of hegemony and helpful definitions see: Walter L. Adamson, *Hegemony and Revolution: A Study of Antonio Gramsci's Political and Cultural Theory* (Berkeley, University of California Press, 1980); Alastair Davidson, *Antonio Gramsci: Towards an Intellectual Biography* (London: Merlin Press, 1977); Chantal Mouffe, ed., *Gramsci and Marxist Theory* (London: Routledge, 1979); Quintin Hoare and Geoffrey Nowell Smith, eds. and trans., *Selections from the Prison Notebooks of Antonio Gramsci* (New York: International Publishers, 1971) Thomas Nemeth, *Gramsci's Philosophy: A Critical Study* (Sussex: Harvester Press, 1980); Leonardo Salamini, *The Sociology of Political Praxis: An Introduction to Gramsci's Theory* (London: Routledge and Kegan Paul, 1981); Anne Showstack Sassoon, ed., *Approaches to Gramsci* (London: Writers and Readers Publishing Cooperative Society, 1982); and Roger Simon, *Gramsci's Political Thought: An Introduction* (London: Lawrence and Wishart, 1982). For examples of research that incorporates the

concept of hegemony see: Dwight B. Billings, "Religion as Opposition: A Gramscian Analysis," *American Journal of Sociology* 96, no. 1 (July 1990): 1-31; Don Dawson, "Educational Hegemony and the Phenomenology of Community Participation," *Journal of Educational Thought* 16, no. 3 (1982): 150–160; David Ferrero, "Antonio Gramsci and His Relevance for American Public Education, *Research and Society* 7 (1994): 41-68; John Fiske, "British Cultural Studies and Television," in *Channels of Discourse: Television and Contemporary Criticism*, ed. Robert Clyde Allen (Chapel Hill: University of North Carolina, 1987), 254 289; Frederick H. Gareau, "International Institutions and the Gramscian Legacy," *Social Science Journal* 33, no. 2 (1996): 223–235; Stuart Hall, "Gramsci's Relevance for the Study of Race and Ethnicity," *Journal of Communication Inquiry* 10, no. 2 (Summer 1986): 5–27; Alan Hunt, "Rights and Social Movements: Counter-Hegemonic Strategies," *Journal of Law and Society* 17, no. 3 (Autumn 1990): 309–328; Donald V. Kurtz, "Hegemony and Anthropology: Gramsci, Exegeses, Reinterpretations," *Critique of Anthropology* 16, no. 2 (1996): 103–135; Bruce A. McConachie, "Using the Concept of Cultural Hegemony to Write Theater History," in *Interpreting the Theatrical Past: Essays in the Historiography of Performance*, ed. Thomas Postlewait and Bruce A. McConachie (Iowa City: University of Iowa, 1989), 37–58; Lila Leontidou, "Alternatives to Modernism in (Southern) Urban Theory: Exploring In-between Spaces," *International Journal of Urban and Regional Research* 20, no. 2 (1996): 178 195; Frank Pearce and Steve Tombs, "Hegemony, Risk and Governance: 'Social Regulation' and the American Chemical Industry," *Economy and Society* 25, no. 3 (1996): 424–454; and, Barry Smart, "The Politics of Truth and the Problem of Hegemony," in *Foucault: A Critical Reader*, ed. David Couzens Hoy (Oxford: Blackwell, 1986), 157–173.

10. Mary Lee Bundy and Frederick J. Stielow, *Activism in American Librarianship, 1962–1973* (New York: Greenwood Press, 1987), 1–2.

11. Mary Lee Bundy, "Information Work for Social Change," 17 February 1973, ALA's Social Responsibilities Round Table Papers (SRRT), University of Illinois at Urbana-Champaign, University Archives.

12. *Intellectual Freedom Manual*, 1996, xxiii.

13. John Swan and Noel Peattie, *The Freedom to Lie: A Debate About Democracy* (Jefferson, NC: McFarland, 1989), 2.

14. *Intellectual Freedom Manual*, 4th ed. (Chicago: American Library Association, Office for Intellectual Freedom, 1992), xiv.

15. Jesse H. Shera, "Plus ça Change," *Library Journal* 95, no. 6 (15 March 1970): 985.

16. Joe W. Kraus, "The Progressive Librarians' Council," *Library Journal* 97, no. 13 (July 1972): 2351–2354. See also Rosalee McReynolds, "Trouble in Big Sky's Ivory Tower: The Montana Tenure Dispute 1937–1939," *Libraries & Culture* 32, no. 2 (Spring 1997): 163–190.

17. *Intellectual Freedom Manual*, 1996, xxiii.

Chapter 1

The 1960s and
the Alternative Press

The 1960s

Historians define "the 1960s" loosely. Some literally frame the 1960s around the decade. Edward P. Morgan, for example, begins his discussion with the sit-down strike in a Greensboro, North Carolina, Woolworth store staged by four African-American student members of the National Association for the Advancement of Colored People (NAACP) on February 3, 1960, and ends with the killings of six students at Kent State and Jackson State universities during their protests against the American invasion of Cambodia on May 4 and May 15, 1970.[1] Others "find it impossible" to cover the 1960s "without entering the 1970s."[2] John Morton Blum, for example, sandwiches the era between President John F. Kennedy's 1961 inauguration and President Richard M. Nixon's 1974 resignation.[3] When historians choose selective chronologies, their interpretations highlight a similar set of personalities, groups, movements, and/or other epoch-making events. In the context of the 1960s, these typically include the administrations of John F. Kennedy, Lyndon B. Johnson and Richard M. Nixon; the assassinations of John F. Kennedy on November 22, 1963, Malcolm X on February 21, 1965, Martin Luther King, Jr., on April 24, 1968, and Robert F. Kennedy on June 4, 1968; the Student Non-violent Coordinating Committee (SNCC) and the Freedom Riders, and the Students for a Democratic Society (SDS) protests; the anti-war, Black Power, gay liberation, free speech, women's, and Youth International Party movements; and finally, the general political climate created by revolts in cities such as Paris, Mexico City, Prague, Belgrade, and Warsaw.[4] But because "the history of social movements often confines itself to the large events," historian Howard Zinn argues that missing from these are "the countless small actions of unknown people that led up to those great moments."[5] In the 1960s, for example, various groups of citizens, e.g., those tired of the social and political indifferences of the Eisenhower years, those involved in the Southern civil rights movement, those morally resentful of the war in Vietnam, or those bitter about a government unable to solve the problems surrounding race and poverty issues in the world's most prosperous nation, launched a series of campaigns across the country, and sought left of center changes in the civil rights movement, the peace movement, and the counterculture.[6] Others resorted to using boycotts, countercultural education, and nonviolent demonstrations.

Historians typically characterize the post–World War II United States using diverse factors such as anticommunism, evolution of foreign policy, dominance of mass media, rise of corporations, emergence of neocapitalism, general economic growth and prosperity, expansion of education, change in the composition of the middle class, and triumphs of scientific and technical research. These socio-political markers allowed a number of groups interested in this period, such as marketing specialists, macroeconomists, education consultants, public policy analysts, and foreign policy experts to depict the post–World War II United States as a rational and progressive society. However, conventional historians regard the postwar social activists as isolated alienated groups lacking a sense of community. Sociologist Daniel Bell defines the demeaning and restrictive conditions that led to social activism as symptoms of the "radical dehumanization of life." He cautions against labeling the postwar society as the "mass" or "modern" society because these labels fail to "reflect or relate to the complex, richly striated social relations of the real world."[7] Robert M. Collins asserts that the interests of many post–World War II social groups did not always match the economic and political ideals of the growing middle class. He argues that "not all Americans shared fully in the post war boom. Blacks, Hispanics, Native Americans, and the elderly remained less well-off than others."[8] In effect, poverty, racism, and segregation were still the realities of 1950s life. Personalized historical accounts, such as those by activist/intellectual Todd Gitlin and alternative press advocate Ray Mungo, also demonstrate the imbalance between post war economic and political ideals. Gitlin, for example, writes that he was "not living in history, but biography" in the 1950s. Indeed, Gitlin was searching for heroes while involved in peace work, hanging out with activist intellectuals, and playing a role in the national drama in the 1960s.[9] Gitlin's experience suggests that the impetus for radicalization in the 1960s had roots in the 1950s experience.

On the margins of 1950s society, the beats and bohemians represented dissent, rejection of established values, and anti-materialism. Percussive language poets, jazz musicians, and readers of *Liberation, Evergreen,* and *The Village Voice* experimented with new forms of culture. Leftist intellectuals read the anti-establishment *Dissent* and *I.F. Stone's Weekly.* More in the mainstream, the nation's youth experimented with new sounds on rock and roll radio and revered rebellious screen idols such as Marlon Brando and James Dean. By 1960, a sizable number of college students gathered in campus corners across the nation, exchanging views on Betty Friedan, the media machine, folk music and existentialism.[10] In the political arena, with the increasing awareness about the struggles of civil rights figures like Rosa Parks and Martin Luther King, Jr., the socio-political agenda of the southern civil rights movement increasingly became the focus of attention of activists involved in sit-ins, or in demonstrations against the "bomb," the cold war, and various manifestations of McCarthyism (e.g., proceedings of the House Un-American Activities Committee [HUAC] and the hysteria of anticommunism). Large numbers of Americans from differing backgrounds began articulating their growing disillusionment with society and their concern about the absence of social responsibility from the American dream. In particular, many young Americans called for an alternative social structure — one that emphasized participatory democracy, equality, and justice for the oppressed.

Zinn writes of his own mid 1950s shift from a liberal believer in the "self-correcting character of the American democracy" to a radical proponent of the belief that something was "rotten" at America's "root."[11] Others shared his viewpoint. For example, several influential social critics began publishing their analyses of America's problems in the mid to late 1950s. In *The Power Elite* (1956), activist sociologist C. Wright Mills argues that the corporate sector, the government, and the military formed an overbearing nucleus of power and urged intellectuals to become social actors for change. In *The Affluent Society* (1958), economist John Kenneth Galbraith examined "the blight of poverty amidst affluence," the emergence of a new social and political community and attitudes, and the need for more public effort and funds to redress social imbalance.[12] Daniel Bell's *The End of Ideology* (1960) also called for social responsibility and political activism.

John F. Kennedy's 1960 election as president — the first Democrat to win the presidency in 12 years — marked a new era for those who called for social change. During Kennedy's administration, some Americans formulated and carefully examined a comprehensive set of reform platforms, including those on affirmative action, civil rights, abolition of the draft, education, health care, housing, military intervention, and poverty. The

1962 "Port Huron Statement" ratified at the first national SDS convention in Port Huron, Michigan; Martin Luther King's "I Have a Dream" speech delivered at the August 28, 1963, march on Washington; President Kennedy's June, 1963, pacific speech delivered at the American University; emergence of the New Left; and various protest sits-ins and anti-bomb demonstrations typically characterize the early 1960s as years during which calls for change were based on optimism about the future. John N. Ingham describes these years as the time of Camelot. There was a brash, energetic feeling of idealism, and the expectation, he says, that a new generation of young Americans — "The *Best and Brightest* the country had to offer — were going to reform America and the world."[13] This optimism, Ingham concludes, was reflected in the growing support for the civil rights movement, and in the numbers of people who joined the Peace Corps.

But even though the emergence of co-ops, communes, free universities, and experimental colleges symbolized the increasing acceptance of alternative lifestyles and learning processes, and even though the alternative press became a powerful voice of the counterculture, the optimism about ending social ills gradually (and probably inevitably) waned. Young leftist sociologist Michael Harrington, for example, documented the prevalence of poverty in largely "invisible" social groups such as ethnic minorities, migrant workers, women running households, and the aged.[14] As structural poverty, the cold war, the arms race, and racism persisted, many people began to recognize the limitations of efforts to usher in changes while working within the system. They became disillusioned by the government's hands-off liberal moral stance and realized that their rhetoric was not producing the changes they desired. A stream of events including President Kennedy's assassination on November 22, 1963; the Gulf of Tonkin Resolution passed by the U.S. Congress on August 7, 1964; the Democratic Party's rejection of the Mississippi Freedom Democratic Party in Atlantic City in August, 1964; the Berkeley Free Speech Movement in the fall of 1964; the urban riots in Harlem and Watts in 1964 and 1965; and, the subsequent escalation of the Vietnam war intensified the growing sense of disillusionment amongst those who wanted change within the framework of democracy. The optimistic talks gave way to new discourses on socialism, anti-capitalism, anti-colonialism, anti-imperialism, and world revolution. Many people's behavior took on a Gandhian style of expressiveness as they acted out a nonviolent civil disobedience agenda. The widespread series of arrests that followed, propelled people into a new phase of protest. Influential people like James Baldwin, Daniel Bell, Norman O. Brown, Paul Goodman, Michael Harrington, Nat Hentoff, LeRoi Jones, Staughton Lynd, Norman Mailer, Herbert Marcuse, C. Wright Mills,

A.J. Muste, I.F. Stone, William Appleman Williams, Malcolm X, and Howard Zinn nurtured an activist ideology. And as Alice Echols claims, "in its rejection of liberalism, its embrace of participatory democracy, and its fusion of the personal and political, 60s radicalism represented a break with politics as usual."[15]

Some scholars term the mid-decade as "the high 1960s" or "the great refusal," because during this time groups like black nationalists, draft resistors, ecologists, feminists, hippies, and New Leftists refused to perpetuate the status quo and chose as their models figures such as Fidel Castro, Che Guevera, Mao Tse-Tung, and Malcolm X.[16] Meanwhile, persistent poverty, segregation, and escalation of the Vietnam War fermented protest.[17] By 1968, the Tet Offensive by the Vietcong, the assassinations of Martin Luther King, Jr. and Robert F. Kennedy, the release of the Kerner Commission report on urban riots, the massive anti-war protests at the Democratic National Convention in Chicago, the first Chicago women's conference, and the revolt in Paris escalated tensions further.[18]

As the mainstream media tracked the Vietnam story and provided sensational coverage of events such as the student occupation of Columbia University in the spring of 1968; the protest against the Miss America Pageant in Atlantic City on September 7, 1968; and the conspiracy charges against the Chicago Eight/Seven in the fall of 1969, the alternative press community also ardently documented its own record of events in publications like the *Los Angeles [CA] Free Press* (95,000 copies a week), the *Berkeley [CA] Barb* (85,000) and *The East Village [NY] Other* (65,000).[19]

According to Farber, the "long subterranean history" of the 1960s alternative press confirms that diverse published opinions have been pushed to the margins of public discourse for many years.[20] Ruth Marie Eshenaur holds that the alternative press is rooted in the protest journalism of the colonial New England papers, the abolitionist press of the anti-slavery movement, the populist and socialist papers of the late 19th and early 20th century, and the 1950s "underground press."[21] Kenneth Cmiel includes artistic modernism and Rousseau's "mid-eighteenth century attack on politeness" as other influences in the history of protest journalism.[22]

In general, three characteristics distinguished the 1960s underground press from other publications: (1) it was mainly the voice of political and cultural communities, (2) it used new offset print technology, and (3) it was a response to the harassment that followed dissent.[23] These distinctive features led Olé editor Douglas Blazek and many others to regard the alternative press as (what Blazek called) a "laboratory" for new ideas and a "weapon" against the tyrannies of "governments, police, bureaucracies and institutions."[24]

The alternative press journals of the late 1950s, like *The Village Voice* (1955), *The Realist* (1958) and others, initially experimented with a variety of unconventional vehicles of expression. Subject matter included psychedelic art, Asian religions, sex, drugs, and rock and roll. From these tenuous and far-out props, the alternative press evolved into a more sophisticated medium in the 1960s, such as *The Los Angeles Free Press* (1964) and *The Berkeley Barb* (1965). During this period, the alternative press also thrived because opponents of the Vietnam War on college campuses, politically radical activists, and advocates of the new drug culture could harness easy to use and inexpensive offset printing methods. Furthermore, liberal Supreme Court decisions on obscenity enabled them to create a newer spirited and unconventional medium.[25] The alternative press thus came to reflect the voices of disenfranchised groups in society like youth, women, ethnic minorities, labor workers, and political radicals.

Partly because of its rapid growth and increasing popularity, and partly as a result of its high interest coverage of events like the conspiracy trial of the Chicago Eight/Seven, the Nixon administration came to consider the alternative press as a record of political and cultural rebellion. Nixon also worried that the alternative press was unifying and strengthening the power of disparate dissenting voices.[26] In 1969, Nixon withdrew some troops from Vietnam, secretly initiated the bombing of Cambodia, and then at home launched a wave of government repression on the antiwar movement. Because the alternative press provided a forum for the united protest, it became one of his targets. Under J. Edgar Hoover's direction, the Federal Bureau of Investigation (FBI) registered the names of alternative press workers on a Security Index, planted agent provocateurs, and finally laid charges and made arrests. By 1970, "the government's draconian campaign of repression" (as Echols puts it), aided by manipulative agent provocateurs, exacerbated factionalism; different activist groups clashed over conflicting agendas.[27] For example, feminist historian Sara Evans points out that as the war intensified FBI harassment escalated, ghettos "exploded," and women activists "demanded that the men in the movement deal with their male chauvinism in their personal, social and political relationships."[28] At the same time, many women, hippies and pacifists rejected the militant politics and the creed of violence practiced by SDS and other New Left factions, especially the Weathermen and Weatherwomen. Others, disillusioned by the many hypocrisies inherent in the movement, receded from the active political scene into more private spaces. Most importantly, however, the SNCC (mostly African-American urban poor) quarreled with the SDS (mostly white Jewish college students) over basic issues like race, class, and culture. Bitter inter-activist group conflict in the 1968 Brooklyn Ocean Hill–Brownsville New York City public school teachers' strike over issues of decentralization and community control of local school districts (and the race-related hate campaigns that surrounded it) indicated that "the radical vision of a participatory democracy with small-scale units and client-centered services presupposed a society, a community of values, that simply did not exist."[29] After the Newark and Detroit riots in 1967, the universal Movement finally splintered into distinct interest groups and "newly minted minorities."[30] Rifts developed within these splinter groups as well. Echols notes that the women's movement "convulsed" when "agents aggravated the conflicts around class, elitism and sexual preference in the early 1970s."[31]

While the 1970 student protests against the American incursion into Cambodia "brought the war back home" and sparked an outbreak of strikes in campuses across the nation, the number of demonstrations and the level of press coverage on protest movements began to experience a steady decline.[32] As the war subsided, the draft waned, students left campuses, and the economic boom (1945–1973) drew to an end, many moderates and liberals forsook their activist roles and moved on to other things. Diehards did hope that Senator George McGovern would defeat Nixon in the 1972 presidential election, but the Senator was overwhelmingly defeated and the national fascination subsequently shifted to Watergate and the White House tapes.[33]

The rise and fall of 1960s library activism took place within this social and political context. Social protest movements in the larger society were paralleled in librarianship as library activists also tried to oppose domination, to support equality, to facilitate participatory democracy, to persuade politicians to take on social issues, and to mobilize the general public to become more active participants in their civil institutions. Librarians became socially aware through involvement in the causes and issues espoused by the alternative press. Some librarians were intrigued by the novelty of the messages in the alternative press, as well as by the freshness of the medium itself. When, for example, publications like *The Oracle* (San Francisco), *The East Village Other* (New York), *The Fifth Estate* (Detroit), *The Paper* (East Lansing), *The Los Angeles Free Press* (Los Angeles), and *The Berkeley Barb* (Berkeley) began attracting national recognition because they questioned the objectivity of the establishment press in the mid 1960s, a subset of American librarians took note.[34]

The Alternative Press

By the mid 1960s, the phrase "alternative press" was common jargon for what James P. Danky and Elliott Shore call an array of publications "produced by non-standard, non-establishment groups or individuals" of left or right orientation who represented the counterculture press, the free press, the fugitive press, the radical press, the small press, and/or the underground press.[35] Topics covered by the alternative press included antimilitarism, art, communications, covert action, culture, ethnic studies, ecology, gay-lesbian-bisexual studies, media, music, peace, political repression, women's studies, etc.[36]

The alternative newspapers and magazines were the products of amateur publishers who did their own writing, printing, layout, publicity and, in many cases, distribution. In some instances, high school students, GI's, groups involved in the Black Power Movement, and homosexuals created their own specialized news services. Other small news services were also formed. Of these, the Underground Press Syndicate and the Liberation News Service were most recognizable and had the widest circulation.

The former was established by *The Village Voice* founder John Wilcok who wanted to create a clearinghouse for subscriptions, for exchanging papers and subscription lists, and for developing a vehicle for national advertising and distribution. The Underground Press Syndicate held its organizational meeting north of San Francisco in the spring of 1967. The Syndicate began by publishing a newsletter to promote circulation. By 1968 it had 15 member papers and a circulation of 150,000. By 1971 it had 125 member papers, another 200 less regular member publications, and a total circulation of close to 1,000,000.

Marshall Bloom and Ray Mungo established the Liberation News Service in Washington, D.C., in late 1967. Bloom had worked with the New Media Project, an organization which linked anti-war and countercultural newspapers and magazines. Mungo was an outspoken pacifist and a critic of the conventional press's analysis of dissident culture.[37] The service they organized supplied alternative press news articles and graphics of a radical perspective to underground, college and community newspapers, their radio stations, and allied organizations. Subscribing papers reprinted many of its news releases. Mungo published a Liberation News Service packet twice a week and made it a regular feature in places like GI coffeehouses, women's centers, and prisons.[38] He also published lists of underground newspapers and magazines. Although the Liberation News Service generally competed with the Underground Press Syndicate, together they increased public awareness of the alternative press.

George Lipsitz observes that along with "record companies, FM radio stations, and clothing, record and head shops," underground newspapers formed the "infrastructure of the *youth culture* economy." Once the alternative press gained this footing, it aroused anger and fear in establishment circles. Lipsitz points out that "contemporary neoconservatives, including William Bennett and Allan Bloom" have identified 1960s rock music as "the product of a *destructive* and *nihilistic* counterculture organized around drug use, antiwar activity and sexual experimentation."[39] Gradually, because of its increasing momentum, the alternative press came under even closer scrutiny by the establishment. According to Mungo, the increased distribution and readership of the alternative press publications only occasionally led to actual increased subscriptions. Sometimes there were even appreciative and sympathetic review articles about them in mainstream publications like the *New York Times, Time* and *Editor & Publisher.* More often, however, there was unwelcome interference in the form of legal, financial, postal, and technical problems, including problems concerning the availability of printing facilities. Finally, there were investigations, censorship, suppression, and legal prosecution.[40] Also (because most alternative publishers primarily used a colporteur or direct street sales) the rising number of arrests of street vendors created distribution problems. In Chicago, for instance, police in the Loop could arrest anyone selling anything other than a daily newspaper. And alternative press publishers were in constant danger of losing subscriptions. In an effort to combat the problem, publishers supplemented street sales by selling through book stores and kiosks as well as by promoting personal and library subscriptions. But subscribers, especially libraries, usually looked for easy methods of acquisition. Librarians, for example, often became annoyed when alternative presses regularly changed houses, printers, and/or even their names.

To counter this problem, the Underground Press Syndicate offered to function as the alternative press vendor. It promised to eliminate tedious correspondence with individual editors regarding subscriptions, addresses, delivery, submission of invoices, publication frequency, cessations, etc. Despite good intentions, however, their efforts failed. Sixty percent of the membership experienced interference by the government (e.g., FBI, CIA or the army) who, most commonly, intimidated printers and advertisers.[41] Local merchants and businessmen often applied political pressure against the alternative press until it became simply unprofitable for the printers to continue the printing of underground newspapers and magazines. Several publishers dealt with as many as 50 printers. Some publishers were forced to cross state lines to print.

Government agents often sabotaged news services, interfered with housing, ransacked offices, stole subscription lists, persecuted editors for exercising normal press freedoms, planted informants, issued threats, and sometimes even resorted to bombings.[42] Numerous formal, informal and manifestly illegal actions by private individuals and groups took place as well. Formal adversarial actions included bans on distribution and sales, organization of opposition by school officials, arrest and/or imprisonment of editors and staff, refusal of press passes and/or suspension or expulsion of staff from educational (and other) institutions. Informal adversarial actions included rejection by distributors, confiscation of published issues, boycott by printers, and resignation of staff. Illegal actions included physical attacks on staff and property.[43] In many instances, local politicians joined in the persecution and harassment of the alternative press to gain exposure and recognition.

Agents of the FBI put pressure on a New York distributor of *Rat* until the distributor refused to work with the publishers. When vendors for Spokane's *Natural* sold the paper on the streets, they were charged with vagrancy. *Rag* and *Kaleidoscope*, two college papers, were banned on their Austin and Madison campuses. Editors of Miami's *Daily Planet* endured 29 arrests on obscenity charges in a one year period. News services also suffered harassment. The FBI ordered the Internal Revenue Service (IRS) to investigate the tax-related documents of the Liberation News Service. The Underground Press Syndicate was subjected to constant surveillance. In 1972, an undercover narcotics agent worked for six months on its staff. A drug raid turned up nothing, but during the search police confiscated subscription lists and damaged files and the Syndicate's library collection. Government officials also targeted papers representing specific political groups. For example, the Buffalo police harassed the staff of the *Black Panther Party Paper* on charges of violating a state criminal-anarchy statute. School officials received anonymous letters (possibly drafted by the FBI) protesting the availability of this paper in the school library and classrooms.

These harassments contributed to the alternative press' rapid attrition. Although the Underground Press Syndicate had over 400 member publications in 1971, by 1973 most no longer existed. Five years later, the Syndicate had only 65 members, 30 percent of whom had joined after 1973. Alternative presses lacked money, could not afford much publicity, took greater risks than the mainstream press, and suffered from continuing harassments and boycotts.[44]

In recognition of the need to disseminate counterculture information, a variety of agencies arose to fill a gap left by the mainstream press's inattention. For instance, Vocations for Social Change was founded in Canyon,

California in 1967, in response to a call to provide information about, as well as jobs for, people involved in radical social change.[45] The initial focus was on alternative institutions like free clinics, free schools, and food and housing co-ops. Eventually the focus shifted to disseminating information to a broader group that included young workers, the unemployed, and all others who were alienated from the institution and the society to which they were assigned, and who were not properly functioning in these places.[46]

Quite often, members of collectives traveled to different communities to publicize their services. In February, 1969, for example, George Brosi spoke about Vocations for Social Change at a conference at Carleton College — a small liberal arts school in Northfield, Minnesota. Brosi pointed out the importance of disseminating information in alternative publications, and stressed the need for the availability of an index to provide access to such alternative materials. In his audience were Rod Stilger, Bill King and Sealy Ann Hicks, three young and hopeful social justice advocates who were studying at Carleton. Almost immediately after his visit, they formed the Radical Research Center (RRC) and began preliminary planning for an index to the alternative press that would help librarians in providing access to "other" viewpoints, and thus encourage them to build alternative collections in libraries.

Stilger, a sophomore "social change" major, quickly took over leadership. Along with King, Hicks and 12 others, he launched the project by starting a letter-writing campaign to alternative publications and prospective subscribers, many of whom he identified from a mailing list sent him by ALA's Round Table on the Social Responsibilities of Libraries. The round table was initiated by a group of dissenting American librarians in 1968, many of whom had an interest in the alternative press.[47] This was the first of many links between RRC and ALA.

Initial support for RRC came from the Carleton College. In March, 1969, Dean Bardwell L. Smith wrote Stilger that such an index "could be of genuine help to the college ... something of real value."[48] Within months, Stilger obtained office space and use of computers, and established national and international contacts. Despite the Dean's aid, however, the Center never developed a formal relationship with the Carleton College. Stilger noted that "all of Bard's support came through me as a personal friend; the supportive relationship of Carleton College was never given form within the formal structures."[49] Apart from a $1,500 Danforth Foundation grant received in the summer of 1969, the non-profit group survived on subscriptions, donations, and a national network of volunteer indexers.

Sometimes this caused problems. With only limited backing, RRC was often required to defend itself against critics from both the left and the right. Activist groups often wanted to know how the information was being disseminated and to whom. Many suspected RRC was a "capitalist rip-off group."[50] Stilger assured movement groups RRC was not feeding information to the right. To this end he was reluctant to compile and share a list of contacts, because he did not want "to make anybody's job easier."[51]

And while the Center began with a list of contacts provided by ALA's Round Table on the Social Responsibilities of Libraries, Stilger was reluctant to be too closely linked to librarianship. He pointed out that RRC was not about doing librarians' work for them, but was motivated by its political agenda. "I see the INDEX as a political (leftist) project and not as another reference tool for the library trade," he said. "Nothing against librarians, mind you, but essentially we're doing this for the sake of the movement, rather than for the sake of intellectual scholarship."[52] Stilger's protestations notwithstanding, however, the Center was still closely linked to libraries. The RRC goals, for example, were to place a copy of the index in every library in the country, to reach more people through libraries, and to encourage librarians to begin alternative press collections. In addition, the Center depended "almost solely on revenue from library subscriptions to survive."[53]

Stilger and King both left Northfield for the summer months and Stilger took the bulk of the files to Portland, Oregon, where he essentially took charge of the organization. Meanwhile King went to Berkeley to set up a make-shift regional office. During the summer, Stilger expanded his operation by enlisting the services of two more people: Mickey Williamson, who started a New England office and became known as the conscience of the organization; and Sylvia Price, who started a New York office and who came to realize that a model index like the *Readers' Guide to Periodical Literature* using Library of Congress Subject Headings was not an adequate guide to index the kind of material the Center covered.[54]

That fall Stilger toured the country to identify alternative periodicals, establish periodical exchanges, recruit volunteer indexers, and collect periodicals for a national resource collection. He also ran the office, pushed for increased subscriptions, compiled a subject heading list, drafted instructions for indexers, and developed computer programs. By late fall, Stilger felt optimistic about the Center's progress and its potential to libraries.[55] But tensions continued within the group. Some felt the Center suffered from Stilger's top-down leadership style and wanted to reconfigure the operation. In December Stilger bowed to this pressure and gave up his leadership role.

Around this time Karen Clark, Fred Olson and a few other new faces joined the Carleton team in Northfield. While Olson and Clark began computer operations for checking in publications, indexing and billing, close to 50 volunteers worked on the index. In February, 1970, just one year after its conception, RRC published the first *Alternative Press Index*. The volume indexed 6,300 articles and contained 15,000 entries. Martin noted that of the 72 periodicals included, more than half were underground newspapers focusing on community news. The RRC borrowed the original subject heading list from ALA's Round Table on the Social Responsibilities of Libraries. The Center revised and enlarged subsequent issues based on the suggestions of indexers. By the spring, 1970, the Center had 500 subscribers, excluding exchange and indexer subscriptions. Individuals and activist groups paid $10.00 per index, whereas libraries paid $30.00. Paid subscriptions came primarily from libraries in cities like New York, Philadelphia, San Francisco, Berkeley, Minneapolis, St. Paul, Madison, and Toronto; almost every major university library subscribed. Many public and college libraries, activist groups, counseling centers, theology, and seminary libraries, and individuals subscribed as well.[56]

After seeing the *Alternative Press Index*'s initial issue, Sanford Berman, an American librarian who was working overseas in Lusaka, Zambia, decided to explore the possibility of launching an index to dissident literature. Berman felt strongly that librarians had the unique combination of skills to produce a more professional and accessible tool. As a well-skilled cataloguer, Berman had a long-standing interest in improving bibliographic access to overlooked materials but had garnered little support from the library community.[57] On May 4, 1970, he wrote to H.W. Wilson Company editor John Jamieson that the first issue of the *Alternative Press Index* was "well-intended" but "in execution, strikingly amateurish and unprofessional." He pointed out various flaws: failure to cover most conservative and many radical and underground titles, the fact that the index included fewer titles than planned, a limited international scope, and lack of author-access.[58] Unless the *Alternative Press Index* improved, he said it could not compete with his proposed project on dissident literature.

On May 14 Jamieson responded that Wilson "reluctantly" decided not to support the publication. He agreed that author-subject access to dissident periodicals was a good idea and that Berman's sample index entries of publications were first rate, but he also observed that libraries holding sizable collections of radical periodicals were few in number. While *Dissent, Human Events,* and *I.F. Stone's Weekly* were established titles, he argued, alternative press titles were likely to be short-lived.[59] The H.W. Wilson Company preferred to work in more stable and less fluctuating fields, he said, and advised Berman to solicit a nonprofit university press or write to the Council on Library Resources for financial assistance.

The profession's response to the *Alternative Press Index* was mixed. Librarian Julie Babcock witnessed "a stink" over the index at the June, 1970, ALA conference in Detroit. "Some of the librarians" present, she said, "were just jealous that they didn't think of it first." Babcock believed they were also bothered by the knowledge that a group of people "could create an index without the aid of a librarian!"[60] Because the *Alternative Press Index* reflected viewpoints concerning contemporary problems and issues that libraries were ignoring, Brooklyn College library activist Jackie Eubanks declared it "an embarrassment to the profession that the *Alternative Press Index* began from an impetus outside the ALA."[61] To her, the emergence of the *Alternative Press Index*, in combination with librarianship's continued neglect of the alternative press, raised the important question — was librarianship "neutral" when it came to the provision of access to *any* form of information?

Notes

1. Morgan, *The Sixties Experience*, 3.
2. Rebecca Jackson, *The 1960s: An Annotated Bibliography of Social and Political Movements in the U.S.* (Westport, CT: Greenwood Press, 1992), xi.
3. John Morton Blum, *Years of Discord: American Politics and Society, 1961–1974* (New York: W.W. Norton, 1991), ix.
4. Morgan, *The Sixties Experience*, 4.
5. Howard Zinn, *You Can't Be Neutral on a Moving Train: A Personal History of Our Times* (Boston: Beacon Press, 1994), 24.
6. Robert Glessing, *The Underground Press in America* (Bloomington: Indiana University Press, 1970), 11.
7. Daniel Bell, *The End of Ideology* (Glencoe, IL: The Free Press, 1960), 21, 25.
8. David Farber, ed., *The Sixties: From Memory to History* (Chapel Hill, NC: University of North Carolina Press, 1994), 13.
9. Todd Gitlin, *The Sixties: Years of Hope, Days of Rage* (Toronto: Bantam Books, 1987), 1–2.
10. *Ibid.*, 28–29.
11. Zinn, *You Can't Be Neutral*, 173.
12. John Kenneth Galbraith, *The Affluent Society*, 4th ed. (Boston: Houghton Mifflin, 1984), xiii.
13. John N. Ingham, *Sex 'n' Drugs 'n' Rock 'n' Roll: American Popular Culture Since 1945* (Toronto: Canadian Scholars' Press, 1989), 153.
14. Michael Harrington, *The Other America: Poverty in the United States*, rev. ed. (Baltimore: Penguin Books, 1971), 2.

15. Alice Echols, *Daring to be Bad: Radical Feminism in America, 1967-1975* (Minneapolis: University of Minnesota Press, 1989), 12.

16. Allan Bloom, *The Closing of the American Mind: How Higher Education Has Failed Democracy and Impoverished the Souls of Today's Students* (New York: Simon and Schuster, 1987), 331.

17. Blum, *Years of Discord*, 1991, ix.

18. Morgan, *The Sixties Experience*, xxi–xxii.

19. Gitlin, *The Sixties*, 343.

20. Farber, ed., *The Sixties*, 269.

21. Ruth Marie Eshenaur, *Censorship of the Alternative Press: A Descriptive Study of the Social and Political Control of Radical Periodicals (1964-1973)* (Carbondale, IL: [s.n.], 1975), 5.

22. Farber, ed., *The Sixties*, 269.

23. Robert Weis, "The Military Underground Press," in *The Magic Writing Machine*, ed. Everett E. Dennis (Eugene: School of Journalism, University of Oregon, 1971), 60–61.

24. Diane Kruchkow and Curt Johnson, eds., *Green Isle in the Sea: An Informal History of the Alternative Press, 1960-85* (Highland Park, IL: December Press, 1986), 119.

25. Eshenaur, *Censorship of the Alternative Press*, 6.

26. *Ibid.*, 84.

27. Echols, *Daring to Be Bad*, 8.

28. Sara Evans, *Personal Politics: The Root of the Women's Liberation in the Civil Rights Movement and the New Left* (New York: Alfred Knopf, 1979), 190–191.

29. Gitlin, *The Sixties*, 352.

30. Peter Collier and David Horowitz, *Destructive Generation. Second Thoughts about the Sixties* (New York: Summit Books, 1989), 15.

31. Echols, *Daring to Be Bad*, 8.

32. Peter N. Carroll, *It Seemed Like Nothing Happened: The Tragedy and Promise of America in the 1970s* (New York: Holt, Rinehart and Winston, 1982), 15.

33. Gitlin, *The Sixties*, 419.

34. Kruchkow and Johnson, eds., *Green Isle in the Sea*, 119.

35. James P. Danky and Elliott Shore, eds., *Alternative Materials in Libraries* (Metuchen, NJ: Scarecrow Press, 1982), 13.

36. These subject groupings are used in the alternative press catalogues of CRISES Press Inc.

37. Laurence Leamer, *The Paper Revolutionaries: The Rise of the Underground Press* (New York: Simon and Schuster, 1972), 44–45.

38. Dennis Carbonneau, Action Council, 1972/1973, ALA's SRRT Papers, Box 2.

39. Farber, ed., *The Sixties*, 213, 228.

40. Ray Mungo, *Famous Long Ago: My Life and Hard Times with Liberation News Service* (Boston: Beacon Press, 1970), 88.

41. Geoffrey Rips, *The Campaign Against the Underground Press* (San Francisco: City Lights Books, 1981), 81.

42. *Ibid.*

43. Eshenaur, *Censorship of the Alternative Press*, 74.

44. "Liberated Librarians," *Workforce* 34 (March-April 1973): 24–25.

45. Dennis Carbonneau, Action Council, 1972/73, ALA's SRRT Papers, Box 2.

46. "Introduction," *Workforce* 34 (March-April 1973): 5.

47. "Alternative Press Index," *SRRT Newsletter* 64 (July 1982): 6.

48. Bardwell L. Smith to Robert Stilger, 7 March 1969, Radical Research Center (RRC) Papers, State Historical Society of Wisconsin, Archives, Box 1.

49. Robert Stilger to Kathy, Art and others, 22 October 1971, RRC Papers, Box 6.

50. Kathy Martin to Augar Publishing Co., 28 June 1971, RRC Papers, Box 1.

51. Robert Stilger to Mike Brown, 3 December 1969, RRC Papers, Box 1.

52. *Ibid.*

53. Mary McKenney to Archives of Social History, 14 November 1970, RRC Papers, Box 1.

54. Robert Stilger to Brothers and Sisters, [n.d.], RRC Papers, Box, 6.

55. Robert Stilger to American Friends Service Committee, 10 September 1969, RRC Papers, Box 1.

56. Movement groups like Center for Alternatives In/To Higher Education; Center for Conflict Resolution; Center for Curriculum Design; Center for Education Reform; Center for Information on Latin America; Center for New Corporate Priorities; Center for Urban Encounter; and, Center for the Study of Democratic Institutions.

57. Dissident Literature, 1969–70, Eric Moon to Sanford Berman, 8 September, 1969, ALA's Sanford Berman Papers, University of Illinois at Urbana-Champaign, University Archives.

58. Dissident Literature, 1969–70, Sanford Berman to John Jamieson, 4 May 1970, ALA's Sanford Berman Papers.

59. Dissident Literature, 1969–70, John Jamieson to Sanford Berman, 14 May 1970, ALA's Sanford Berman Papers.

60. Julie Babcock to John Benson, 1 August 1970, RRC Papers, Box 1.

61. "Proposal for an Alternative "BIP" National Task Force," prepared by Jackie Eubanks, [n.d.], ALA's SRRT Papers, Box 8.

Chapter 2

The Ethos of
Intellectual Freedom

In the opening pages of the 1996 edition of the American Library Association's *Intellectual Freedom Manual*, Judith F. Krug and James A. Harvey attempt to dispel two myths — that although librarians had begun grappling with the concept of intellectual freedom in the late 19th century, ALA has never endorsed "a uniform definition" of intellectual freedom, and that "intellectual freedom has always been a major, if not the major, part of the foundation of library service in the United States."[1] According to Charles Busha, librarians "use the term intellectual freedom as the antithesis of censorship" and they believe in "library users' rights to read, watch, or listen to material" of their choice "without supervision or restraint from public officials, public opinion, institutional repression, private groups, or individuals."[2] Democratic societies endorse this concept of intellectual freedom because it mirrors the Jeffersonian principle that free people make their own choices and self-govern.

But in order for intellectual freedom to move beyond rhetoric and function in day-to-day life, a full range of information on any given topic or issue must be available to the voting public. When a full spectrum of opinion is not fairly represented, forms of censorship occur. Krug and Harvey define censorship as "not only deletion or excision of parts of published materials, but also efforts to ban, prohibit, suppress, proscribe, remove, label, or restrict materials." In effect, censorship violates the notion of intellectual freedom because it hinders peoples' ability to make informed decisions.[3]

Krug and Harvey maintain that "the catalyst spurring librarians to take initial steps toward supporting intellectual freedom was the censorship of specific publications."[4] When ALA was founded in 1876, the concept of intellectual freedom did not figure into the identification and selection of library materials, which, in retrospect, was mostly a process of inclusion and exclusion based on dominant ideology and culture.

Library historian Wayne Wiegand notes that early library selection tools were standard bearers of bibliographic access to mainstream media. In 1893, ALA produced the first in a series of bibliographies that listed book titles deemed suitable for small public library collections. In 1900, H.W. Wilson Company began publishing *Reader's Guide to Periodical Literature*, which indexed predominantly mainstream journals. In 1905, ALA supplemented its bibliography with a monthly book review journal called *Booklist* that reviewed a small fraction of newly published books.[5] And in 1908, H.W. Wilson published the first issue of what eventually became *Fiction Catalog*, which listed titles culled from ALA bibliographies, Pittsburgh Public Library selections, and Newark Public Library's list of "the best one hundred novels."[6] These classic library sources were not rooted in the notion of intellectual freedom, because their contents did not represent a broad range of available published materials. For example, Wiegand asserts that in its infancy, *Booklist* helped librarians build collections of "the best reading materials — past and present — that Western society had to offer."[7] The question is — best according to whom?

In *An Active Instrument for Propaganda*, Wiegand links the nature of censorship activities to a profile of library professionals. He argues that between 1887 and 1910, librarianship developed as a feminized profession largely run by men. While the nation's growing number of libraries were staffed by women of the "right character and who knew books," it was the men — mostly "white Anglo-Saxon, apolitical Protestants reared in middle-class families"—who ran America's large public libraries.[8] Because each library's staff shared roughly the same characteristics, library collections were often homogeneous as well. In effect, the nature of library collections closely reflected the values of the people that built and shaped them.

While librarians in theory could select from a wide array of published media by the turn of the century, in practice most did little to extend their selection sights beyond the prevailing literary, intellectual, and cultural canons. The average librarian, however unconsciously, practiced a paternalistic form of selection that supplied the public with sets of so-called "best reading" library materials. Meanwhile, other — and especially controversial — works like Theodore Dreiser's *Sister Carrie*, Eleanor Glyn's *Three Weeks*, Thomas Hardy's *Tess of the D'Urbervilles*, George Bernard Shaw's *Man and Superman*, and Mark Twain's *The Adventures of Huckleberry Finn* and *Tom Sawyer* were excluded from key bibliographies and library collections, at least until the literary establishment accepted them as part of the canon.[9]

The idea of the library's playing a part in the crafting of the nation's culture through the process of collection development helps illustrate how institutions shape culture and ideology. One of the key characteristics of hegemony, for example, is that power is distributed across a network of civil institutions.

By 1916 the public library had become a nearly ubiquitous civil institution, and once America entered the war in 1917, the federal government began to exert direct authority over the selection of library materials for enlisted men. Wiegand observes, for example, that the Army declared German language, pacifist, and labor union-related materials unfit for consumption of trainees. In *Forbidden Books in American Public Libraries, 1876-1939: A Study in Cultural Change,* Evelyn Geller examines the American public library's shift from censorship in the late 19th century to freedom of access advocacy in the mid–20th century. She concludes that World War I not only focused attention on the issue of the freedom to read, but also spurred librarians to become "more decisive guardians of the public taste."[10] When, for example, librarians cooperated with the state in prohibiting access to subversive materials, they entered an overt phase of censorship activity. Likewise, when librarians cooperated with the state in promoting access to patriotic materials, they became, "an active instrument for propaganda."[11]

Library scholar David A. Lincove's research about the American public library and propaganda in the 1930s and the eve of World War II picks up where Wiegand's research leaves off. Like Wiegand, he tracks libraries and their social context by exploring public library censorship practices. In particular, he examines the political propaganda used in World War I and its subsequent dramatic increase in the 1920s and 1930s. Lincove sets the historical context for library censorship practices by examining the reasons underlying the increased use of propaganda. First, he suggests that a growing fear of communism combined with an increased recognition of the power and influence of the mass media gave the nation's leaders reasons to worry. In particular, they feared that propaganda from Europe and Asia threatened western democracy. Second, Lincove suggests that an increasing number of Americans agitated for domestic reforms that stemmed from domestic problems, many of which were associated with economic depression.[12]

Some librarians, many of them new to the profession, supported the domestic calls for reform. They also demanded changes within librarianship itself. They wanted more participation in running the nation's libraries and called for librarians to reconsider the way they handled "the growing presence of politically and socially sensitive literature."[13] These librarians asserted that the prevailing selection criteria prejudiced librarians against such materials and so they called for a shift away from the paternalistic best books approach and towards an emphasis on the freedom to read.

Stanley J. Kunitz, editor of the *Wilson Library Bulletin* from 1928 to 1943, whom Geller calls "the herald of change," strongly supported the concept of intellectual freedom in the 1930s.[14] Kunitz called upon librarians to be active participants in filling information gaps, base their selection decisions on intellectual freedom, and represent all sides of issues. His opinions often conflicted with those of his own publisher, the H.W. Wilson Company. While Kunitz appeared to garner a lot of support from progressive librarians, a pacifist subset argued that librarians should take a public stand on the issue of peace. Library pacifists supported the purchase of pacifist propaganda, but they were not entirely in favor of a purist moral stance on intellectual freedom and the accompanying position of library "neutrality." At the 1935 annual conference of the Pacific Northwest Library Association, for example, Seattle public librarian William Tucker proposed that the Association pass a resolution which called on librarians to oppose war, fascism, and any other harmful attacks on American culture. His suggestion caused a considerable stir, but ultimately failed. Many argued the resolution would involve librarians in non-library matters. But the pacifists did not give up their fight. Many joined the Progressive Librarians' Council, formed in 1939. The Council incorporated the pacifists' stance into a more general demand for social responsibility in librarianship. However, because their definition of social responsibility conflicted with the idea of library "neutrality," their ideas proved controversial. Lincove notes that while progressive librarians believed that the public had a right to choose its own reading materials, the library establishment feared that supporting the notion of intellectual freedom would promote an antidemocratic ideology.[15]

When Archibald MacLeish became Librarian of Congress in 1939, he addressed the issue of advocacy versus "neutrality." Although he opposed library censorship and was critical of right-wing radicals who censored unAmerican materials, at the same time he did not hesitate to call for "an intellectual and political offensive against Fascist propaganda."[16] MacLeish believed librarians needed to become more proactive educators so that the public could read literature with a critical eye, identify propaganda for what it was, and ultimately make informed and democratic decisions.

This proactive interpretation of the library's cultural role in society deviated from the status quo. Up until 1939, ALA held no official position on intellectual freedom and censorship. The 1922 "Code of Ethics," for example, outlined etiquette, not professional functions.[17] Meanwhile, librarians selected materials based on the cues they took from the academic and literary establishment. At its 1939 annual conference in San Francisco, however, ALA took unprecedented action and adopted a policy statement on intellectual freedom, i.e., the Library's Bill of Rights. The Association modeled the document on the Des Moines, Iowa, Bill of Rights for the Free Public Library, drafted by Library Director Forest Spaulding and adopted in 1938. Christine Jenkins points out that "no single event has been specifically identified as the catalyst for this policy adoption ... that the rise of fascism in Europe and the consequent rise in public awareness of the dangers which totalitarian regimes posed to books, libraries, and the freedom of speech and the press," all contributed to a growing concern in ALA.[18] Most accounts of the history of the Library's Bill of Rights (Jenkins' included) also cite the reaction to the publication of John Steinbeck's *The Grapes of Wrath* in 1939 as a factor that contributed to its adoption by ALA. Librarians received mixed messages about the book. And once it became the "target of censorship pressures around the country" and was banned by various libraries in Illinois, New Jersey, and California, both on account of its so-called "immorality" and because of the "social views advanced by the author," ALA responded.[19]

The Library's Bill of Rights began with the following statement: "Today indications in many parts of the world point to growing intolerance, suppression of free speech, and censorship affecting the rights of minorities and individuals." "Mindful of this," ALA's Council adopted three policy statements to direct free public library services. The first policy stated that library materials should be selected based on their value and intrinsic interest to the community, not on the race, nationality, political or religious views of authors. The second, directed that library materials should "fairly and adequately" represent all sides of social issues. The final statement pertained to a democratic open-use policy for library meeting rooms, so that all community groups would have equal access.[20]

The adoption by ALA of the Library's Bill of Rights marked a turning point in the history of American libraries. From then on, the principle of intellectual freedom defined the library's responsibility to society. But because society continued to change, so too did the profession's understanding of the library's role in "social change and education."[21] From its inception in 1939 to its 1960s incarnation, the Library's Bill of Rights shaped librarianship's developing professional ideology and the status of its responsibilities towards intellectual freedom and censorship.

Once intellectual freedom emerged as the central ethic of a self-declared "neutral" library profession in 1939, the rhetoric of the Library's

Bill of Rights immediately began to affect practical professional issues. At its 1940 annual conference, the Association formed the Committee on Intellectual Freedom to Safeguard the Rights of Library Users to Freedom of Inquiry. The committee was created to recommend policies regarding intellectual freedom, in particular those concerning violations of the Library's Bill of Rights. Its existence, however, indicated that while the Library's Bill of Rights served as a guideline, ALA did not require its enforcement.[22] Furthermore, the need to establish a committee showed the text of the Library's Bill of Rights led to different interpretations.

University of Washington librarian Bernard Berelson found immediate fault with the Library's Bill of Rights. He asserted that the stance of library "neutrality" was defective and asked how American librarians could take positions on freedom and democracy and still call themselves impartial.[23] In so doing, he urged librarians to recognize failings in the Library's Bill of Rights, to understand that they were not "neutral" individuals, and to know that it was possible to take stands on social issues. Berelson's views were controversial because of the widespread belief that partisanship led to censorship and thereby violated the idea of intellectual freedom; that librarianship required a "neutral" vision.

While some librarians debated heady philosophical subjects such as library "neutrality," partiality, intellectual freedom, and social responsibility in the early 1940s, the discussions had little impact on the typical library practitioner. Despite the existence of the Library's Bill of Rights, the Committee on Intellectual Freedom, and all the philosophical discussions, "the code of freedom adopted in 1939," as Geller puts it, "was the expression of an ideology rather than a norm."[24]

In the mid–1940s, under the direction of the University of Chicago's Graduate Library School professor Leon Carnovsky, the Committee on Intellectual Freedom requested that ALA revise the Library's Bill of Rights. The Committee wanted to add an amendment to Article I that read, "Further, books believed to be factually correct should not be banned or removed from the library simply because they are disapproved of by some people." The ALA Council approved the amendment in October, 1944, and thereby proclaimed the Association's first official position on the banning or removal of materials.[25] Despite the amendment, however, the Library's Bill of Rights remained largely rhetorical.

Under David K. Berninghausen's direction (newly appointed chief librarian for Cooper Union for the Advancement of Science and Art), in 1948 the Committee on Intellectual Freedom suggested that four changes be made to the Library's Bill of Rights. The impetus for these revisions was the perception that "there was no longer the pre–World War II need to point out" growing censorship practices; that "in the developing cold war, those factors justifying the 1939 policy were even more evident." The first revision pertained to the inherent relationship between intellectual freedom and library materials selection. The committee proposed that ALA declare intellectual freedom a responsibility of library service. The second revision recommended that ALA improve upon the 1944 amendment, in particular, that the phrase "books believed to be factually correct" be changed to "books ... of sound factual authority." Despite the change, however, the phrase remained problematic. The direction did not indicate who ultimately determined a work's factual authority. The third revision recommended adding an article calling upon librarians to challenge book censorship "urged or practiced by volunteer arbiters of morals or political opinion or by organizations that would establish a coercive concept of Americanism." The last sought to add an article in which ALA declared its professional responsibility to work with "allied groups" in the name of intellectual freedom. Later that year, ALA's Council approved all of the recommendations and renamed the document the Library Bill of Rights. Also, Berninghausen's committee shortened its name to Intellectual Freedom Committee. The new statement on intellectual freedom differed from former versions by enlarging its scope and making librarians responsible for challenging censorship and cooperating with allied institutions.[26]

Soon after ALA's adoption of the revised document, the New York City public school system banned the *Nation* magazine from its libraries because it contained unfavorable references to the Roman Catholic church. As chair of ALA's Intellectual Freedom Committee, Berninghausen publicly opposed the ban, and began collaborating with other civil groups like the Ad Hoc Committee to Lift the Ban on the *Nation*. American library historian Louise S. Robbins suggests these actions marked librarianship's entrance into a public debate on censorship and alerted the society at large to the profession's willingness to work with external forces, such as those who joined in the fight against censorship. While the ban was not revoked until 1957, the formation of a united cultural front was a logical first step to combat censorship.[27]

After World War II, the House Un-American Activities Committee continued its efforts to chase so-called communists in government, labor unions, foundations, schools, and other institutions. In 1947, President Harry S Truman implemented a national loyalty program for government workers and shortly thereafter state legislatures also introduced loyalty oaths to prevent the spread of communism.[28] Between 1949 and 1953, Wisconsin Senator Joseph R. McCarthy and his cohorts imposed a blanket of conformity. Intellectuals (professors, teachers, librarians, et al.) who deviated from the status quo were persecuted.[29] McCarthy's focus on the U.S. Information Services Libraries abroad, Robert B. Downs writes, resulted in "the burning of some books that were labeled as Communist propagandas, the resignations of numerous librarians, and finally, to the closing of a considerable number of libraries because of reduced congressional support."[30]

Originally, ALA charged its Intellectual Freedom Committee with recommending policies regarding intellectual freedom, in particular those concerning violations of the Library Bill of Rights. After 1948, however, the Committee expressed interest in taking actions that promoted intellectual freedom for librarians, as well as for the public. This new responsibility proved difficult to enforce because ALA lacked the infrastructure to defend librarians who put their jobs on the line in the defense of intellectual freedom. Despite the Library Bill of Rights and the Intellectual Freedom Committee, ALA was unable to provide the kind of legal and financial support needed to back librarians. A notable example involved Ruth W. Brown, a Bartlesville, Oklahoma, librarian.

In February, 1950, members of the Bartlesville chapter of the American Legion accused Brown of circulating subversive library materials. Despite the existence of the Library Bill of Rights and verbal support from her public library board and ALA's Intellectual Freedom Committee, public pressure from community leaders forced her dismissal in July, 1950. The Ruth Brown case showed inherent problems with the Library Bill of Rights. The document, as Robbins put it, "seemed merely a few words on paper incapable of supporting librarians in trouble."[31] The next year, the American Legion pressured the Peoria Public Library to take three films out of its collection — *The Brotherhood of Man, Boundary Lines* and *Peoples of the U.S.S.R.* — despite the fact that ALA's Audio-Visual Committee recommended each. The 1948 Library Bill of Rights had not made reference to non-print materials. Thus in 1951, ALA changed the text to address "all materials and media of communication collected by libraries."[32]

In late 1950, the Montclair, New Jersey, chapter of the Sons of the American Revolution pressured public libraries in the state to label literature which "advocated" or "favored" communism (or which was issued by communist or communist affiliated organizations), to limit loan periods for these publications, and to record names of individuals who consulted them. Montclair public librarian Margery Quigley quickly turned to the Intellectual Freedom Committee for guidance, and in July, 1951, ALA adopted its "Statement on Labeling." The "Statement on Labeling" said ALA had a responsibility to oppose labeling of library materials because:

(1) librarians did not "advocate" or "endorse" the intellectual content of library materials; (2) no individual librarian could label library materials without bias; (3) labeling prejudiced the reader; (4) labeling violated the Library Bill of Rights; and (5) librarians were opposed to censorship.[33]

Not everyone agreed. Director of the Detroit Public Library (and former ALA president) Ralph Ulveling argued that the normal interpretation of the Library Bill of Rights, which favored the free flow of information, "kept channels for enemy propaganda open." Ulveling wanted subversive library materials labeled and segregated into non-circulating main branch reference collections instead, in order to reflect democratic values. At the 1952 midwinter conference, ALA reaffirmed its commitment to intellectual freedom, to democratic values, and to the public's freedom to read what it liked. The discussion surrounding library material labeling illuminates how the rhetoric of the Library Bill of Rights was shaping librarianship's professional ideology and status.[34] The ALA gained professional standing as a self-proclaimed social arbiter of intellectual freedom.

To profile the Library Bill of Rights and educate librarians about intellectual freedom ethics, in the early 1950s ALA sponsored preconferences on intellectual freedom and disseminated special educational kits and literature to librarians. A 1953 ALA preconference focused on book selection, at which Lester Asheim urged librarians to take more charge of their professional jurisdiction by concentrating on selection, not censorship.[35] On June 18, 1953, the American Book Publishers Council adopted a seven-point "Freedom to Read Statement," which the ALA Council endorsed on June 25, 1953. The points instructed publishers and librarians to make diverse views available, to enforce obscenity laws (but not to take non-legal measures to determine "taste" for others), to contest encroachments upon the freedom to read by individuals or groups, and to enrich the meaning of the freedom to read by supplying the fullest range of books possible, but to recognize that they need not endorse the ideas presented in library materials. Librarians and publishers were also instructed not to reject a book solely based on either the author's personal history or political affiliations, or force a reader to accept subversive characterizations of a book.[36] The statement promoted pluralist democracy, and thus struck a positive chord with the country's media.[37] Perhaps for the first time in librarianship's history, the media knew that the profession held intellectual freedom as a central professional ethic.

Jenkins notes that as right-wing pressure groups gained strength during the McCarthy era, their efforts "increasingly focused on challenging, attacking, and seeking to censor books and other materials, particularly those written for and available to young readers in classrooms and libraries." Thus, the American Association of School Librarians adopted the School Library Bill of Rights in the 1955 ALA midwinter meeting. The policy statement instructed school librarians "to place principle above personal opinion and reason" in the selection of materials that supported the curriculum, stimulated educational growth, allowed students to make "intelligent judgments in their daily life," and represented opposing views on controversial issues as well as religious, ethnic and cultural diversity.[38] After the adoption of the School Library Bill of Rights by the ALA Council on July 8, 1955, Wisconsin Senator Joseph R. McCarthy's death in 1957, and the increasingly "settled" pattern of the Cold War, the profession gradually turned its attention to other concerns.[39] But even though the oppressive atmosphere began to lift, challenges to library materials did not stop. In 1959 Marjorie Fiske showed that the practice of self-censorship was quite common in the profession. For example, in anticipation of external challenges, she discovered many California librarians had screened out potentially controversial materials during the selection process.[40]

Desegregation was also a major issue in the 1950s. In 1961, ALA's Special Committee on Civil Liberties recommended the Library Bill of Rights include a statement that "the rights of an individual to the use of a library should not be denied or abridged because of his race, religion, national origin or political views." When Council approved the amendment on February, 2, 1961, it constituted the first change in the profession's policy statement on intellectual freedom in ten years.[41]

During the 1960s, members of the alternative press movement pushed for positive social changes by making hard-to-come-by or suppressed information more accessible to the public, especially to disaffected social groups who suffered from lack of information. As a response to this push, a group of librarians worked to improve access to the alternative press as a means of effecting community change. Thus, the alternative press movement, a product of the 1960s, prompted the profession to reexamine its concept of intellectual freedom, as well as its responsibility to society.

But as some members of the profession turned their attention to a review of intellectual freedom, they met four obstacles. First, as a concept intellectual freedom was not historically wedded to librarianship. Second, censorship was a long-standing characteristic of library practice. Third, the concept of social responsibility undermined ALA's purist "neutral" stance on intellectual freedom, as stated in the Library Bill of Rights. Fourth, the tension between "neutrality" and social responsibility heightened in the 1960s when librarians denounced the legacy of bias in materials selection and forced the profession to reassess its responsibility to society and reconcile the weight of the status quo with the demands of social dissent. In practical terms, given the nature of library collections, could librarianship claim a "neutral" stance? In philosophical terms, should the library, as a social institution, serve as an advocate for social justice?

In the context of intellectual freedom and the ideological framework of the Library Bill of Rights, the issue of library "neutrality" was problematic throughout the 1960s. For example, despite the 1961 amendment to the Library Bill of Rights, problems remained. Criticism of the idea that librarians could evaluate the validity of published materials was prompted by an incident in which a Catholic librarian in Belleville, Illinois, excluded a Protestant document because it lacked "sound factual authority."[42] The incident illustrates how the phrasing of the Library Bill of Rights led to its misuse. In effect, it was possible for librarians to use the Library Bill of Rights as a justification for the exclusion of library materials, or as the director of the Minneapolis Public Library Ervin J. Gaines once put it, as a "shield for their prejudices."[43] This loophole was not addressed until 1967, when the statement was revised. The new directive instructed that "no library materials should be proscribed or removed from libraries because of partisan or doctrinal disapproval."[44]

In an 1996 essay titled "The Library Bill of Rights — A Critique," First Amendment scholar Gordon B. Baldwin states that the 1967 revised directive to reflect "all points of view" created drafting problems that arose from framing a policy in "neutral" terms. "The breadth of the LBR [Library Bill of Rights] invites making decisions." He asserts that "a book selector can justify why an item does not match community needs, that it isn't hard to dress decisions in non political terms which may mask politics and moral sensibilities."[45] Baldwin shows how both Library Bill of Rights versions in the 1960s left censorship loopholes and invited further exploration of the "all points of view" rhetoric.

First, the Library Bill of Rights acknowledged a library's responsibility to inform on the issues of the day and furthermore implied that libraries had a role to play in them. Second, in its indication that the balanced collection was the ideal, the Library Bill of Rights implied that imbalance in library collections should be redressed. Social responsibility advocates argued that while the revised article in the 1967 version of the Library Bill of Rights called upon librarians to "provide books and other materials presenting all points of view concerning the problems and issues of the times," most library practitioners were slow to collect alternative press materials.[46]

Because professional library literature provided scant attention to the alternative press, 1960s librarians confronted few reminders of their own shortsightedness. Professional journals did contain an occasional article or bibliography about the alternative press. For example, Bill Katz's *Library Journal* column, "Magazines for Libraries," featured alternative titles and informed the profession about publications like the *Freedom of Information Center Report No. 226 on the Underground Press* and the *Directory of America's 490 Most Controversial Periodicals*. But unless librarians read advertisements in the alternative press, screened the Liberation News Service checklists, or perused "little mag" directories, they were unlikely to come across much mention of these sources.

In 1970, University of California–Davis librarian Noel Peattie began publishing an alternative library journal called *Sipapu* and found that only librarians like himself—those concerned with "self-publication"—were even aware of the alternative press in the 1960s. Peattie was shocked to find, for example, that while *Library Journal* editor Eric Moon published two anthologies on 1960s librarianship—*Book Selection and Censorship in the Sixties* and *Library Issues: The Sixties*—the first did not contain any mention about the alternative press. Furthermore, well into the mid–1970s, "*Library Literature* cross-referenced UNDERGROUND NEWSPAPERS to NEWSPAPERS, and thus discouraged any search for the sub-class."[47]

Most librarians, despite their professional training, knew little about or had little understanding of the alternative press.[48] Jackie Eubanks was one of the few who did. Because of her suspicion that "built-in WASP hang-ups" contributed to a form of censorship that grew from ignorance about the kind of information being produced, Eubanks believed that the profession had a responsibility to educate librarians about publishing.[49] She argued that because the average librarian did not read the alternative press, professional education was a key factor in determining what s/he had learned about the alternative publishing community. Eubanks identified two important points. First, the typical library student began a professional education that was steeped in mainstream culture. Second, the library school experience did little to change the student's narrow cultural focus.

Library educator Mary Lee Bundy, who supported the social responsibility stance in librarianship, went a step further. She asserted that "restrictive barriers" kept non-white and non–middle class people from entering the library education system and that the profession managed to confine itself to maintaining the status quo by running schools that did little to produce community information specialists.[50] In particular, she noted lack of education about the need to provide information about government activities, including new government programs, official corruption, misinformation, and community issues. "Library educators as a group," Bundy argued, "never seriously addressed their social commitments."[51] Library academics failed to initiate federal funding for minority groups, to produce scholarly research that underpinned the social responsibility of librarianship, or to address the issue of the canonization of the status quo in library collections.[52]

Not surprisingly, many of the 1960s library activists radicalized on the job, rather than in school. For example, Celeste West recounted from her library school experience at Rutgers in the 1960s that while some students were "very interested in the rise of the counter-culture press," instructor Mary Gaver was the only one who "taught us to read between the lines of *Publishers Weekly.*" Rather than educating students, "library schools just seem to blank out" when it came to the alternative press. "Shaking down independent voices and earmarking funds" for the alternative press were skills that could be taught at library schools just like the courses on rare book collecting or database management.[53] But they were not taught.

In *The Freedom to Lie: A Debate About Democracy,* Swan explains why selection procedures for alternative press products could not be developed in the same way as establishment press products. "The products of the commercial and academic marketplace are given preference over those works which are outside of that relatively normalizing sphere." With little effort, he adds, "this point can be extended to include all of our standard indexes and other access tools, inevitably given preference over the few counter-cultural reference works." Although Swan states that librarians shape library collections and reference sources in an effort to increase the availability of some materials at the expense of others, he is careful to emphasize that "selection and collection development which favor one community's world view over all others is not *ipso facto* censorship." However, Swan's analysis of the rhetoric of the Library Bill of Rights shows how the document fails to account for the "cultural and ideological screening" that underlines the acquisitions process. The librarian who follows the Library Bill of Rights direction to provide library resources on the basis of community demands or needs, he states, "will inevitably violate" the subsequent direction not to exclude materials. Despite conscientious efforts to expand the community's horizons, Swan concludes, the librarian "also mirrors to some degree the prejudices and limitations of that community."[54]

Librarians had little opportunity to select alternative literature in the 1960s precisely because they conscientiously followed the collection development procedures taught in library school programs. Procedures like heavy reliance on review media, for example, worked in favor of the mainstream press because they served to "filter out" non-mainstream materials.[55] The work of library scholar Judith Serebnick, book review editor for *Library Journal* from May, 1969 to February, 1972, revealed the role that reviewing plays in the collection building process. Her research indicates that key review media, like *Booklist, Choice, Kirkus Reviews, Library Journal, New York Times Book Review,* and *Publishers Weekly* mostly dealt with large mainstream publishers. As a result, the alternative press was not reviewed as often as the mainstream press and certainly less so in the standard trade journals.[56]

Thus, collection development constituted an enclosed circle of activity. First, library students entered library programs with little knowledge of the alternative press. Second, they failed to learn more about it in the process of their professional education. Third, when they adhered to professional guidelines and used standard review journals, they encountered scant coverage of the alternative press.

Once they became practicing professionals, librarians generally ordered new materials from vendors — single sources for many materials — because it cut down on paperwork. Vendors, however, avoided the alternative press materials because they did not care to deal with smaller press runs, to locate addresses of out-of-the- way houses, and to fuss with frequent title changes, unusual formats, and irregular publication schedules. Besides, the alternative press was not indexed by major commercial indexers. In effect, products of the alternative press were not collected because they were not reviewed or indexed, and they were not reviewed or indexed because they were not known.

So the circle completed and enclosed itself. As a result of the selection criteria for who was accepted into library programs, the establishment nature of library education, and narrow collection development standards and practices that favored the works of large, mainstream, commercial publishers, 1960s library collections did not represent all points of view. "I began to notice that librarians (including me) are trained to buy largely from big business publishers," Jackie Eubanks recounted, "not from groups like (for example) the National Welfare Rights Organization."[57]

When Eubanks and librarians like her came to realize the use of mainstream sources (Random House, *New York Times, Life,* etc.) not only favored establishment cultural interests but economic, social and political ones as well, they brought the issue of unbalanced library collections to light. Consequently, they forced the profession to reexamine the notion of intellectual freedom, the claim to library "neutrality" and the rhetoric of the Library Bill of Rights. Although these issues were the subject of previous discussions, the climate of the 1960s, especially with the emergence of the alternative press movement, gave them a new urgency. Dissenting librarians not only reexamined the impracticality of library "neutrality" exposed by Bernard Berelson years before, but also carried through on his advice by taking public stands on social issues.

In *There's No Such Thing As Free Speech, and It's a Good Thing, Too,* Stanley Fish argues that the belief in liberal concepts such as "fairness," "neutrality," and the "marketplace of ideas" is flawed. While liberal thought, he asserts, is based on the idea that a point of view is irreducible, "the liberal strategy is to devise (or attempt to devise) procedural mechanisms that are neutral with respect to point of view and therefore can serve to frame partisan debates in a nonpartisan manner." But, while the marketplace of ideas is supposed to monitor the contest between conflicting agendas without any consideration of their intellectual content, the fact that the structure of the marketplace has to be set up suggests that ideological considerations do come unconsciously into play — that organization "necessarily favors some agendas."[58]

Peattie holds that historically a great many public libraries, like those of New York City and Cleveland, provided successful literacy and educational programs to enable immigrants to gain citizenship. Naturalization procedures required immigrants, for example, to have a knowledge of the Constitution and of democratic principles. He concludes that the movement toward social responsibility in the 1960s was a natural extension of this type of outreach library service, because in the 1960s, not just immigrants, but a whole variety of people required improved library services.[59] But when 1960s library activists began to redress imbalance in library collections, the professional establishment responded with accusations of bias and censorship in library materials selection. The next chapters examine this issue and the struggle for formulating an acceptable definition of librarianship's professional jurisdiction.

Notes

1. *Intellectual Freedom Manual,* 1996, xix.

2. Charles H. Busha, ed., *An Intellectual Freedom Primer* (Littleton, CO: Libraries Unlimited, 1977), 12.

3. *Intellectual Freedom Manual,* 1996, xx.

4. *Ibid.*

5. Wayne Wiegand, *An Active Instrument for Propaganda* (New York: Greenwood Press, 1989), 1-2.

6. Evelyn Geller, *Forbidden Books in American Public Libraries, 1876–1939: A Study in Cultural Change* (Westport, CT: Greenwood Press, 1984), 95.

7. Wiegand, *An Active Instrument,* 2.

8. *Ibid.*, 2-3.

9. Geller, *Forbidden Books*, 80-88.

10. *Ibid.*, 110, 59.

11. Wiegand, *An Active Instrument*, 136.

12. David A. Lincove, "Propaganda and the American Public Library from the 1930's to the Eve of World War II," *RQ* 33, no. 4 (Summer 1994): 511.

13. *Ibid.*

14. Geller, *Forbidden Books*, 148.

15. Lincove, "Propaganda," 511–515.

16. *Ibid.*, 520.

17. Geller, *Forbidden Books*, 124.

18. Christine A. Jenkins, "The Strength of the Inconspicuous: Youth Services, the American Library Association, and Intellectual Freedom for the Young, 1939–1955" (Ph.D. diss., University of Wisconsin–Madison, 1995), 146.

19. *Intellectual Freedom Manual*, 1996, xxiii.

20. *Ibid.*, 6-7.

21. *Ibid.*, xx.

22. *Ibid.*, 7.

23. Bernard Berelson, "The Myth of Library Impartiality: An Interpretation for Democracy," *Wilson Bulletin for Librarians* 13, no. 2 (October 1938): 87–90.

24. Geller, *Forbidden Books*, 192.

25. *Intellectual Freedom Manual*, 1996, 7.

26. *Ibid.*, 8–9.

27. Louise S. Robbins, "Champions of a Cause: American Librarians and the Library Bill of Rights in the 1950s," *Library Trends* 45, no. 1 (Summer 1996): 32–33. See also David K. Berninghausen, *The Flight from Reason: Essays on Intellectual Freedom in the Academy, the Press, and the Library* (Chicago: American Library Association, 1975).

28. Busha, ed., *An Intellectual Freedom Primer*, 41–42.

29. Blum, *Years of Discord*, 16.

30. Robert B. Downs and Ralph E. McCoy, eds., *The First Freedom: Critical Issues Relating to Censorship and Intellectual Freedom* (Chicago: American Library Association, 1984), 7.

31. Robbins, "Champions of a Cause," 34. See also Robbins, Louise S., "Racism and Censorship in Cold War Oklahoma: The Case of Ruth W. Brown and the Bartlesville Public Library," *Southwestern Historical Quarterly* 100, no. 1 (1996): 19–46.

32. *Intellectual Freedom Manual*, 1996, 10.

33. *Ibid.*, 113–115.

34. Louise S. Robbins, *Censorship and the American Library: The American Library Association's Response to Threats to Intellectual Freedom, 1939–1969* (Westport, CT: Greenwood Press, 1996), 54–55.

35. See Lester Asheim, "Not Censorship, But Selection," *Wilson Library Bulletin* 28, no. 1 (1953): 63–67.

36. *Intellectual Freedom Manual*, 1996, 137–140.

37. Robbins, "Champions of a Cause," 41–42.

38. Jenkins, "The Strength of the Inconspicuous," 559, 671.

39. Robbins, "Champions of a Cause," 43.

40. Lowenthal, Marjorie Fiske, *Book Selection and Censorship: A Study of School and Public Libraries in California* (Berkeley: University of California Press, 1959).

41. *Intellectual Freedom Manual*, 1996, 10–11.

42. *Ibid.*, 11-12.

43. Wedgeworth et al., "Social Responsibility," 36.

44. *Intellectual Freedom Manual*, 1996, 13.

45. Gordon B. Baldwin, "The Library Bill of Rights — A Critique," *Library Trends* 45, no. 1 (Summer 1996): 8.

46. *Intellectual Freedom Manual*, 1996, 13.

47. Bundy and Stielow, *Activism*, 47.

48. Bill Katz to Sanford Berman, 13 April [1970], ALA's Sanford Berman Papers.

49. "Selection of Library Materials," Position paper prepared by the Book Selection Sub-Committee, San Francisco Bay Area Chapter Social Responsibilities Round Table, January 1971, ALA's SRRT Papers, Box 4.

50. Mary Lee Bundy, "Information Work for Social Change," 17 February 1973, ALA's SRRT Papers, Box 2.

51. Bundy and Stielow, *Activism*, 94.

52. Stanley Fish, *There's No Such Thing as Free Speech, and It's a Good Thing Too* (New York: Oxford University Press, 1994), 307.

53. "A Conversation with Celeste West," 3–6.

54. Swan and Peattie, *The Freedom to Lie*, 29–31.

55. Edward S. Herman and Noam Chomsky, *Manufacturing Consent: Changes in the Labor Process Under Monopoly Capitalism* (Chicago: University of Chicago Press, 1982), 2.

56. Judith Serebnick, "An Analysis of Publishers of Books Reviewed in Key Library Journals," *Library and Information Science Research* 6, no. 3 (1984): 289–303; "Book Reviews and the Selection of Potentially Controversial Books in Public Libraries," *Library Quarterly* 51, no. 4 (1981): 390–409; "Selection and Holdings of Small Publishers' Books in OCLC Libraries: A Study of the Influence of Reviews, Publishers and Vendors," *Library Quarterly* 62, no. 3 (July 1992): 259–294.

57. Noel Peattie, *A Passage for Dissent: The Best of Sipapu, 1970–1988* (Jefferson, NC: McFarland, 1989), 138.

58. Fish, *There's No Such Thing*, 16–17, 297.

59. Patricia Glass Schuman, comp. and ed., *Social Responsibilities and Libraries: A Library Journal/School Library Journal Selection* (New York: R.R. Bowker, 1976), ix–x.

Chapter 3

Calling for Change, 1967–1969

In the late 1960s, a number of American librarians argued that library collections lacked balance, that a purist moral stance on intellectual freedom was an example of hands-off liberalism, and that the library served mainstream social sectors, not the whole community. As a result, they had little faith in the establishment stance of library "neutrality" and its accompanying vision of intellectual freedom. Instead, they believed that the library should become an active agent for social change and that the concept of intellectual freedom should incorporate the premise of social responsibility.

The establishment portrayal of a "neutral" library reinforces Louise S. Robbins' proposition that the concept of pluralist democracy played a large role in shaping the profession's notion of intellectual freedom in the 1950s. During the McCarthy period, champions of library "neutrality" believed that academic freedom and the freedom to read were threatened from the right. But in the 1960s and 1970s, the library establishment believed that the threat to intellectual freedom also came from the New Left. Thus, they perceived the concept of social responsibility that emerged in librarianship in the late 1960s as a New Left tactic that threatened the traditional "neutrality" and purpose of the American Library Association.

Librarians who advocated social responsibility used the issue of the alternative press to redress a perceived imbalance in library collections, to provide enhanced information services to a broader public, to make the library more relevant to a changing society, and to show that long-standing library practices put the library profession in conflict with its own Library Bill of Rights. Much of this activity emanated from San Francisco Public Library's Bay Area Reference Center (BARC), established in 1967. The experimental Center provided support reference services to 17 North

Bay Cooperative Library System libraries scattered across six counties, "with some as far away from San Francisco as 125 miles in suburban communities across the Golden Gate Bridge." The Reference Center occupied a small room just off the Main library's second floor general reference department and communicated with most of the cooperative institutions via facsimile transmissions, nationwide communication systems, and "the latest designed photocopying gear." From its start, BARC began looking to non-commercial book publishers to find information on new areas of interest and in its first year launched a monthly newsletter titled *Synergy* to serve as a reference tool and disseminate news of the project. *Synergy's* "Update" section listed outstanding new additions to the San Francisco Public Library reference collection, while another section included a bibliography of topical importance "not obtainable through usual channels."[1]

San Francisco was a hotbed of social activity in 1967. From the city's 65,000 person anti-war demonstration held concomitantly with the Spring Mobilization Committee's New York City protest, to the influx of thousands of people for the "Summer of Love" activities, the Bay community manifested social change.[2] Celeste West, *Synergy's* first editor (renowned as much for her intelligence and feminist viewpoints as her large frame glasses and floppy hats), commented on the relationship between San Francisco's transformation and the local library scene. She described the city as "a trend-mecca — whether it be communal living, campus riots, gay liberation, independent film making... You name it and we've got it." But what San Francisco had, she argued, was not reflected in library collections unless somebody took the time to pull together "the elusive printed material."[3] Thus, *Synergy* began examining the nature of library card catalogs, indexes, and selecting tools because its staff believed that such tools were mostly "rear-view mirrors" that provided little or no bibliographic access to the public's current information needs.

Synergy's staff believed that because librarians were not sufficiently trained to create access to or learn about where to find many forms of information, they were unable to fulfill their professional mandate to present balanced/multiple points of view. The passive nature of library practice grounded on a myth of "neutral" service understated this information access problem. Because librarians were followers and not leaders in the information marketplace, alternative press related topics received attention only when big publishers sensed profit. To illustrate this point, West tracked the lag time between discussions of women's liberation in the alternative press and their appearance in mainstream library literature. The mainstream library press, she noted, "slumbered along" for nearly five years before recognizing it in about 1970. The April, 1970, issue of *Amer-*

ican Libraries included an article titled "The Disadvantaged Majority: Women Employed by Libraries" by Anita R. Schiller, a research associate at the University of Illinois Library Research Center. And in May, *Library Journal* ran a feature titled "The Liberated Librarian? A Look at the *Second Sex* in the Library Profession" by Salem (Massachusetts) State College librarian Janet Lois Freedman.[4]

Synergy consistently included information about neglected topics. The April-May, 1968 issue, for example, criticized conventional library literature's lack of attention to subjects like astrology, Native Americans, the women's liberation movement, ecology, the drug revolution, library service to prisoners, the occult, the family, the underground press, and the criticisms of the establishment. In subsequent issues, *Synergy* provided coverage of these and other topics. But *Synergy* stood for more than just information access. Under West's direction, it called on librarians to become "pivotal agents to enforce" the Library Bill of Rights, to support a free press, and to develop a new professional attitude by shifting from "conserving and organizing" information to "generating or promoting it."[5] *Synergy* defined an alternative library culture that worried less about the library as a keeper of the cultural record, and more about the library as an active agent for change.

By the summer of 1967, other librarians began adopting *Synergy's* philosophy. For example, at the ALA conference in San Francisco a group of librarians picketed a meeting, cosponsored by the Adult Services Division and the Council on Foreign Relations, at which Maxwell D. Taylor delivered a pro-war speech titled "U.S. Foreign Policy in S.E. Asia." Approximately 150 people (students, hippies, and librarians) rallied outside the conference hotel waving signs that read "Books Not Bullets" and "This is a Taylor-made Demonstration." Inside, librarians demonstrated at the entrance to Taylor's banquet room.[6] The protest showed an emerging political movement within librarianship in general, and ALA in particular.[7]

Then in December, Bundy published a report in *Wilson Library Bulletin* on factors that influenced public library use, and concluded that the profession had failed to meet its responsibility to a changing society. While "extraordinary educational, political, economic, social and technological changes" had occurred and the culture in which libraries functioned had "dramatically altered," the public library had "stood still, caught in the straitjacket of its traditional view of itself and the world, by its historical commitments, and by its clienteles."[8] Coincidentally, on December 1, 1967, ALA took an unprecedented step and opened its Office for Intellectual Freedom to protect commitment to the Library Bill of Rights by individual librarians — both in their professional and personal lives.

The Office for Intellectual Freedom was born of a 1965 recommendation by the Intellectual Freedom Committee to ALA's Executive Board that "an office be established at Headquarters through which legal support [for librarians] could be provided." After the Office for Intellectual Freedom opened on December 1, the Intellectual Freedom Committee focused solely on policy development.[9] Library activists were not appeased by the opening of ALA's new bureau.

By 1968, ten ALA members began informally meeting to discuss an alternative library agenda within the Association structure: Dorothy Bendix (Graduate School of Library Science, Drexel Institute of Technology), Bessie Bullock (Brooklyn Public Library), Verner Clapp (president, Council on Library Resources, Inc., Washington, D.C.), Kenneth Duhac (Division of Library Extension, Maryland State Department of Education), Norman Finkler (Montgomery County, Maryland, Department of Public Libraries), Rachel Gross (Huntington Valley, Pennsylvania, Public Library trustee), Allen T. Hazen (Columbia University School of Library Service), Evelyn Levy (Enoch Pratt Free Library), H. Thomas Walker (Maryland Division of Library Extension), and Benjamin Weintraub (Graduate School of Library Service, Rutgers). Uncomfortable with ALA's "neutral" position on social concerns, they exchanged views about lobbying the Association "to demonstrate a sense of responsibility" on non-library issues.[10] Most were unwilling to separate their politics from their work, most wanted the library profession to take a stand on social issues, and most based their proactive stance on the Library Bill of Rights.

Library Journal columnist Leonard H. Freiser dubbed the activist group the "Bendix-Duhac establishment" after Dorothy Bendix — the group's thoughtful "guiding spirit" of the library social responsibility movement — and Kenneth Duhac — its impassioned "eloquent spokesman" — took leadership roles.[11] Both were seasoned librarians, researchers, and ALA members who recognized that instituting rapid changes in the Association required unusual tactics. The Association had 14 divisions, 58 state, regional and territorial chapters, 12 affiliated organizations, and a total membership that exceeded 35,000. It was the world's oldest and largest national library association and its complex structure and slow pace presented an impediment to anyone who wanted quick action.[12]

While *Synergy* exemplified the important connection between the new librarianship and the social message of the alternative press, it was not sufficiently influential to carry the movement forward. And while library activists had a common interest in this press and often made contacts and connections through it, they still lacked a mechanism for organizing their more general social justice efforts. Thus, Bendix formed a plan to radicalize the profession through the formation of a new ALA round table. In May, 1968, just weeks before the summer conference in Kansas City, she initiated a coalition called the Organizing Committee for ALA Round Table on Social Responsibilities of Libraries. Because ALA Bylaws, specifically Article VII, Sec. 1, stated that at least 50 signatures were required to establish a round table, the committee drafted a petition on June 11, which stated that the proposed round table's function and responsibility were to provide a forum and propose activities to improve the understanding of contemporary social issues.[13]

By June 19, Duhac had received 78 signatures — enough to forward the petition to ALA's Committee on Organization (COO). Committee chairman Robert Sheridan (director, Levittown, New York Public Library) received the petition on June 19, just five days before the conference began. By June 24, after nearly 270 ALA members had signed the petition, COO determined it had merit and began the process of gathering Divisional opinions (e.g., Adult Services Division, Children's Services Division, Library Education Division, Reference Services Division, etc.) for basing its ultimate recommendation to ALA's Executive Board and Council.

More than 6,500 librarians arrived in Kansas City in the third week of June to face, among other things, "90-plus degree temperatures and sputtering air conditioning." They "shuffled through the heat" with a "round-eyed, panting expression" and dragged their feet six blocks to the Kansas City Public Library opening reception on June 22 and the 809 meetings which followed on subsequent days. To many, conference activities seemed normal. The Friends of the Library section was "spellbound" by luncheon with speaker Alex Haley, the Newbery-Caldecott section attended a "sparkling affair" at the Imperial Ballroom at the Muehlbach Hotel, and the Program Evaluation and Budget Committee (PEBCO) met for long hours, "day and night," in an effort to finalize the budget for the next fiscal year. And an unusually large number of attendees "shivered in the blast of a suddenly over-eager air conditioner" at the first Council session on June 25.[14]

But the 1968 conference proved to be anything but normal. The first hint of dissent came when Intellectual Freedom Committee chairman Ervin J. Gaines (director, Minneapolis Public Library) addressed the ALA Council on June 25. Because the protection which ALA provided to its members in the battle for intellectual freedom was often insufficient, he argued, "the Association, has, in effect, cut its members adrift and let them survive as best they could." To address this shortcoming, he presented a resolution that called for support of librarians who upheld intellectual freedom principles expressed in the Library Bill of Rights. In addition,

Gaines asked the Intellectual Freedom Committee to explore the possibility of establishing a support fund for librarians. His motion passed to "resounding applause from both [the] Council and [the] audience."[15]

The second hint of dissent came when PEBCO chair Mary V. Gaver presented committee recommendations for the Association's future, including one that "no new divisions, sections, and subsections, as well as round tables, committees, or other subunits of the Association, be created in 1968-69 except in cases of extreme urgency." Not long into this meeting, the general membership and the Council members recognized that the conference would not be routine. That evening "the rumor mills" set into motion as conversations carried on past midnight in "some smoke filled rooms."[16]

By the time the Membership meeting got under way the next afternoon, no veteran ALA conference goer "could fail to detect a new spirit and tempo" and a "distinct stirring" in the air.[17] The session took place in the huge Municipal Auditorium where "a sizable crowd, laden with shopping bags filled with exhibit hand outs, nearly filled the main floor and most of the side boxes."[18]

When Duhac moved to form a new round table that addressed social responsibilities of libraries, he requested the Council and others to act quickly to avoid ALA's normal delays. In particular, he wanted the Membership to instruct Council to request COO to report their decision to the Executive Board at this conference. He also requested that any COO or Executive Board decision on the round table be reported to Council at its June 28 meeting.[19] A "parade" of speakers then supported his motion.[20]

Charles O'Halloran (state librarian, Missouri State Library) said that the proposed social responsibility group "could be a kind of conscience of the Association." Robert Johnson (librarian, University of Arizona) noted, "we are debating something, as before with integration, which should be undebatable." Emily Copeland (head, Department of Library Service, Florida A&M University) asserted that the proposed round table was needed to open up communication, because "We say hello, how are you, fine and all that, but we don't really understand each other or our problems."[21] Others, such as leading library civil rights activist E.J. Josey (New York State Division of Library Development), argued that the establishment of such a group was necessary to move ALA out of business-as-usual.

Most of the opposition to Duhac's motion came from people who argued against moving the ALA machinery at "an unseemly pace." In particular, COO chairman Robert Sheridan objected to pressure placed on his committee. Duhac's motion, however, "finally passed easily" and at 5 p.m. ALA President Foster E. Morhardt (director, National Agriculture Library,

United States Department of Agriculture) attempted to meet with Council to discuss the Duhac motion, but he had no quorum. "Cocktail parties clearly beckoned," *Library Journal* noted. The periodical also observed that, "with few exceptions (such as the integration battles of the early 1960s)," never had a Membership meeting created such "a ripple of interest or dissent."[22]

At nine o'clock the next morning, the Council held a special session to discuss the formation of a social responsibilities round table. Morhardt presided. After COO chairman Sheridan reported action taken at the Membership meeting, initial opposition came from councilors who believed that ALA should use its "normal machinery." Sheridan himself said Duhac's motion was "an attempt to exert pressure" on his committee, and that it put the Council in a position of "bowing to the most brazen power play" the Association had witnessed in ten years.[23] Many Council members agreed with Sheridan's reluctance to abandon due process.

Verner Clapp stated that while he supported the round table formation, he was also in favor of following established procedures and would therefore vote against the motion. Gaines argued that if Council adopted Duhac's motion it would set a precedent hard to resist in the future, and that "to abrogate" the normal machinery even a little bit was "to begin the long slow descent to anarchy." He then indicated that it was inappropriate for ALA to take sides on issues that lay beyond its "professional horizons." He also denigrated petitioners as "all hot-eyed and panting" and likened the previous day's debate to a "revolt against the iron-booted tyranny of bureaucracy."[24]

Other Council members deemed Duhac's motion problematic because ALA's existing organizational structure already provided the requested forum. While some councilors argued that nothing prevented any organized ALA unit from scheduling meetings on the subjects in question, others insisted that Duhac's request would unduly stress the Association's finances.[25] Howard Rovelstad (director of libraries, University of Maryland) wondered if the proposed round table might influence or effect ALA's "extremely favorable tax status." He feared the Internal Revenue Service (IRS) might revoke it if ALA engaged in non-educational activities.[26] Preserving the tax-exempt status had its costs, Robert McClarren later wrote in a 1970 issue of *American Libraries*: The ALA had to limit lobbying efforts, be nonpartisan, and not devote "a substantial amount of its resources to influence legislation."[27]

But not everyone at the special Council session opposed Duhac's motion. As one of the original petitioners, Evelyn Levy argued that signees did not intend "any kind of power play," nor did they want to "start a revolution." She noted that the Membership deserved an opportunity to discuss the library's place in society and its responsibilities. Jovian Lang expressed surprise that the Council underestimated and misread the "type of revolution that is occurring on certain campuses and other places in the United States." While he conceded petitioners appeared "much worked up," he disingenuously added they were not "emotionally involved." In his view the "so-called revolution" inherent in the petition was a "very controlled and sensible one" and he suggested that it was a testing ground for ALA's governance. For ALA to ignore it, he cautioned, would lead to trouble.[28]

After floor discussion, the Council agreed that the proposed time limit for approving the new round table would most likely not allow the petitioning group to formulate its purpose statement and meet other obligations necessary to launch a new Association activity. The Council also determined that the round table needed a more complete responsibility statement to identify areas of overlap with other ALA units and ALA needed more time to examine the impact such a unit might have on its tax-exempt status. Council then approved the round table's formation. By a vote of 62 to 57, it chose June 28 as the date by which the round table should be established.

At the second scheduled Council meeting on June 28, Sheridan announced that the Council would re visit the subject of a round table on social responsibilities at ALA's 1969 midwinter meeting. Duhac showed "cool patience" in an attempt to control an "overheated situation" and thanked COO for the prompt consideration of his petition. He added that from the beginning, the group intended "to work in a responsible fashion within normal channels."[29] Finally, he announced that a meeting would be held that afternoon to discuss the functions, purposes, and responsibilities of the proposed round table.

But Ralph Blasingame (associate professor, Graduate School of Library Service, Rutgers) was incensed. In what *Library Journal* called a "pungently critical"[30] final speech as ALA's Council Treasurer, he complained that ALA was an old Association controlled by old people, and that "the same names and faces turn up on committees, on offices, on Council, year after year." He argued that ALA was a bureaucracy ruled by members of other bureaucracies who were "marvelously able to ignore the climate of membership, to alter policies without seeming to and to locate the treasured young people who are prone to socialization." Finally, he stated that discussions of major issues in the Executive Board meetings were too often "challenges and defenses of the status quo rather than searches for new or even different courses of action."[31] *Library Journal* reported that Blasingame's speech sent "shock waves" around the large arena. For the remainder of the conference "it was unquestionably the top corridor discussion item," while Blasingame "appeared more and more the lone heretic among the top hierarchy."[32]

Later that day, a group of approximately 100 ALA members attended the first meeting of the proposed Round Table on Social Responsibilities of Libraries. Attendees discussed a number of sensitive subjects: more accountability from ALA elected officials, the needs of the public at large, the Association's operational structure, details of recruitment, and intellectual freedom. They also passed a hat around to collect support for organizing efforts.

The stir in Kansas City did not go unnoticed by ALA's incoming president. In his inaugural speech near the close of the conference, Roger McDonough referred to the "considerable psychological distance" between "those of us who came out of the genteel librarianship" and "the younger element" in the profession.[33] But Eric Moon, *Library Journal*'s editor, argued a generation gap existed not in ALA's membership, but in its Council.[34] With the exception of Council meetings, he maintained, demands for change voiced at Kansas City were "broadly based, coming in some cases from high places in the ALA hierarchy."[35] Patricia Schuman (New York City Community College) asserted that while not all the activists were young, many junior ALA members "were already establishment."[36] And Jesse Shera observed that the one problem with the call for change in ALA was that "we do not know whom we are criticizing, for we do not know where the power center in ALA lies, or who the Establishment is." "We assume," he wrote, "it is the Executive Board, but the profession has grown and with this growth in numbers has come a lessening of the individual voice, an increasing delegation of authority to the hands of the selected few, and the ever-present problems of making democracy work."[37] On July 1, E.J. Josey wrote Bendix that the Organizing Committee for ALA Round Table on Social Responsibilities of Libraries needed to "avoid sounding and acting like the Council." He believed the round table should exert pressure "through every conceivable mechanism to create an intellectual confrontation" that would force ALA to become more socially responsible.[38]

On September 21, the Organizing Committee held a meeting at Drexel Institute of Technology that drew about 100 librarians from "as near-by as New York City and as far away as Missouri and Florida."[39] President McDonough attended the meeting briefly and pledged his support, but after he left, attendees got down to the business of defining social responsibility and determining its relationship to librarians, libraries and ALA. All agreed to focus on seven questions — (1) What did social responsibility mean? (2) What were the group's social responsibilities? (3) What were the social problems of the library and of librarians? (4) What were the functions of the round table? (5) What were the priorities of the round table? (6) What was to be done next? and (7) How would a relationship with other round tables be established?[40] Discussion of these questions led the group to several conclusions. It agreed to address ALA members both as private citizens and as librarians, to try to get ALA involved in the total community and social issues, to attract and involve younger and less active ALA members, to put pressure on COO and ALA's president to establish the round table, to initiate regional activity, and to convince people it was serious by providing concrete examples of what the round table would do.

In response to the latter, Emily Copeland, an African-American ALA member who had expressly traveled from Baltimore to discuss race, noted that although ALA had insisted on the integration of state library associations, it did not guarantee the right of black librarians to be involved in Southern library associations. This issue alone, Copeland noted, exemplified the need for social responsibility in the profession.[41] Immediately, George Hathaway (Brooklyn College) suggested that a group of New York city librarians form an experimental regional round table concerned with race to be a model for a broader based organization on the social responsibilities of libraries. Patricia Schuman, Joan Marshall (Brooklyn College), Jackie Pelduz (Brooklyn College), Betty-Carol Sellen (Brooklyn College), and Kathleen Weibel (student, Columbia University School of Library Service) volunteered, and after they returned to New York, created the New York Round Table on the Social Responsibilities of Libraries (NYS-RRT) and began to meet weekly in order to determine a course of action.[42] Soon, Marilyn Berg (New York Public Library), Miriam Braverman (student, Columbia University School of Library Service), Jean Coleman (Bookmobile Service Trust), John Clune (Kingsborough Community College), Roberta Consgrove (student, Pratt Institute Library School), Sanford Goin (librarian, Holt, Rinehart and Winston), Barbara Shapiro (New York Public Library), and Janet Siegel (New York Public Library) joined the team.[43]

The New York SRRT focused on finding a viable demonstration project, but when volunteers contacted several local agencies, they were surprised to discover that the city's social activists had no idea how librarians could be of use. Only after an Urban League representative suggested NYS-RRT might want to work alongside other librarians did things start to fall into place. The group's members then focused on the New York City public school teachers' strike over issues of decentralization and community control of local school districts (i.e., Ocean Hill–Brownsville). The dispute had strong racial overtones. Parents were mostly poor and black, teachers mostly white people who belonged to a union led by Albert Shanker, a well-known liberal, white, Jewish trade unionist. To favor community control was often interpreted as anti–Semitic, to oppose it was often interpreted as anti-black. Meanwhile, hate literature openly circulated in both Jewish and black Brooklyn districts. The NYSRRT resolved to improve access to information about the strike because many librarians worked in the school system and the fields of librarianship and education were both feminized service professions. Also, the strike seemed appropriate for a trial project because it was an opportunity to apply library skills to a community need.

Members of NYSRRT began gathering handbills, leaflets, articles, mimeographed sheets, and petition statements. They also attended meetings, approached organizations, and even visited picket lines. They then compiled all this information into biweekly bibliographies which they duplicated and ultimately disseminated through interlibrary loan from the New York Community College of the City University of New York to libraries, librarians, parent groups, and other organizations such as the United Federation of College Teachers and the Commission on Human Rights.

In January, 1969, advocates for an ALA Round Table on Social Responsibilities of Libraries traveled to ALA's midwinter conference in Washington, D.C. They arrived with a report on the successful NYSRRT project, fortified with the support of the Library Association of the City University of New York and news that the California Library Association had also created a committee on the social responsibilities of libraries. Although they were prepared to do battle with ALA's establishment, it proved unnecessary.

In his midterm report at the first Council session, President McDonough said he was "glad to report some substantial progress" towards a more responsive ALA, "particularly in terms of the formation of the Round Table on the Social Responsibilities of Libraries." Although COO's recommendation for the establishment of the round table was not on the agenda until the second Council session, McDonough's support forecast the outcome. On January 30, the Council voted unanimously to approve the formation of the Round Table on Social Responsibilities of Libraries (RTSRL), informally called SRRT. However, COO cautioned Council that the round table could not set ALA policy or incur expenses on behalf of ALA, and could be dissolved once its purpose had been met. These "admonitions," reported Library Journal, "came from the ALA Bylaws" and were "carefully spelled out" in Sheridan's recommendation from COO.[44]

Although at Kansas City "some councilors expressed strong antipathy to the very idea of the round table," six months later RTSRL received unanimous support. Sellen speculated on the reason —"the term of office of all the antipathetic councilors" had expired following the Kansas city meeting.[45] She may have been right, but one "council old-timer, a back bench conservative," told *Library Journal* that he regretted not opposing the idea on the floor, but was convinced the round table "can't do anything anyway." *Library Journal* saw it all differently. While "the young, the babies of the profession and ALA" were given "a nod" at midwinter, "it will be a muted voice from that new round table if it lives completely within the proscriptions of ALA Bylaws and the Statement of Purpose that ALA gave it."[46]

The next day RTSRL held its first official organizational meeting. Bendix served as temporary chair and opened the meeting by thanking librarians who had come to Washington on their own time and money. She also thanked COO for speedy action in establishing the round table. The people at the head table were then introduced.[47] Schuman, Hathaway, and Sellen presented a NYSRRT report which led to a lively and at times adversarial discussion of the controversial New York City teachers' strike. Afterwards, when Bendix pointed out that ALA bylaws required all round tables to have a formal structure, attendees engaged in a lengthy debate about how to organize the round table.[48]

For an hour or two the group faltered until Duhac angrily observed, "We're acting like an ALA group already, let's take some action to get organized now."[49] Arthur Curley (director, Palatine, Illinois, Public Library) then nominated Duhac to be RTSRL's temporary or Steering Committee chair, but Duhac refused both posts. Instead, he moved that the group elect an Organization Committee of seven members (including a chair) to set up RTSRL's permanent organization, a By-Laws Committee, and a Program Committee to prepare for ALA's summer conference in Atlantic City. The motion passed. At this point, William T. DeJohn (community affairs librarian, Missouri State Library) volunteered to serve on the Organizing Committee, and urged those interested in joining him to move to the front of the room so they could be seen. Nina Ladof (director, St. Charles County, Missouri, Library) then moved that the large number of volunteers be permitted to get the group down to seven and to select a chair, while the rest of the attendees start a general discussion on RTSRL's areas of concern. The motion was seconded and passed.[50]

Except for the Organizing Committee volunteers, attendees then got down to the business of identifying social issues most important to their new round table. Their lengthy list of concerns read like a catalogue. Josey suggested the round table address the problems of black librarians; Henry

Kaperstein (Free Library of Philadelphia) addressed inner-city needs; Mary Ann Russell (librarian, Arlington, Virginia, County Public Library) thought that library education lacked social awareness; and Joan E. Clark (New York State Library) argued for more autonomy for neighborhood and branch libraries. Others spoke about service to prison inmates and migrant workers, the stagnancy of the library institution, as well as of war and peace. Meanwhile, once again the group passed around a shopping bag to collect contributions.

Eventually the Organizing Committee returned with a membership: William T. DeJohn (chair), Duhac, Betty-Carol Sellen, Marjorie Barker (Prince George's County, Maryland, Memorial Library), Charles Weisenberg (Los Angeles Public Library), Margaret Turanski (Free Library of Philadelphia), and Marshall Leventer (position unknown).[51] With the exception of Duhac, no one else had been a member of the "Bendix-Duhac establishment." By the time conference attendees left Washington, RTSRL had secured a place in ALA, selected its Organizing Committee, and begun the lengthy process of identifying key social concerns for librarians.

After midwinter, RTSRL members began consolidating their position in ALA. Schuman (Program Committee chair) arranged a RTSRL session for the summer Atlantic City conference and Eubanks (By-laws Committee chair) planned a report on RTSRL's structure. DeJohn authored "READY FOR ACTION!"—a short information bulletin which stated that the round table would function both as an ALA conscience and as a pressure group by promoting discussion on the library's role in society, supporting information exchange between ALA units, and stimulating ALA's responsiveness to society's needs.[52] The RTSRL mailed the document "to all those interested in the ALA Round Table on Social Responsibilities of Libraries" on March 13.

But the ALA administration's spirit of accommodation had limits. An official ALA report on aids to collection building published in the *ALA Bulletin* failed to mention *Synergy*.[53] That may have been an oversight. But three other incidents occurred that winter that convinced library activists that in order to define the library's role in society, intellectual confrontations had to take place within ALA. It all started in Missouri where on February 12, 1969, several SDS members handed out copies of two alternative publications—*The New Left Notes* and *The Movement*—from a booth in the University's Student Union building. Their alternative press work was activist, but not radical. By this time, for example, more radical members of the student movement had splintered off from the SDS. However, after the dean of students ordered them to stop distribution of these "vulgar" publications and an official University student publication titled *The Free*

Press Underground reprinted an "obscene" cartoon and an article from The *New Left Notes* on February 19, the situation escalated. Campus police ordered *The Free Press Underground* employees, some of whom were SDS members, to leave the University grounds. After they began selling the paper on a public sidewalk nearby, county sheriffs placed four under arrest and seized the paper.[54]

That weekend Joan H. Bodger, children's consultant to Children's Services at the State Library of Missouri and one who routinely conducted public workshops on censorship, drafted a protest. But before making the missive public, she cleared it with Associate State Librarian Susanna Alexander and State Librarian Charles O'Halloran. *The Columbia Tribune* published Bodger's protest on February 26. Within days other Missouri papers were flooded with editorials and letters condemning Bodger, Alexander, and O'Halloran.[55]

In response the State Library Commission started an investigation. Although O'Halloran defended Bodger by citing principles of intellectual freedom outlined in the Library Bill of Rights, the Commission asked Bodger to stop censorship workshops, which had heretofore been part of her job. Bodger felt unable to carry out her professional duties and on April 7 she submitted a resignation letter that stated that "the Commission has tied the hands of the State Library and forced the State Librarian to *suggest* that I refrain from my normal duties." But the Commission refused to accept Bodger's resignation and instead dismissed her on April 8.[56] The Missouri State Library Association rallied to Bodger's defense.[57]

In the midst of the Bodger affair, another event occurred, this one at the University of Maryland where School of Library and Information Studies (SLIS) students and faculty were meeting over the issue of inner-city recruitment, and where at about the same time 30 activist students from ten schools had gathered "to identify themselves and their ideas to one another."[58] For two days in March, students discussed how library schools and library education needed to change, to diversify, and to become more relevant to society. Their meeting ran well past midnight, and eventually wandered into a broader call for the library's involvement in social change. At the conclusion of the meeting, the gathering planned to appeal to those already in the profession who desired change. Their immediate aim was to organize a national conference of library school students and other like-minded librarians. James C. Welbourne (president, Maryland SLIS Student Group) initiated action and circulated a letter of concern to 14 other library schools.[59]

Before the library school representatives met in Washington in June, a spring symposium on "Public Library Service to the Black Urban Poor" held at Wayne State University issued a document titled the "Friday the 13th Manifesto" which stated "the social crises of the cities have brought people into conflict with the Establishment," that librarianship "reflects the values and attitudes of the Establishment," and that "present" priorities were established in response to the articulated needs of the power structure not the unarticulated needs of those outside the power structure. The missive concluded that because "the library profession has been neither neutral nor objective," it must immediately adopt a "philosophy of *advocacy* in every respect of its service to the urban poor."[60]

As a result of the College Park meeting, the "Friday the 13th Manifesto," and "discussions and the confrontations going on at other campuses," the Congress for Change (CFC) was born.[61] On June 19, *Wilson Library Bulletin* noted, 180 "youngish people dedicated to smashing the status quo" came to Washington, D.C., from library schools in New York, Pennsylvania, and Maryland. About 30 years old on the average, the "shaggy-faced, long-haired, or wide-eyed [students] behind giant, steel-rimmed, tinted sunglasses,"[62] jammed into "a plasticplush meeting room" in the "mangy" Manger-Annapolis Hotel.[63] According to *Wilson Library Bulletin's* reporters, they were "properly threadbare in chinos or summery culottes," and wore yellow buttons with black lettering that read "Libraries to the People."[64] *Library Journal* editor John Berry described them as

> a mere hundred, arrogant enough to take on a 93-year old, 40,000 member association; naive enough to expect that others would believe with them that its services and servants were tired and worn, that its connections with society and community were somehow false, somehow so tenuous as to be irrelevant.[65]

With "a very light touch" James C. Welbourne presided over a 36 hour "floating debate" that moved from the Smithsonian auditorium to hotel rooms to Federal City College. *Wilson Library Bulletin* noted "there was not a potted palm or silver punch bowl" in the hotel, and that it was "a welcome change just to be talking about poverty and the disadvantaged without being surrounded by cut flowers and Hiltonian opulence that have come to form the setting for most library conferences."[66] The group participated in general sessions, workshops and all-night discussions on how social movements applied to library education and careers. In particular, the unstructured meeting included among its topics the Berkeley Free Speech Movement, Vietnam, anti–ballistic missile systems, ALA election reform, library education, and recruitment. On all issues, delegates expressed a diversity of opinions and agendas. Despite their differences, however, they agreed on a set of statements to be presented at ALA's upcoming Atlantic City Membership meeting, and called themselves the CFC.

Unlike RTSRL, the Congress for Change was intended neither to become part of ALA's structure nor to be an ongoing pressure group. Rather it was a one-time event designed to bring concerned individuals together. As RTSRL member Carolyn Forsman once put it, the CFC "was more an experience than an organization."[67] Its purpose was strictly to make waves in Atlantic City. And "without a cooling off period," many CFC delegates went directly to the ALA conference. Some library activists suspected that members of the "old Guard" gathered on the "elitist Atlantic City" board walk and waited anxiously to hear from them. Perhaps they heard that the "radicals" were coming to make demands.[68]

When the conference started, about 10,250 librarians congregated in Atlantic City. No ALA conference had drawn so many members before and the scale of everything was big — there were 700 exhibit booths, dinners for 3,000 people, and divisional meetings for 1,000 and 2,000 ALA members. Despite the grandiose atmosphere, however, John Berry noted, "we had less time for old convention pleasures, all night card games or marathon cocktail parties — it was an action meeting."[69]

On June 25, between 3,000 and 4,000 people flocked to the first Membership meeting at the convention hall's Grand Ballroom to hear a long discussion on ALA's structure and purpose. While Albert P. Marshall (Lincoln University, Missouri) and Lester Stoffel (Suburban Library System, West Springs, Illinois) presented parallel motions on the establishment of a committee to study the Association's goals and future, incoming ALA president William S. Dix (Princeton University) announced that such a committee — the Activities Committee for New Directions for ALA (ACONDA) — had already been recommended to him by the Executive Board in their June 23 meeting. After "the basic issues involved in changing the ALA were sunk in a malodorous parliamentary quagmire,"[70] ACONDA's statement of purpose and committee selection procedures were established. The Executive Board would nominate 12 members. The President would select the first six on his own and another six from JMRT and RTSRL nominations. The President would also appoint a thirteenth person as ACONDA's chair. In effect, the committee's composition would be a curious mixture of ALA's "radicals" and "mossbacks."[71] As a result, ACONDA was soon called the "Dix Mix."[72]

The ACONDA marked ALA's first major organizational response to the Kansas City and Washington, D.C., conferences. *Wilson Library Bulletin* reported that although probably few CFC/RTSRL members knew it,

Dix "shared most of their concerns." He had fought McCarthy's attacks on libraries, chaired the Intellectual Freedom Committee from 1951 to 1953, and chaired the joint committee with the American Book Publisher's Council in the drafting of the "Freedom to Read Statement."[73]

After the ACONDA announcement, outgoing President McDonough presented the CFC to the packed general Membership meeting. Welbourne then introduced CFC delegates, some of whom read statements agreed to at their organizational meeting, all of whom revealed that like RTSRL, CFC delegates would not separate politics from work when it came to "race, violence, war and peace, inequality of justice and opportunity."[74] Syracuse University Graduate School of Library Science student Leila Davis, a CFC delegate who did not belong to ALA, read the first statement. She arrogantly announced that the CFC was a temporary alliance organized to prompt ALA to be more relevant and flexible, and demanded that the Association take substantive action on reforming itself by midwinter or CFC members would discourage professionals from joining ALA.[75] Membership booed because, as Edward G. Holley observed, "ALA was, right now, listening to the voices of the young ... was willing to change...."[76]

Second, Daniel Boone Regional Library (Columbia, Missouri) librarian and ALA member John Goddard read a CFC statement which addressed the issue of lack of support for librarians embattled in intellectual freedom issues. The statement echoed an action program proposed by the Intellectual Freedom Committee. Ellen Gay Detlefsen, a recent graduate of the Columbia University library school and a student ALA member, then presented curriculum-centered proposals for immediate consideration and implementation by ALA's Board of Education for Librarianship and the American Association of Library Schools. She suggested that the accrediting process lacked relevance to contemporary professional needs and that standards were too low. She also urged that accreditation be turned over to the American Association of Library Schools, where both students and new professionals would participate in writing new standards as well as in the accreditation process.[77]

Thomas Bonn, another Syracuse student but also an ALA member, read the fourth CFC statement. He requested that the Board reconsider the conference site. To support his request, he cited events at the 1968 Democratic Convention and the political machinery that ran Chicago as his reasons. Renee Feinberg from New York asked ALA not to support the nation's anti-ballistic missile systems program. Social responsibilities round table member Christine Patterson followed with a CFC statement condemning the nation's participation in the undeclared war in Vietnam. Then, Welbourne read the "Friday the 13th Manifesto" and announced that CFC delegates supported "the intrinsic right of every individual to participate fully in the decisions which affect his life." He then urged ALA professionals to take responsibility for encouraging and serving the public in its search for "self-determination."[78]

New York librarian Billie Wilson read the seventh and final CFC statement. She called ALA "stagnant" and unresponsive to librarians and the problems they faced. Wilson also stated that young members could not see meaningful ways to participate in the Association and finally requested that by midwinter ALA tackle various issues, including enforcing its standards in various states, backing the Intellectual Freedom Committee proposals with a support fund, establishing sanctions against institutions which did not adhere to the Library Bill of Rights, considering the previous year's recommendation for election reform, publishing a detailed breakdown of election results in the *ALA Bulletin*, doing more in terms of exploring manpower possibilities (especially for paraprofessionals), and reevaluating recruitment policies for minorities.[79] The CFC had thrown down the gauntlet. A resolution that all CFC statements be printed in the *ALA Bulletin* passed immediately, while the remaining CFC resolutions were not put to a vote until the second Membership meeting.

Surrounded by this atmosphere, RTSRL drew a crowd of 300 librarians at its June 26 business meeting, where DeJohn "continued to display the cool ease and authority that had carried him" through CFC, the conference, and the many late night informal sessions.[80] He began the meeting with a brief description of the action taken at the midwinter conference, including the establishment of RTSRL's By-Laws and Program Committees. But most of the meeting dealt with mapping out the round table's four-level structure. While other ALA round tables were run by Steering Committees, RTSRL resolved to take direction from an Action Council in order to highlight action-oriented work. The RTSRL also agreed that its Action Council should increase from seven to ten elected members, chosen from volunteers who placed themselves for nomination by platform statements. In order to fill the Action Council positions, DeJohn asked the existing members who wished to serve for another year to stand. Seven wanted to remain; only two more were needed. Patricia Schuman and Ruthanne Boyer (Deerfield, Illinois, Public Library) were eventually elected. Then, RTSRL voted unanimously to retain DeJohn as RTSRL Action Council Coordinator, quite unlike other ALA round tables, which were directed by a chair or a president.

In addition to the Action Council, RTSRL discussed three other units. First, DeJohn announced that the Clearinghouse Committee (Schuman, chair) — charged with managing communications for ALA and non–ALA members via a national quarterly publication titled *SRRT Newsletter*—needed five more people. George Hathaway, Billie Wilson, Joan Goddard, Diana Vescelius (Akron Public Library), and Ruby O. Woods (position unknown) were elected. Second, instead of ALA's usual round table Standing Committees, RTSRL opted to create task forces at the will of any group of members. These task forces would be problem-oriented, would go out of existence at the end of each year unless purposely continued by interested members, and would be comprised of volunteers, not appointees. Task forces were established on library education, intellectual freedom, black librarians, community participation in libraries, humanization of library personnel, ALA reorganization, and publishing. Third, RTSRL decided to encourage non–ALA members to affiliate with the round table through local groups.

DeJohn next addressed the need to nominate six members to ACONDA. He asked for volunteers who would be willing "to read the ALA Constitution, work like hell, and travel."[81] Of the 13 RTSRL members who volunteered, the six selected were George Alfred, Jackie Eubanks, Arthur Curley, William Hinchcliff, Gordon McShean, and Patricia Ternes. Finally, Ellen Gay Detlefsen reported on CFC platforms, after which RTSRL moved that DeJohn present CFC resolutions as individual motions at the next day's Membership meeting.

That same evening, while over 2,000 members squeezed into the Traymore Hotel's Grand Ballroom to hear the culmination of the Newbery-Caldecott children's book award activity, in a room at the Dennis Hotel Schuman hosted what many delegates considered "by far the most interesting and provocative" convention program.[82] The RTSRL had asked for a room to seat 600, but 800 people pushed in "to see what the young rebels — who had been meeting late each night and causing some minor tremors — were up to." Another 500 were turned away at the door. While some skeptics came expecting "haranguing," instead they witnessed a "dazzling" session titled "The Failure of Libraries: A Call to Action." Major Owens (commissioner, Community Development Agency of the Human Resources Administration of the City of New York) moderated the program and set the evening's tone. He spoke about the need for librarians to make themselves relevant to society and asserted, "it is our duty and obligation to participate and to register as much influence as possible for peace and against the barbaric war in Vietnam." Owens later "brought down the house" when he asked "Meanwhile, back at the library schools — what is being done?"[83]

A provocative multi-media essay on the rape of the American Indian caught the crowd's attention before John H. Black (chairman, Student Association Council, Columbia University School of Library Service) took the floor. Black urged library schools to open their doors to "let down the admissions barriers and allow people from poverty and ghetto areas" to receive library training and help their communities. Then Geraldine Clark (Bureau of Libraries, New York City Board of Education) presented an audio-visual piece on the grape picker's strike in California. In her accompanying speech, she attacked the "current library practices that support the upper and middle class white culture and measure all others against that standard." The program's closing words were "hard-hitting" to the "establishment gathered in the room." Brigitte L. Kenney, a research associate at the University of Mississippi Medical Center, asked later, "What brought so many? Curiosity or real concern? We will never know, but no one in that room could fail to be touched by what was being said."[84]

At the June 27 Membership meeting, ALA's Executive Director David H. Clift read a request from Robert Johnson (University of Arizona) that called for cancelling the 1970 site for ALA's midwinter meeting in Chicago because of the way the city had handled incidents during the Democratic National Convention in 1968. While some members voiced the opinion that a cancellation would be an effective protest to the city's government, others worried that such an act might endanger the city's support of the Chicago Public Library. The request was turned down by 578 to 299 votes.[85] Next, DeJohn asked that CFC position statements be read as resolutions and that, this time, membership vote on each. The first resolution passed — ALA election candidates would make platform statements and election results would be counted and publicized. The second CFC resolution — that ALA take a stand against the war in Vietnam — caused such a lengthy discussion it had to be postponed until after the second Council meeting at noon of the same day.[86] Later that afternoon, over 500 people turned up for the final Membership session. "Tempers grew loud and ugly" over the resolution to oppose the Vietnam war, which was defeated 294 to 208.[87] Next, three more CFC proposals came up for debate and were disposed of as follows: first, membership defeated the anti-ballistic missile system motion; second, it voted that ALA turn over library school accreditation to the American Association of Library Schools; and third, it voted to examine and revitalize ALA's recruitment policies for minorities. Thus in the two years since the San Francisco protest, library activists had made some substantial progress. Because they had become "more sophisticated and varied in their responses" to social issues, Carolyn Forsman noted, they had moved from "hastily formed picketing to petitions," to resolutions at Kansas City and Atlantic City, to "planned political pressure, investigation, reports and fund raising."[88] Furthermore, they had garnered support from varied sources.

"I think you have performed a most constructive service for your-selves, for the ALA, and for librarianship generally," R.R. Bowker company president George M. McCorkle wrote DeJohn after the conference. "It is good to feel the winds of change blowing and I think a great many people at Atlantic City shared that feeling. All of you are to be congratulated, and I hope you will keep your movement going as successfully as it has started."[89] In *Library Journal*'s August issue, Berry thanked Schuman and her Program Committee for the "outstanding" RTSRL program and also extended thanks to CFC for assistance during the conference, "especially during the program and membership meetings." At the same time, however, he posed a provocative question: "Can a traditional professional liberalism, a long-standing definition of purpose for ALA, and a library institution based on both, accommodate the demands of a society in revolution?"[90]

One month after the conference convened another library organization was born. Librarians for 321.8 was founded by a group of Washington, D.C., ALA members who continued the push towards democratization. Indeed *Library Journal* suggested that the ALA organization adopt this Dewey Decimal because it stood for "participatory-democracy."[91] Librarians for 321.8, for example, chaired by John Forsman (Federal City College, Washington, D.C.), disseminated a list of proposed reforms for ALA which included a requirement that candidates for ALA Council and the presidency provide platform statements, a provision for sanctions against librarians who violated the Library Bill of Rights, and a budget for more staff positions at the Office for Intellectual Freedom.[92] The group's effort preceded ACONDA's discussion on the Association's future obligations and priorities at ALA's headquarters in Chicago on September 26 and 27.

Both ALA President Dix and Executive Director David Clift attended the two-day Chicago sessions during which ACONDA's terms of reference and proposed schedule of activities were discussed. Frederick Wagman (former ALA president and director of libraries, University of Michigan) presided over a group consisting of Albert P. Marshall (director of libraries, Eastern Michigan University), David Kaser (director of libraries, Cornell University), Glenn F. Miller (assistant director, Orlando Public Library), Katherine Laich (assistant city librarian, Los Angeles Public Library), William Hinchcliff (Media Services, Federal City College), Arthur Curley (director, Montclair, New Jersey, Public Library), Keith Doms (director, Free Library of Philadelphia), George J. Alfred (by now with the Walden Branch Library, San Francisco), Shirley Olofson (librarian, Information Center, University of Kentucky), J. Maurice Travillian (director, Marshalltown, Iowa, Public Library), and John G. Lorenz (deputy Librarian of Congress).[93] Alfred, Curley, and Hinchcliff represented RTSRL. Laich, Miller, and Olofson represented JMRT.

The following areas were identified by ACONDA as needing ALA's attention: (1) ALA's social responsibilities, social relevance, and its commitments to fundamental values such as library service to the disadvantaged and international concerns; (2) Manpower, library education, ALA membership's welfare, and recruitment with an emphasis on people interested in service to disadvantaged minority groups; (3) Intellectual freedom, including the development of better procedures for the support of librarians under pressure or attack for upholding the Library Bill of Rights; (4) Further democratization of ALA, including more participation by younger members, in particular, and greater responsiveness to members' concerns, in general; (5) Legislation; and (6) Planning and research.[94] Because ACONDA had to prepare a preliminary report for ALA's midwinter conference, it determined that the first draft of this report be completed and disseminated by January 1 to the whole body for study. Accordingly, ACONDA organized itself into various subcommittees, each concerned with one of its priorities for action. Subcommittee chairs were designated as follows: Alfred — Social Responsibilities, Curley — Intellectual Freedom, Laich — Democratization, and Travillian — Legislation and Planning and Research.

The areas of concern of ACONDA closely resembled issues already identified by RTSRL's Task Force on Reorganization, which recommended the following short term goals: (1) to change the status of all committees from standing to ad hoc (i.e., emphasis on task-completion, not perpetuation of membership); (2) to shift the priorities of ALA towards (a) intellectual freedom (b) recruitment for the profession (c) research and evaluation, and (d) enforcement of professional standards through sanctions; and (3) to reorient the organization to make it the American *Librarians* Association instead of the American Library Association. The remaining directives pertained to exercising democratic prerogatives, supporting members on current critical issues, and effecting positive social change.[95]

The overlap between the two sets of recommendations indicated that RTSRL participants had been influential during ACONDA's talks and were being taken seriously. Some individuals, however, were uneasy about where ACONDA would lead. They worried that specific agenda items — especially the Association's social responsibilities — were non-library issues that compromised library "neutrality." In later years, David K. Berninghausen referred to ACONDA as the "first official attempt to discard the principle [of intellectual freedom]."[96] But soon after ACONDA's September sessions, it became apparent to other ALA members that the Association's concept of intellectual freedom needed re-examining. In October, 1969, for example, Carolyn and John Forsman sent a circular to Dix, *Wilson Library Bulletin*, and several other library journals asking that ALA's Executive Board consider suspending the Missouri State Library, its Commission, and the State Librarian from the Association because of their action in the Bodger incident. They also asked that ALA re-examine its commitment to intellectual freedom.[97] The Forsmans wanted ALA to provide librarians with job protection — a benefit Joan Bodger failed to receive.

Coincidentally, reports of the dismissal of T. Ellis Hodgin as city librarian in Martinsville, Virginia, on July 25 began surfacing in the library press. Hodgin believed that his constitutional rights were violated and that he was dismissed because, based on his beliefs as a private citizen, he had joined a lawsuit that challenged the constitutionality of a religious education course at his daughter's school. His attorney, Robert P. Dwoskin, noted that up to July 22 there had been no complaints about Hodgin's direction of the library, that Hodgin had recently received a two-step raise, and that the dismissal was made without reason.[98] Several Pittsburgh area library professionals formed the National Freedom Fund for Librarians to raise money for Ellis. Meanwhile, in initiating the Program of Action to support the Library Bill of Rights (approved by the Council in Atlantic City, 1969, and based on the Intellectual Freedom Committee's Resolution approved in Kansas City, 1968), it became apparent to ALA's leadership that a support and defense fund "was not only a necessary adjunct, but a logical next step."[99] Executive Director Clift asked for a careful review of the concept of intellectual freedom and ALA's role in its promotion and defense, after which he directed the Association's legal counsel "to proceed with steps necessary and appropriate to establish a support fund to aid persons who resign under duress or are fired from their positions because they stood up for principles of intellectual freedom."[100] The need for a support and defense mechanism for librarians, first voiced in 1938, had finally been addressed by the ALA hierarchy.

As Krug and Harvey explain it, "soon after the adoption of the Library Bill of Rights (1939) and the establishment of the Intellectual Freedom Committee (1940), "the profession realized that more than just information sources were needed to foster the practice of intellectual freedom in libraries." For example, at ALA's 1948 conference, Council received a proposal for implementing "a *policing* effort to publicize censorship problems and bring pressure upon authorities to correct conditions conducive to censorship." This proposal took 20 years to put into effect. Thus, it was in 1969 that ALA developed its Program of Action in Support of the Library Bill of Rights to study complaints about censorship incidents that were reported to the Intellectual Freedom Committee. For example, in 1969 the Intellectual Freedom Committee and the Office for Intellectual Freedom were charged with studying such complaints to determine if they were within the scope of the Library Bill of Rights. If they were, both groups were instructed "to attempt to mediate, arbitrate, or provide appropriate assistance to effect a just resolution of the problem." If such a resolution was not arrived at, "a fact-finding team" was then to investigate further.[101]

The ALA Executive Board approved the establishment of an ALA sister organization called the Freedom to Read Foundation at its November meeting in Chicago.[102] The Foundation was incorporated as a not-for-profit organization in Chicago and its purposes were patterned on the ACLU Foundation and the NAACP Legal Defense Fund, but oriented to the support of librarians and the freedom to read. These purposes were: (1) to promote and protect freedom of speech and freedom of press, (2) to promote the library's role as the repository of the "world's accumulated wisdom," (3) to protect the public's access rights to the "world's accumulated wisdom," (4) to support the inclusion of legally obtained works in library collections, and (5) to supply legal counsel to libraries and librarians who suffer legal injustices because of their defense of freedom of speech and/or press.[103] Thus, the Foundation was created independent of ALA's legal and financial jurisdiction so that it could serve as a means for supporting the Library Bill of Rights through legal precedents for the freedom to read and as ALA's response to "librarians who increasingly wanted defense machinery to protect their jobs from jeopardy when they undertook to challenge violations of intellectual freedom."[104]

To maintain the link to ALA, the Foundation's executive director served the dual role as the director of ALA's Office for Intellectual Freedom. The ALA Executive Board appointed Judith F. Krug (director of ALA's Office for Intellectual Freedom) as the Foundation's executive director and designated eight persons to serve on its Board of Trustees until spring elections were held: Jackie Eubanks, Alex P. Allain (trustee, St. Mary Parish Library, Franklin, Louisiana), Sanford Cobb (vice-president, general manager and editor-in-chief, Trade Publishing Division, Rand-McNally), Robert B. Downs (dean, Library Administration, University of Illinois), LeRoy C. Merritt (dean, School of Librarianship, University of Oregon), Carrie C. Robinson (school libraries consultant, Alabama State Department of Education), Joseph H. Reason (director, Howard University Libraries), and C. Lamar Wallis (director, Memphis Public Library).

Meanwhile, the H.W. Wilson Company gave *Synergy* the Library Periodical Award "for a highly contemporary, off-beat, consistently communicative, NOW-oriented publication which, in imaginative format and sprightly content, matches its milieu, while giving useful service to its clientele."[105] *Synergy* staff used the positive publicity to continue driving their message home. Issue 24 (published in December, 1969) covered the women's liberation movement and provided commentary on the New Left's exploitation of women, the objectification of women by underground papers and the "low and sinking status" of women in the library profession.[106] As the year drew to its close, *Synergy* continued with its alternative press and library culture activities and RTSRL (already the largest ALA round table with 1013 members) pressed forward and planned for ACONDA. Thus, two years after a small group of Bay Area librarians began to spur interest in the alternative press and argue that librarians needed to address social issues, the American Library Association had a formal conduit for its members to tackle social responsibility.

Notes

1. Richard Cronenberg, "SYNERGIZING Reference Service in the San Francisco Bay Region," *ALA Bulletin* 62, no. 11 (December 1968): 1379, 1384.

2. Morgan, *The Sixties Experience*, xix–xx.

3. Celeste West, "Stop! The Print Is Killing Me," *Synergy* 33 (1971): 3.

4. Janet Lois Freedman, "The Liberated Librarian? A Look at the *Second Sex* in the Library Profession," *Library Journal* 95, no. 9 (1 May 1970): 1709–1711.

5. Celeste West, "Congloms: Stalking the Literary-Industrial Complex," *American Libraries* 13, no. 5 (1982): 299; "A Conversation with Celeste West," 3-6.

6. "San Francisco '67," *Library Journal* 92, no. 14 (August 1967): 2708.

7. Carolyn Forsman, "Up Against the Stacks: The Liberated Librarian's Guide to Activism," Affiliates, List of Correspondence, 1970-1973, ALA's SRRT Papers, Box 11.

8. Mary Lee Bundy, "Factors Influencing Public Library Use," *Wilson Library Bulletin* 42, no. 4 (December 1967): 382.

9. *Intellectual Freedom Manual*, 1996, xxx–xxxi.

10. Subcommittee Report — Social Responsibilities prepared by George J. Alfred, A.P. Marshall and Shirley Olfoson, [n.d.], ALA's SRRT Papers, Box 1.

11. Leonard H. Freiser, "The Bendix-Duhac Establishment," *Library Journal* 93, no. 16 (15 September 1968): 3105; "Business Not Quite as Usual." *Library Journal* 93, no. 14 (August 1968): 2798-2799.

12. "The American Library Association," *ALA Bulletin* 61, no. 10 (November 1967): 1155.

13. SRRT Organization Movement, Dorothy Bendix, 1968-69, ALA's SRRT Papers, Box 12.

14. "Growing Pains and Generation Gaps: Kansas City Conference," *ALA Bulletin* 62, no. 7 (July-August 1968): 817–818.

15. *Ibid.*, 827.

16. *Ibid.*, 829, 817.

17. "Business Not Quite as Usual," 2797.

18. "Growing Pains," 830.

19. Council Meetings, Transcripts and Minutes, ALA, 87th Annual Conference, Kansas City, Missouri, June 23–36, 1968, ALA's SRRT Papers, Box 2.

20. "Business Not Quite as Usual," 2799.

21. *Ibid.*

22. *Ibid.*, 2799–2800.

23. Council Meetings, Transcripts and Minutes, ALA 87th Annual Conference, Kansas City Missouri, June 23–26, 1968, ALA's SRRT Papers, Box 6.

24. *Ibid.*

25. By virtue of ALA's tax-exempt status, it received grants from the Rockefeller, Ford, and Carnegie Foundations, as well as the Council on Library Resources.

26. Council Meetings, Transcripts and Minutes, ALA 87th Annual Conference, Kansas City Missouri, June 23–26, 1968, ALA's SRRT Papers, Box 6.

27. Robert McClarren, "Tax-Exempt Status," *American Libraries* 1, no. 6 (June 1970): 607.

28. *Ibid.*

29. *Proceedings of the 87th Annual Conference 1968 American Library Association Kansas City, Missouri June 23–29, 1968* (Chicago: ALA, 1968), 14–15.

30. "Business Not Quite as Usual," 2797.

31. "Growing Pains," 832–833.

32. "Business Not Quite as Usual," 2805.

33. *Ibid.*, 2808.

34. Eric Moon served as *Library Journal*'s editor from 1959 to 1968.

35. Eric Moon, "The Generation Gap," *Library Journal* 93, no. 14 (August 1968): 2775.

36. Patricia Schuman, "Perception Gap," *Library Journal* 95, no. 10 (15 May 1970): 1781.

37. Jesse Shera, "The Playgirl of the Western World," *Wilson Library Bulletin* 42, no. 5 (January 1968): 529.

38. E.J. Josey to Dorothy Bendix, 1 July 1968, Anne Sweat, Pre-SRRT, 1968, ALA's SRRT Papers, Box 1.

39. Betty-Carol Sellen, 1970–87, ALA's SRRT Papers, Box 11.

40. Anne Sweat, Pre-SRRT, 1968, Organizing Meeting of Round Table on Social Responsibility of Libraries, ALA's SRRT Papers, Box 1.

41. Betty-Carol Sellen, 1970–87, ALA's SRRT Papers, Box 11.

42. Bill DeJohn, Affiliates, including newsletters, 1967–71, The Social Responsibilities of Libraries: The New York City Round Table Experience, ALA's SRRT Papers, Box 1.

43. Bill DeJohn, Affiliates, including newsletters, 1968–1971, ALA's SRRT Papers, Box 1.

44. "Wait 'Til Atlantic City," *Library Journal* 94, no. 6 (15 March 1969): 1104–1105.

45. Betty-Carol Sellen, 1970–81, ALA's SRRT Papers, Box. 11.

46. "Wait 'Til Atlantic City," 1104–1105.

47. Ruth Warncke (deputy executive director, ALA), Patricia Schuman, Betty-Carol Sellen, George Hathaway, Diana McMullen (Free Library of Philadelphia), and Anne Sweat (assistant coordinator of Adult Services, Prince George's County Memorial Library, Laurel, Maryland).

48. DeJohn Correspondence, 1969–70, Organizational Meeting of the ALA Round Table on Social Responsibilities of Libraries, ALA Midwinter, Washington, D.C.—January 31, 1969, ALA's SRRT Papers, Box 1.

49. "Wait 'Til Atlantic City," 1111.

50. DeJohn Correspondence, 1969–70, Organizational Meeting of the ALA Round Table on Social Responsibilities of Libraries, ALA Midwinter, Washington, D.C.—January 31, 1969, ALA's SRRT Papers, Box 1.

51. *Ibid.*

52. Bill DeJohn Correspondence, 1969-70, "Ready for Action," ALA's SRRT Papers, Box 1.

53. *"Know Your ALA: Services to Members and Aids to Collections,"* ALA *Bulletin* 63, no. 1 (January 1969): 54–57.

54. Barbara Papish, Walter Bergen, Herbert Markham, and Patricia Vandiver.

55. David K. Berninghausen, "Appendix A: The Bodger Report: A Landmark Case for ALA," in *The Flight from Reason* (Chicago: ALA, 1975), 139–156.

56. "Mrs. Bodger Resigns," *Wilson Library Bulletin* 44, no. 3 (November 1969): 275.

57. John Berry, "Channels for Change," *Library Journal* 95, no. 4 (February 15 1970): 611.

58. "The ALAiad, or, A Tale of Two Conferences," *Wilson Library Bulletin* 44, no. 1 (September 1969): 80.

59. Bundy and Stielow, *Activism*, 125.

60. Correspondence, Clearinghouse, 1969–70, ALA's SRRT Papers, Box 7.

61. *Ibid.*

62. "The ALAiad," 80.

63. Bundy and Stielow, *Activism*, 123.

64. "The ALAiad," 80.

65. John Berry, "The New Constituency," *Library Journal* 94, no. 14 (August 1969): 2725.

66. "The ALAiad," 81, 80; *Proceedings 1969 of the Midwinter Meeting Washington, D.C. January 26–February 1, 1969 and the 88th Annual Conference Atlantic City June 22–28, 1969* (Chicago: ALA, 1969), 58.

67. Forsman, "Up Against the Stacks," 11.

68. "The ALAiad," 82, 90.

69. John Berry, "Channels for Change," *Library Journal* 95, no. 4 (15 February 1970): 611.

70. *Ibid.*

71. Raymond, "ACONDA and ANACONDA," 357.

72. "A Great Show — In Two Parts and a Cast of Thousands," *ALA Bulletin* 63, no. 7 (July-August 1969): 947.

73. "The ALAiad," 91.

74. Kenneth Duhac, "A Plea for Social Responsibility," *Library Journal* 93, no. 14 (1968): 2798.

75. "A Great Show," 932.
76. "The ALAiad," 86–87.
77. *Ibid.*, 932–933.
78. *Ibid.*, 933–935.
79. *Ibid.*, 935.
80. "A Great Show," 961–962.
81. *Ibid.*
82. *Proceedings*, 1969, 66.
83. "The ALAiad," 85, 67.
84. *Ibid.*, 67-68.
85. *Proceedings*, 1969, 71.
86. In this Council meeting, the Intellectual Freedom Committee proposed a Program of Action in Support of the Library Bill of Rights to open ALA's door to complaints concerning Library Bill of Rights violations, and to provide mechanisms for examining and acting on these complaints. The Council approved the Program, but voted down an accompanying proposal to secure funds for action regardless of its tax-exempt status.
87. "The ALAiad," 90.
88. Forsman, "Up Against the Stacks," 12.
89. George M. McCorkle to William DeJohn, 18 July 1969, ALA's SRRT Papers, Box 7.
90. Correspondence, Clearinghouse, 1969–70, Action Memo #2, August, 1969, ALA's SRRT Papers, Box 7.
91. John Berry, "Electing an ALA Council," *Library Journal* 95, no. 9 (1 May 1970): 1683.
92. "Librarians for 321.8," *SRRT Newsletter* 2 (1 September 1969): 5.
93. Action Council Business, 1972–1973, ALA's SRRT Papers, Box 11.
94. "Activities Committee on New Directions for ALA," *ALA Bulletin* 63, no. 10 (November 1969): 1383.
95. "ALA Interim Report," *American Libraries* 1, no. 3 (March 1970): 238–241.
96. Action Council Business, 1972–1973, ALA's SRRT Papers, Box 11.
97. "ALA Asked to Act on Bodger Case in Missouri," *Wilson Library Bulletin* 44, no. 2 (October 1969): 136.
98. "The Month in Review," *Wilson Library Bulletin* 44, no. 9 (May 1970): 901.
99. Judith F. Krug, "Intellectual Freedom," *American Libraries* 1, no. 4 (April 1970): 336.
100. "Green Light on Intellectual Freedom Support Fund," *Wilson Library Bulletin* 44, no. 1 (September 1969): 6.
101. *Intellectual Freedom Manual*, 1996, xxxii–xxxiii.
102. *Ibid.*, xxix.
103. Krug, "Intellectual Freedom," 337.
104. *Intellectual Freedom Manual*, 1996, p. xxxv.
105. *Synergy* 24 (December 1969): 25.
106. Peggy Barber, "Ladies in Waiting," *Synergy* 24 (December, 1969): 24.

Intellectual Freedom and Social Responsibility, 1970

The Freedom to Read Foundation Board of Trustees met in Chicago on January 17, 1970, to draft its Constitution and Bylaws. By this time, however, the question of how the American Library Association should act on behalf of individual members in trouble over matters of intellectual freedom was preempted by what Robert Sheridan called "a membership dilemma." In an article in the January issue of *American Libraries,* Sheridan asserted that in Atlantic City, ALA "found itself faced with an identity crisis," and that it was time to determine "whether the Association's primary purpose is library service or service to librarians (or both if they can survive in one envelope.)"[1] His article was timely. The question of ALA's purpose became a focal point of the Association's midwinter (January 18–24) conference in Chicago.

Although all of the approximately 1,800 members who checked in at Chicago's aged Sherman House Hotel suffered record breaking subzero temperatures, some became seriously ill. For example, Executive Director Clift and the Rev. James Kortendick (Catholic University) were carted out on stretchers and taken to the hospital. Erv Eatenson (Notable Books Council chair) spent three days in the hotel doctor's care. And Frederick Wagman departed before the conference closed to struggle through a week of respiratory infections at home.[2] Nonetheless, ALA reported that the "feverish days in that dingy hotel" carried over the urgent feeling of previous conferences and "marked a decided turning point for a budding profession."[3] And *Wilson Library Bulletin*'s "Month in Review" summary stated that the "atmosphere of tension, hostility, and polarization in the City of Law and Order was almost as visible to conferees as the steam and soot trapped in the frozen air of the Loop."[4]

The ongoing trial of the Chicago Eight/Seven, just four blocks away from the Sherman House, meant that police with billy clubs and uniformed security officers were much in evidence around the conference hub. The National Call for Library Reform, a coalition which evolved from the Congress for Change and Atlantic City conference activism, braved the cold and staged a protest march to the Federal Building, where dissenting librarians called for the "right, principle, and constitutional guarantees of free speech and due process," and cited many examples of free speech infringements, including police brutality against demonstrators at the 1968 Democratic National Convention, the Chicago Eight/Seven trial, oppression of Black Panther members, the "apparent" police murder of Fred Hampton, and the mishandling of Bobby Seale's due process rights. Members of the National Call for Library Reform were predominantly members of the Round Table for Social Responsibilities of Libraries, the CFC, and Librarians for 321.8 with an interest in restructuring ALA, forming a national union of library workers, strengthening library unions, reforming library education, promoting community participation, opening up discussions on the social and political issues of war, racism and poverty, and strengthening intellectual freedom. They called on ALA not to meet in Chicago or any other city that "exemplified the repressive forces" of society. Meanwhile, underground press worker and ALA member Tom Forcade "haunted the conference, an apparition in Yippie garb." And police intervened at the Chicago Public Library, where the Illinois RTSRL sponsored a film about local police riots and where guerrilla theater performers acted out several scenes. Thus, a local newspaper headlined, "Librarians get good look at cops in action."[5]

But the midwinter conference also included some new ALA business. At its January 20 meeting, in "an unprecedented move to expedite" the recommendations of the Activities Committee for New Directions for ALA at the Association's upcoming Detroit conference, "Council passed a motion to set aside a fund of up to $50,000." The money was to be allocated to various ALA units according to ACONDA's recommendations for action. In addition, ALA approved the founding of a Black Caucus, chaired by E.J. Josey.[6] The Caucus primarily concerned itself with "the second class citizenship of blacks in ALA, the profession, and society" and remained independent of any other aspect of ALA's structure because its members felt the need for self-determination.[7] Effie Lee Morris (coordinator, Child Services, San Francisco Public Library) read a document called the "Black Librarians Caucus Statement of Concern" to the Council. It pointed to the small number of African-Americans serving on ALA's Council and noted there still was no African-American president in the Association's history. It also addressed discrimination in promotion and hiring, lack of recruitment, and institutional racism as practiced by libraries.[8] The Caucus successfully brought to the Council a resolution in support of Carrie

Robinson, "a black librarian who had brought suit against the state of Alabama, charging discrimination in promotion."[9] The resolution called for "censure of libraries and/or librarians ... who ... through either services or materials ... supported racist institutions." *Wilson Library Bulletin* reported that "some caucus spokesmen" took the Executive Board's recommendation to refer the resolution to the Intellectual Freedom Committee for implementation and action "as just another stalling tactic." But the Executive Board withdrew this motion and the resolution passed 135 to 2.[10] Thereafter, the Caucus aligned itself with the general social responsibility movement groups within ALA in areas of mutual concern. Some were evident in Chicago, where throughout the conference RTSRL members held committee meetings and concurrently tried to appear at the open ACONDA hearings and Intellectual Freedom Committee meetings.

"In a room surrounded by draped cubicles not too far removed from the side-show booths at the county fair," ACONDA presented its *Interim Report of the Activities Committee on New Directions for ALA*, with attendant Subcommittee background papers, to the members. The committee then asked the membership to "come tell us what you think." The unstructured discussions that followed, presided over by Wagman (until his early departure) and Laich, lasted three days. Tape recorders were placed by ACONDA in little booths surrounding the hearing room so that the shy, or "those that couldn't get a word in edgeways during oratory time," could comment. These recorders produced a dozen sound reels.[11] Obviously, ALA members had a lot to say about the new Freedom to Read Foundation, the defense of intellectual freedom, and its importance as an ALA priority.

The most serious criticism pertained to the Hodgin case and was specifically directed at William North (ALA's legal counsel) and Judith F. Krug. Many argued the Foundation set its purpose in such a way as to protect library patrons' right to get information from Hodgin, while Hodgin would only be protected if fired because of a censorship incident.[12] Critics also objected to the fact that ALA's Executive Board designated the Foundation's Board of Trustees without consulting interested groups. Mostly, however, they worried about the issue of intellectual freedom, which would likely be a major priority in ACONDA's final report. It was clear the Freedom to Read Foundation was not yet ready to offer direct financial assistance to librarians who lost their jobs in the defense of intellectual freedom. And until the Foundation garnered the resources for a defense fund, the National Freedom Fund for Librarians had to remain in existence. Plainly ACONDA needed to develop a comprehensive definition of intellectual freedom for ALA.[13] Although ACONDA members had arrived in Chicago expecting they were "halfway home in their charge to offer up some new directions for ALA," they went home "in a state of shock" at how much work remained to be done before the summer conference.[14]

The end of midwinter seemed like a good time for RTSRL to reflect not only on how ALA treated issues of intellectual freedom and social responsibility, but also on how the round table fared during its first year. The members of RTSRL observed that the *Newsletter* had successfully convinced some "well-meaning, but inactive, librarians that social responsibilities can and are being confronted by librarians as librarians."[15] They recalled that over 200 librarians participated in the Vietnam Moratorium demonstrations in Washington, November 13–15, 1969, and that affiliate groups launched many efforts to bring in social change. Furthermore, they recounted how task forces were created to address a wide spectrum of issues, such as ACONDA, evaluation of library outreach programs, availability of black literature reprints, community participation, the status of minorities in the profession, and intellectual freedom.

The Task Force on Intellectual Freedom was a partner with ALA's Office for Intellectual Freedom and its Intellectual Freedom Committee on a number of issues. Originally the task force intended to deal with matters concerning intellectual freedom within librarianship; ALA was supposed to help develop a defense fund for librarians, then incorporate the Freedom to Read Foundation to set legal precedents for the freedom to read. The creation of the Task Force on Intellectual Freedom constituted RTSRL's most important accomplishment because it inter-related the concepts of intellectual freedom and social responsibility, and triggered some ALA members to wonder whether the Association should shift its focus from institutions to individuals.

While ALA maintained the stance that social responsibility and intellectual freedom were dichotomous, and that it should retain an institutional membership focus, RTSRL members disagreed. They wanted ALA to be more responsive to the needs of librarians, including female, minority, gay, and lesbian librarians. They were also involved in organizing library school students and librarians in their intellectual freedom disputes. And after the Atlantic City conference, they were prepared to engage ALA's establishment in a debate. Unfortunately, however, ALA experienced a serious budget crisis. Socially oriented programs came under increasing scrutiny and RTSRL members and their activities became the subject of intense professional debate. In response, ACONDA's Subcommittee on Social Responsibilities of Libraries (George J. Alfred, chair) began efforts to sustain RTSRL's position in ALA.

The ALA Council had commissioned ACONDA's Subcommittee on Social Responsibilities of Libraries to explore improved library service for the disadvantaged and report its recommendations at the Detroit conference. Alfred and his colleagues interpreted this directive as an opportunity to disseminate a broader social responsibility agenda. To some extent, social and political conditions such as "a favorable job situation, the availability of federal funding, and pressures on institutions from outside" helped to facilitate the climate in which the library movement could find expression.[16] For example, Bundy and Stielow argue that the idea of improving library service to the disadvantaged was a part of the "War on Poverty" and "The Great Society" discourse of the Kennedy and Johnson administrations. The federal government "bypassed" local governments and set up spending programs for poor urban communities, while libraries also established their own poverty programs. The Library Services and Construction Act (first passed in 1956 as the Library Services Act) and the 1965 Higher Education Act were key sources of funding for library services to the disadvantaged. Josey also noted that the advent of new programs for minority communities that resulted from federal funding programs was a major impetus for library activism and the increasing concern for social responsibility in libraries.[17]

With respect to library service to the disadvantaged, the Subcommittee decided that a comprehensive definition of intellectual freedom was insufficient, and that the omnibus term "social responsibility" also needed defining. George J. Alfred, Albert P. Marshall, and Shirley Olofson collaborated on a three page ACONDA document titled *Subcommittee Report: Social Responsibilities*, in which they identified two conflicting definitions of social responsibility held by ALA members. The first reflected a traditional interpretation in which the library functioned as a provider of factual material on all sides of issues. In this interpretation, the library housed and preserved information and kept, but did not promote, ideas. The second reflected the new, activist interpretation — "the relationships that librarians and libraries have to non-library problems that relate to the social welfare" of society. Because the group believed that intellectual freedom complemented rather than opposed social responsibility, it opted to use the second definition to begin the process of improving library service to the disadvantaged. The group agreed that ALA needed to "re-think and re-allocate traditional library sources of income" and improve legislation, information, practical advice on topics such as workshops, publications, and recruitment, and finally consulting services.[18]

The New York SRRT group's demonstration project on community control of school boards showing social responsibility in action had served as a model the Subcommittee wanted to emulate. But because many ALA members considered the demand that ALA demonstrate a sense of social responsibility towards many issues — "specifically non-library issues" — controversial, the Subcommittee recognized that the new activist interpretation of social responsibility would prove highly problematic.[19] For example, many librarians were reluctant to abandon librarianship's claim to a "neutral" stance and they were afraid of the social, financial, and legal repercussions that could result from ALA's involvement in social issues. The Subcommittee resolved that it needed to find ways to allay these two fears.

With respect to library "neutrality," the Subcommittee noted that because librarians reacted subjectively to many issues (e.g., intellectual freedom and racial integration) it saw no reason not to validate the activist definition of social responsibility. Furthermore it asserted that the old definition had lost its value, was unrealistic and served to shelter libraries from rather than expose them to social changes. With respect to involving ALA in social issues that threatened ALA's tax-exempt status, the Subcommittee set out to determine if this fear was justified. Because the American Association of University Professors (AAUP) also enjoyed a tax-exempt status, the Subcommittee contacted AAUP and found out that it experienced no threat to its tax-exempt status, despite a 1969 IRS review of its activity in defending faculty member's rights (academic librarians included). The Subcommittee decided there was no reason to fear that ALA's tax-exempt status would be jeopardized by helping librarians threatened with loss of academic freedom or political interference. Ultimately, ACONDA's *Subcommittee Report: Social Responsibilities* stated that ALA's social responsibilities "be defined in terms of the contribution that librarianship as a profession can make in the effort to ameliorate or even solve the many critical problems of society." Here the report outlined both direct and indirect action, both programming and making "freely available the full range of data and opinion on all aspects of such problems."[20]

While ACONDA was preparing its paperwork, the Radical Research Center published the first volume of the *Alternative Press Index* in February, 1970. It showed librarians and non-librarians that standard library tools like *Books in Print* gave only limited access to current alternative media. Library activists were embarrassed that librarians and library schools had done nothing to address the pressing need for indexes to non-mainstream periodicals. Their mood worsened after the outcome of Hodgin's trial.

A jury of "staunch citizens of southernmost Virginia" assembled March 24 and 25, *Wilson Library Bulletin* reported, "to hear the case of Hodgin vs. [Thomas] Nolin" — the former city librarian of Martinsville, Virginia, and the latter, its city manager. In his summation, the prosecution attorney argued that "Hodgin's record as a librarian was unquestioned" and that "the only event which intervened was the July 18 filing of a suit to prevent the Martinsville schools from continuing religious education, to which suit Hodgin was party." Defense attorney Jackson Kiser maintained that "the power of the city manager was complete"—citing that the Martinsville city charter, the date of the religious education suit, and Hodgin's firing were coincidental—and that "poor judgment as an administrator was the chief reason for dismissal." After the judge instructed the jury that "they must find for the defendant unless the *preponderance* of evidence pointed to the religious education issues as the cause of firing," the jury deliberated for half and hour and found for the defense.[21]

But ALA reformers continued their efforts. Position papers were secured from nearly every candidate for ALA's 1970 Council election because of Librarians for 321.8's push for participatory democracy. The group also nominated its own set of candidates. For the first time in *Library Journal's* memory, "an opposition slate" ran "against the choices of the ALA Nominating Committee."[22] In its May 1, 1970 editorial, *Library Journal* announced that it backed the 321.8 candidates because their activist mandate represented adaptation in ALA and because the 1970 election represented "one of the many tests of the Association's willingness to accommodate change." The editorial also stated that choices about the other candidates would be made on the basis of their responses to key questions, such as: Did ALA have the "duty to espouse a concept of intellectual freedom that goes beyond censorship and the freedom to read to include the exercise of all their constitutional rights?" Was it time for ALA to strengthen its position in support of special library services "to the black and brown minorities in America?" Could ALA reform itself without fundamental constitutional and structural changes? Were candidates' "age, costume, type of library, state or region important?" Should groups like Librarians for 321.8, RTSRL, the CFC, the National Freedom Fund for Librarians, or library school students be represented in ALA's governance?[23]

The Round Table was not idle between conferences. Members worked continuously toward their goal of making the round table the conscience of the association. Its Action Council responded to many requests from library schools, professional organizations, and local groups on social action topics. Members formed task forces on women's liberation, a bibliography on the peace movement, and library school student organizing. Furthermore, the round table served as the umbrella organization for numerous affiliates, including Librarians for 321.8, the Black Caucus, National Freedom Fund for Librarians, and Librarians for Peace.[24]

Affiliated groups were popular, Carolyn Forsman noted, because they offered "more freedom and less structure" than RTSRL. But because memberships overlapped and activist groups cooperated in areas of mutual benefit, they also lacked a means to organize.[25] Furthermore, because RTSRL could not include non ALA-members, the National Call for Library Reform initially set up a post office box in Pittsburgh to solicit names of potential activists. The RTSRL later absorbed it into its Clearinghouse and furnished current mailing lists of library people interested in social action to share with other organizations. Task forces of the Round Table, affiliates, and other groups often used these lists whenever there was a need for action, monetary support or organization at the grass roots level.

Social responsibility advocates liked RTSRL's Clearinghouse lists. Mary McKenney, a trained librarian who worked for the Radical Research Center, noted that the Center received a lot of inquiries because of the lists and expressed pleasure that at last like-minded people across the nation were connecting the social responsibility movement in librarianship to the alternative press movement.[26] For others, however, the alternative press remained a mystery. James O. Lehman (Eastern Mennonite College, Harrisonburg, Virginia) published a survey of what 101 American colleges used as selection tools in May, 1970. He found that librarians favored *Choice, Library Journal, New York Times, Saturday Review, Publishers Weekly, Booklist,* and *Wilson Library Bulletin* as selection aids. Survey respondents seemed unaware of the alternative press review media as a tool for the library selection process.[77] Lehman's conclusions came as a reminder to library activists like Arthur Curley that despite the directives in the Library Bill of Rights, some librarians failed to stretch their imaginations beyond the mainstream horizons. In Curley's opinion, for example, "to take no action (or to delay action) in support of change, is tantamount to taking action in support of the status quo." And when outdated library practices led to episodes like failing to assist a librarian under attack, he asserted, "we serve notice that the Library Bill of Rights is a hollow document."[28]

The next month, *Library Journal* published an article by Curley, in which he argued that ACONDA had produced a "predictable backlash," and that "one hears more and more the mournful plaint" voiced by Robert Sheridan in January that "we can't decide what ALA can do until we decide what ALA is." Unfortunately many ALA members "were not interested in answers," but "would bat the question around in the security of the status quo from now on until they retire from the field with their applecarts intact." The so-called "rivalry between library-service and service-to-librarians," he concluded, "was false because the two went hand in hand." Curley believed the "way to prod" the "silent majority into more active participation" was to act on the pressures for change voiced by ALA members who cared enough about the Association to speak out and for ALA to experiment with new actions before ruling them out. He looked forward to the Detroit conference.[29]

The June 1, *SRRT Newsletter* urged people to attend the conference and "spy, interrogate, snoop, report ... and inspire socially responsible round table games."[30] Also, NYSRRT's Committee for a More Responsive ALA prepared and distributed a document entitled *Free in Detroit! A Disorientation Handbook for the ALA Convention*, which notified members that they could identify social change agents in conference hallways by various lapel buttons that read "F*ck Censorship," "Libraries to the People," "R,R,RIP IT," "American Ladies Association," and "321.8."[31] They also planned to pressure ALA to focus on the needs of its African-American, female, gay and lesbian members, and for starters, RTSRL scheduled a two-day preconference (June 26 to 27) titled "In Search of Soul"—a look at "black" Detroit. Obviously, librarians advocating social responsibility planned to be visible at the Detroit conference.

John Berry added to the mood. In his June 15 *Library Journal* editorial he praised librarianship's activists. "The 1970 graduating class, and those that will follow it," he wrote, "are the most promising in years." Their commitment to librarianship and their role in a "vital, valid social movement in America," Berry added, "may force us to change, or lose them from our field."[32] In contrast, Ervin J. Gaines did not think it wise for librarians to abandon their traditional "neutral" stance on social issues. He asserted in the same issue that it was his duty "as public librarian to collect information to the maximum extent possible, to make it freely available to everyone, and to assist people to find and use that information to the best of my ability." Thus "by omission," he said, "such a creed implies that librarians as librarians will not promote good causes."[33] Less than two weeks later, "In Search of Soul" got the "long, hot conference" off to a fiery start.[34] Major preconference events included: (1) a guided tour of Detroit's inner-city by Highland Park College students; (2) a presentation/slide show by Father William Cunningham (co-director, Project Hope, Detroit) on "what it means to be black" in Detroit; (3) a paper by Winnifred Moffet Crossley (consultant in public library service to children, Michigan State Library) on "Community Meetings on Reading Black and White Program," which attempted "to highlight the library as a socially conscious community agency"; (4) a discussion led by Detroit "people's lawyer" Kenneth Cockrel on "power and control in American society"; and (5) an evening panel/dinner/sensitivity-training session titled "On Fomenting a Library Revolution." The latter featured four African-American librarians—James C. Welbourne

(University of Maryland School of Library and Information Science), Bob Wright (also University of Maryland library school), Ella Yates (Montclair, New Jersey, Public Library), Bill Miles (Buffalo and Erie, New York, County Public Library)— and one white librarian — Andy Armitage (University of Maryland library school)— all of whom "put it straight for the fifty or so participants attending."[35] The panel purposefully enraged the audience with questions like, "Are you watching the freaks on display" and "Why aren't you out there making a revolution instead of just talking about it?"[36] The evening's major message confirmed the Black Caucus's will to operate independently of any aspect of ALA's structure.[37] And on the whole, "In Search of Soul," reported *American Libraries*, "was, in a way, a weathervane of what was to follow the next week — the words and the emotions were only indicative of the depth of the problems facing librarians."[38]

Approximately 8,850 librarians and 700 exhibitors registered at the ALA's annual conference. "Delegates were physically comfortable in most hotels, and, if they could survive street temperatures of up to 100 degrees, they could enjoy a day in the spacious, bright, and air-conditioned Cobo Hall." The conference received "first-rate" publicity, including outgoing President Dix's June 26 NBC-TV "Today Show" interview by Barbara Walters and four *New York Times* reports by journalist Henry Raymont. The conference also marked a turning point in ALA history. The organization's role had been largely educational, but in Detroit ALA's Membership and the Council voted on "some radically new directions," such as "implementing socially conscious library service and protecting its members from injustices related to their work."[39]

The first general conference session was marked by a "departure from tradition."[40] In place of a formal program of "awards, acknowledgments, greetings, and receptions," the session set the stage for ACONDA's report. It included a review of ALA activity since Kansas City, a slide show depicting ALA activity in the 1960s, a showing of Charles Braverman's film *The Sixties*, and speeches from ALA's President Dix, Treasurer Robert McClarren (North Suburban Library System, Morton Grove, Illinois), and Executive Director Clift. But before Membership discussed ACONDA, David K. Berninghausen delivered a paper titled "Should ALA Take a Stand on an Issue of Public Interest" at the first Membership meeting on July 1. The direct interests of librarians should be separated from the direct interests of citizens, he said. "New voices in ALA that urge members to perceive social problems are on firm ground when the appeal is to librarians as citizens," he argued, but "there are not grounds at all for their insistence that the critical social problems of the world are the problems of librarians as *librarians.*"⁴¹ Berninghausen then called for a vote not to discuss two RTSRL resolutions (one on the Southeast Asian War and the other on voting rights for 18-year-olds in the United States) on the grounds that "ALA should take positions on those issues that directly affect *only* the professional activities of librarians and libraries." Membership agreed 1220 to 118. Geoffrey Dunbar (Serra Regional Library System, El Centro, California) later called Berninghausen's argument "the big-gun in the Detroit professionalists' arsenal."⁴²

But the "professionalists" were not done. Learned Bulman (East Orange, New Jersey, Public Library) attempted to remove ACONDA's report from debate by moving to hold it back for further study and then a mail vote by Membership. Peter Hiatt (Indiana University) offered a substitute motion to accept the ACONDA document only as "an interim report to be debated and sent back to ACONDA for further work." Hiatt's motion "produced an impassioned speech" from Curley, who argued that "ACONDA was fulfilling Membership's charge in presenting a final report in Detroit." To his relief, the substitute motion was defeated. Next, Laich sparked a considerable response when she read ACONDA's major recommendations. The Membership meeting lasted an unprecedented 15 hours and spread over three days.

The Recommendation 1 of ACONDA — that ALA "continue to be an organization for both librarians and libraries, with the overreaching objective of promoting and improving library service"— passed. Recommendation 2 — that ALA's "highest current priorities be reorganized and officially established as: social responsibilities; manpower; intellectual freedom; legislation; planning, research, and development; democratization and reorganization"— sparked much discussion about "the specter of the loss of tax exemption for ALA." After some time, Renwick Garypie (Sioux City, Iowa, Public Library) reminded attendees "that we are debating a recommendation to Council for this matter ... we're really not doing anything. I for one have faith that that body will not move dangerously fast and furiously in implementing this recommendation." President Dix interceded. He stated that it would be unfortunate if Membership did not take the ACONDA recommendations seriously, debate them, and make decisions. After a short discussion, Membership approved ACONDA's second recommendation and recessed until the following morning.⁴³

At the July 2 Membership session ACONDA's Recommendation 3 — that "substantially increased amounts" of ALA's budget be directed toward implementation of the above-stated priorities"— passed after more deliberation over ALA's tax-exempt status — "both a red flag and a red herring in ALA affairs."⁴⁴ Membership adopted Recommendation 4a(1)(a)— that

"ALA define the broad social responsibilities in terms of (a) the contribution that librarianship can make in ameliorating or even solving the critical problems of society"—but only after several attempts by members to delay the vote. Recommendation 4a(1)(b)—that ALA define its broad social responsibilities "in terms of (b) support for all efforts to help inform and educate the people of the United States on these problems and to encourage them to read the many views on, and the facts regarding, each problem"—elicited numerous responses. William Emerson (Palos Verdes, California, Library District) expressed frustration for many members when he said that unless individuals had "real substantive changes to make," they should "refrain from" making amendments and substitutions that "are delaying the whole process." Ultimately, after Membership approved an amendment to replace the word "read" with the word "examine," the Recommendation passed.[45]

Berninghausen took exception to Recommendation 4a(1)(c)—that ALA "define the broad social responsibilities of ALA in terms of (c) the willingness of ALA to support the guidance and support of its members on critical issues"—and moved that the words "of direct and demonstrable relevance to librarianship" be included. This suggestion triggered a lengthy debate about ALA's role in society. Eventually, members settled a second revised version of Recommendation 4a(1)(c)—"define the broad social responsibilities of ALA in terms of (c) the willingness to take a position on current critical issues." Later they amended recommendation 4(a)2 to read "establish an ALA office for Library Service to the Disadvantaged and Unserved."[46] When membership took up ACONDA's lengthy Recommendation 4 on Democratization and Reorganization, they resolved by a vote of 475 to 413 to refer it back to ACONDA for more analysis and refinement.

After a dinner break, Membership turned its attention to ACONDA's intellectual freedom recommendations. The first Recommendation 4c(1), stated that ALA "expand the staff and budget of the Intellectual Freedom Office to enable it to engage in a nation-wide informational program opposing censorship and in support of intellectual freedom, to conduct workshops for state and regional associations, and to help libraries develop educational programs." Robert Wedgeworth immediately moved that the Recommendation be amended to read: "provide the means to help meet the cost of living and, on an interim basis, the cost of living for members discharged or forced to resign, because of their defense of intellectual freedom or in violation of their personal rights of freedom of expression."[47] His amendment pertained to a fund within ALA's formal structure—the library activists' suggestion to keep the functions of the Freedom to Read

Foundation within ALA. Membership defeated the motion 350 to 199. Thus, reported *Wilson Library Bulletin*, "most members seemed to feel that the Freedom to Read Foundation should be allowed to function, at least for a trial period," but its critics saw it as an "overreaction."[48] Black Caucus chair E.J. Josey announced: "I am deeply grieved and saddened by this vote. And I am also further saddened by the counsel I must offer my fellow librarians who feel that this Association is not really interested in intellectual freedom in terms of real support for librarians who defend intellectual freedom." Angry that the vote showed both the Library Bill of Rights and the ethic of intellectual freedom to be empty rhetoric, he asked RTSRL members and other librarians to join in a walk out. One hundred members followed him, although some returned just a few moments later through a separate entrance. In the meantime, some of the remaining librarians questioned the activists' lifestyles and termed their protests childish.[49]

E.J. Josey was no child. In 1970, he was 46 years old, had worked as a professional librarian since 1953, had attained a strong record of contribution to library service and to ALA, and had edited numerous "respectable" library publications such as the *Delaware Library Association Bulletin*. Later described as "the ultimate insider who retains the outsider's point of view" and as the profession's leading civil rights activist, the "gentleman from Georgia who wore neat, clean gloves over his hard fists" was neither young, naive, nor inexperienced.[50]

The ACONDA Recommendation 4(c)2 sought to extend the scope of the Freedom to Read Foundation from ALA to individuals. It called on ALA to:

> make close and careful evaluation of the ability of the Freedom to Read Foundation to fulfill express needs of ALA for a means of providing grants to help meet the cost of legal action and, on an interim basis, the cost of living for members discharged or forced to resign because of their defense of intellectual freedom or in violation of their personal rights of freedom of expression or action; and if, within a reasonable time, the foundation proves unable to reach a satisfactory level of performance, and further, if there is evidence to indicate that performance would be improved by bringing the functions of the Foundation within the Association, then action should be taken to that end.[51]

After RTSRL indicated its support for the Recommendation, the National Freedom Fund for Librarians volunteered to dissolve and donate its assets if ALA created a defense fund. And although Membership passed the recommendation, *Library Journal* noted, the support fund issue persisted as a "hotly debated and bitterly contested" ALA item because it raised old questions from past conferences concerning ALA's "responsibility, tactics, financing, and that perennial specter, the tax-exempt status."[52]

When Membership reconvened the next afternoon, Tyron D. Emerick (North Platte, Nebraska, Public Library) immediately moved that all approved agenda not yet considered by Membership be scheduled for ALA's midwinter meeting. The motion passed. Thus, only after three days of meetings and "a great deal of squabbling and parliamentary maneuvering," ACONDA proposals were on their way to the Council.[53]

A key issue at the Atlantic City conference was whether ALA should "take a stand"; but in Detroit the question became "on what" should ALA take a stand."[54] Paul Bixler (Antioch College) was puzzled that while social responsibility "was clearly the source" for ACONDA's "inauguration and the stimulus for its enormous labors, the Subcommittee statement came at the tag end of the whole report, not as an introduction."[55] And when Council debated 4(a)1(c), which allowed ALA to take positions on current issues, Ervin Gaines proposed a statement that would limit items to those involved with libraries and library service. Margaret Monroe (University of Wisconsin) proposed a simpler substitution — require position statements to indicate relevancy to librarianship. Her amendment passed roughly 100 to 35, although she and approximately 35 other Council members including Kenneth Duhac, Eric Moon, Effie Lee Morris, and Carrie Robinson opposed it. Supporters included Ervin J. Gaines, Mary Gaver, and Robert McClarren, and library activists Evelyn Levy, Richard Moses (Roger Williams College Library), and Virginia Lacy Jones (Atlanta University). In contrast, about 60 Council members including President Dix, Robert B. Downs, Foster Morhardt, Frederick Wagman, Everett T. Moore (University of California–Los Angeles), and Ralph Ulveling (Wayne State University) abstained.[56]

Ultimately, the Council resisted "the idea of an office devoted to social responsibilities" although, *Wilson Library Bulletin* pointed out, "a few hours before they had named that as one of the Association's priorities."[57] Instead, the Council approved an Office for Library Service to the Disadvantaged and Unserved, but gave it no specific charge or money. It also passed, what *Wilson Library Bulletin* called, the "innocuous" Recommendation 4(c) on intellectual freedom, accepted only the general ACONDA statements of principle, but deferred those requiring implementation. It then established its own ALA Ad Hoc Council Committee on ACONDA (ANACONDA) to discuss the remaining items in ACONDA's final report, directed ANACONDA to submit a report by midwinter, and voted not to take final action on the complete ANACONDA report until late fall, 1971. Thus "professionalists" successfully deflected ACONDA's final report. Although ACONDA's life would be short, it had already left a legacy: "ACONDA had done its work well," *Wilson Library Bulletin* reported. It had held hearings at midwinter and solicited a wide spectrum of views, it had published its preliminary document in *American Libraries*, it had consulted ALA staff, and it had held "open" meetings." But ACONDA tried to focus on new directions, as charged by ALA's membership at Atlantic City, and this "enraged the establishment" in Detroit. "Probably nobody knows," the *Bulletin* surmised, "the true effect of the delay," or the impact of confusion surrounding "TAX EXEMPT STATUS."[58]

Some ALA members agreed that ACONDA's formation had been a positive step that awakened librarians, as one ALA member put it, to ask what they could do for civil liberties and intellectual freedom.[59] On the other hand, many critics agreed with Berninghausen that ALA had "no business taking a stand on issues where the words libraries and censorship were not present."[60] John M. Carter reminded *American Libraries* readers that "ALA is a microcosm of the polarization of American society," and that a lot of ALA members "cannot understand what is happening to their profession." Neither, he suspected, "can they understand what is happening to their world." After attending a Detroit RTSRL rap session, Carter reported that "there is no pastime more thoroughly enjoyed by the young of America than blowing the minds of their elders." And after he "talked with some of the elders of librarianship" about their view on RTSRL and new directions for ALA, he found their response to be the "standard hackneyed criticism of the young: that they have no sense of history, that they find it much more satisfying to tear down than to build up, that they are attempting to infuse into the library profession issues which have no relevance to libraries, and that their hair is too long." One elder, Carter claimed, asked him "What is the future of ALA?" Another asked him, "with tears in his puzzled eyes — 'What the hell does Vietnam have to do with libraries, anyway?'"[61]

While ACONDA had supporters and critics, still others remained neutral. Richard Moses put an intriguing spin on the situation. He suggested that RTSRL was "foreseen and encouraged" as a "foil" for ACONDA. In his scenario, RTSRL and ACONDA would thwart each other and "capitalize on ALA's natural custom to delay, defer, relay, refer ... keep the cement mixer grinding so that issues could be entwined, entangled, mingled, and blended." Ultimately, he concluded, the status quo would look like a set of new directions.[62]

But issues of social activism preoccupied more than just Membership and Council meetings at the Detroit conference. Discussions on new directions also dominated RTSRL, RTSRL-affiliate, Intellectual Freedom Committee, and Black Caucus meetings, as well as in the President's Program. Rooms were made available for a "blacks-only Caucus," a "late-night women's liberation meeting," and a meeting of homosexual and bisexual librarians, "which, like so many fugitive groups, was under RTSRL's wing." Whereas the RTSRL meetings drew, to some extent, an elitist and exclusive underground group in Atlantic City, the "enlarged and wide-open RTSRL meetings, [programs,] and receptions" drew thousands in Detroit.[63]

After RTSRL members elected Patricia Schuman as the new Action Council Coordinator, she immediately welcomed volunteers for a new Task Force on Alternative Books in Print. The Task Force evolved out of RTSRL's interest in the Radical Research Center's efforts and the lack of information about small groups working for social change and what they were publishing. Eubanks spoke about her embarrassment that the *Alternative Press Index* began outside ALA and urged those in Detroit not to allow the same end to come to other materials produced by groups in struggle for change.[64] As an active RTSRL member, a volunteer indexer for the Radical Research Center, and a veteran in the alternative press movement, Eubanks took a leadership role in the new task force, which represented RTSRL's response to the *Alternative Press Index* and a direct link to the Radical Research Center.

The RTSRL also established two other task forces in Detroit — the Task Force on the Status of Women in Libraries and the Task Force on Gay Liberation. The first organized during the conference and passed a resolution that called for equal opportunity for women to be placed on the Membership meeting agenda. But because ACONDA preempted the entire agenda, no action was taken on this resolution. The Task Force on Gay Liberation addressed the importance of providing guidance about collecting materials needed by gay and lesbian patrons. Other goals of the task force included preparing and disseminating relevant bibliographies, sponsoring educational programs concerning cultural bias in library classification schemes and subject headings, and finally introducing an annual gay book award.

In what *Library Journal* called an "impressive" and "eloquent" President's Program, Dix delivered a "classic reinstatement of the liberal democratic philosophy applied to libraries and librarianship" that not only stated his own position, but also "captured the ALA conference."[65] And in her July 3 inaugural speech, incoming ALA President Lillian M. Bradshaw (Dallas Public Library) urged ALA members to use their "collective strength and performance" to achieve "an Association built upon the spirit of our time and a library greatness that can respond to a restive world."[66]

But *Wilson Library Bulletin* asserted that Bradshaw's speech was "general and cautious," that she had "a tough act to follow," that ALA members remained deeply divided on the issue of how to respond to social changes, and that she had "yet to show by deed and statement that she is particularly interested in the wishes of the RTSRL groups and other reform elements."[67] But by this time, RTSRL was ready to champion the cause.

Schuman wasted no time planning RTSRL's future following the conference. On August 4, she wrote William DeJohn that she worried about being dependent on ALA's approval: "Do we operate as any other cog in the ALA machinery, or can we really be vital, effective, free from red tape?"[68] The RTSRL, she wrote, must avoid "the roles others ascribe to us," and noted that DeJohn's own recent RTSRL memo was "replete with what ALA will *allow* us to do." Furthermore, Schuman worried that at the upcoming midwinter conference RTSRL would integrate itself "a bit too quickly into the ALA rut," and suggested RTSRL occupy a suite so that it was free to do its "own" thing. Finally, she opposed any alliance with the Junior Members Round Table (JMRT) because she believed that RTSRL should retain "total control" and not be "coopted too soon."

Schuman's fears were not unfounded. Many ALA members had no desire to see changes in ALA. For example, Hoyt R. Galvin (Charlotte and Mecklenburg, North Carolina, County Public Library) asserted that "except for the small minority of the membership who have sought to turn ALA into a politically active organization and thereby dilute" ALA's energies, "for the majority there is little that is basically wrong with the organizational structure of ALA."[69] But RTSRL also had allies. *Synergy*, for example, complemented efforts of the alternative press by covering ALA's gay liberation movement and by providing a bibliography of gay periodicals in its October issue. It also addressed job discrimination based on sexual orientation, homosexuality as a topic within conventional classification schemes and subject heading lists, freedom and equality for other minority groups within ALA, and bibliographic resources for marginalized groups.[70] Furthermore, as part of its effort to provide information about the alternative press and alternative library activity, *Synergy*'s staff lobbied for the "Great Unreviewed," which constituted "60%+ of all books published."[71] Because standard reviewing journals like *Kirkus Reviews*, *Publishers Weekly* and *Choice* did not cover the alternative press, *Synergy* tried to fill the void. It encouraged subscribers to read intensively in their areas of specialty and to get involved in self-publication.

Meanwhile, the Task Force on Alternative Books In Print worked on a strategy to make libraries and their collections relevant for their publics.[72] First, the Task Force proposed to compile a list of non-serial publications available from underground movement presses and allied organizations left out of *Books in Print*. Second, it planned to revise ALA exhibit policies which reinforced the concept that "the biggest are best" and which charged "too much for the small publisher to afford to exhibit at ALA meetings."[73] Initially the Task Force planned to create an adjunct to regular reference tools that would enhance library and bookstore access to media produced by nonprofit, anti-profit, counterculture, Third World, and other activist groups.

When *Synergy*'s October issue went into distribution, Eubanks and fellow New Yorker Mimi Penchansky of Queens College had just completed a letter campaign to over 1,500 organizations, many of which had been listed in the *Directory of the American Left*. They had identified 250 non-serial materials for the Task Force on Alternative Books in Print's proposed publication project—*Alternatives in Print*. Next, they adopted the *Alternative Press Index* subject headings and persuaded Ohio State University library director Hugh Atkinson to get the university press to publish it.[74]

The Task Force opted for an academic publisher for several reasons. First, commercial publishers judged the proposed publication unprofitable and not sufficiently market tested. Second, alternative press publishers did not have enough start-up capital to get the project off the ground. Third, ALA's publishing procedures were too arduous for a project intended to move quickly. Joan Marshall (Brooklyn College), an RTSRL member, was especially angry with ALA and library leaders for not picking up projects rejected by commercial publishers. She believed ALA needed to support the alternative press.[75]

Round Table members like Marshall, Eubanks, and Penchansky were deeply committed to providing access to the alternative press because they recognized librarians' traditional inability to balance collections by ignoring relatively inaccessible materials. They had no illusions about the profession's "neutrality" and believed that ALA-accredited library schools trained students to build collections using mainstream selection tools and venues. In their view, the Task Force on Alternative Books in Print offered an opportunity to counter the effect of conventional training. Eubanks cited her own experience at library school as an example.

Throughout her University of Chicago library education, she noted, she had passively accepted many traditional views. Only on the job did she learn to "hear and respect the real questions" put to her as a reference librarian at Brooklyn College Library. This experience persuaded Eubanks that many librarians made purchases "in a fog" and needed to pay more attention both to the types of information to which patrons needed access and to the political economy of publishing. She believed the prevailing mode of education to be insufficient because the models on which the purchasing policies were based were commercial. Eubanks was disheartened, for example, that library schools lacked courses in publishing and the book trade, and that the collections and acquisitions courses were too often "concentrated entirely on the freedom to read issue" and seen "entirely from a civil libertarian standpoint." In her opinion, librarianship's commitment to the dissemination of information, as expressed in the Library Bill of Rights, was largely ineffective. If librarians really wanted to convey information to the public, she believed, they needed to get involved in publishing.[76]

With Eubanks at the helm, the Task Force on Alternative Books in Print lobbied to get small and alternative presses into the standard library indexes, catalogs and bibliographic references. It also launched a campaign to change ALA's policies on the leasing of exhibit-hall space so that ability to pay would replace set fees. Because small presses had less money to spend on booth space they were often excluded from library conferences. Large commercial publishers were a regular presence.[77] Initially the Task Force used RTSRL as a vehicle for setting up small press displays at ALA conferences. On varying occasions, displays at RTSRL's exhibit-hall booth were regarded as a part of RTSRL's programs. Eventually the Task Force succeeded in getting ALA's approval for a special section of less expensive exhibit space where small presses could afford to exhibit.[78] The Task Force also set up exhibits at smaller regional library conferences, at meetings of the American Booksellers Association, and at the National Women's Studies Association. Furthermore, when Eubanks and other Task Force members attended national and international book fairs, they took RTSRL materials with them.

While the Task Force on Alternative Books in Print stood out as the RTSRL group most involved with the alternative press, RTSRL's general goal — to make libraries more relevant to the public — provided the impetus for other task forces to address issues of access. The Ethnic Materials Task Force (later an ALA round table), for example, sought to make ethnic materials by and for Blacks, Puerto Ricans, American Indians, Asian Americans, and Chicanos more accessible to patrons and to make the materials better known to other librarians. The Task Force produced lists of publishers who were producing ethnic materials as well as descriptions of the kinds of information that was being published — e.g., short stories, poetry, fiction, informational guides, etc. Task Force members spoke with publishers to develop better working relationships and invited them to participate in ALA programs. Other task forces focused on literature for women, gays and lesbians, labor workers, political prisoners, migrant workers, etc. And all benefited from the efforts of the Task Force on Alternative Books in Print, which functioned as a central part of both RTSRL's structure and its mission.

Meanwhile, after the invasion of Cambodia and the Kent State killings in the spring of 1970, the Radical Research Center office became strike headquarters on the Carleton College campus, a new role that distracted the Center from working on the *Alternative Press Index*. Gathering and indexing became more difficult; so did getting the index in print. "We had a major hassle with a local rip-off printer," Mary McKenney noted, who kept the April-June index for six weeks. When the printer finally returned it, he had done no work on it at all.[79] As a result, Volume II, no. 2 did not appear until after Christmas. The problem in printing the index reflected the larger context of political repression. Similar situations cropped up on campuses all over the nation, where other groups who opposed the Vietnam war went through similar experiences. In response, the Center began searching for a new location where it could operate with autonomy and without harassment.

Although RTSRL had managed to push ALA into the thick of the alternative press movement, many librarians resisted. For some ALA members, rejecting the alternative press could have been a conscious choice. For others, however, it might have been a manifestation of professional insecurity. In *The Culture and Control of Expertise*, Michael F. Winter identifies several factors that contribute to librarianship's "cycle of occupational underdevelopment" and professional insecurity. These include an underdeveloped knowledge base or intellectual capital, low commitment to scholarly work, "a lack of control over the use of knowledge in the way in which doctors and lawyers, for example, have exclusive rights to certain uses of medical and legal knowledge," and librarians' lack of control or authority over their clients, i.e., librarians do not "dictate the correct view of the client's need."[80] The publishing history of "one of the most often read works in library literature"—*Prejudices and Antipathies: A Tract on the LC Subject Heads Concerning People* (by Sanford Berman)—supports Winter's analysis.[81]

Sanford Berman earned his library degree from the Catholic University of America in 1961. By 1970, he had worked in libraries in the United States, Germany, Zambia, and Uganda. Berman had an avid interest in radical literature and a talent for library acquisitions as well as cataloguing and classification. His involvement in the library movement largely developed through his interest in the alternative press. For example, he read *Synergy* regularly, he corresponded with the Radical Research Center's

Mary McKenney, he published his own alternative bibliographies, and he drew attention to and criticized undemocratic library practices. In early 1969, for example, Berman sent a letter to *Library Journal* from Zambia arguing that the Library of Congress' subject heading list enshrined and perpetuated "a racist/colonial bias." He further requested RTSRL to undertake a study "of the extent to which our major cataloguing and classification schemes are white, imperialist and Christian-oriented," and to make suggestions for improvement.[82]

On May 12, 1970, ALA's Publishing Services' senior editor, Richard A. Gray, asked Berman about his "provocative" letter. Gray agreed that subject headings were "saturated with Western chauvinism," argued that such research was "urgently needed," encouraged Berman to undertake a comprehensive study of the ethnic prejudices, and indicated that ALA Publishing was "seriously interested" in such a work. Gray warned Berman, however, that the study would be controversial, but that in his view "a good lively controversy" was just what ALA needed "to counteract the prevailing tone of dullness in professional literature.[83] Berman accepted Gray's challenge. Berman intended to harness the concept of social responsibility for the proposed publication, and while he recognized the study would not only "jolt" the profession to reconsider "one of its most basic tools in a more discriminating analytic manner," he also suspected it would infuriate many people.[84]

Berman's tract was not designed as "an attack" on the Library of Congress editors, but as a means to increase librarians' awareness that "inherited assumptions and underlying values" influence their work. He argued, for example, that the entry of works in library catalogues under the term "NIGGER" was "obviously biased." Thus, he asserted, "if librarians defend their right as educators to present all points of view in their collections, they must accept their obligation to provide an approach to their collections that is equally without bias, and which does not reinforce the psychological, sociological, economic, political, etc. assumptions and prejudices of their readers." Ultimately, his manuscript focused on the "realm" of subject headings "that deal with people and cultures — in short, with humanity," and included revised headings for subjects such as race, nationalities, faiths, ethnic groups, politics, peace, labor, law enforcement, man, woman, sex, children, and youth.[85]

In August, 1970, Gray wrote Eubanks that the Association intended to publish Berman's manuscript after "suitable revisions," but that because of her involvement with the alternative press, and because he was under "current pressures for new directions" within ALA, he sought her counsel and advice.[86] Eubanks agreed to read the manuscript. Meanwhile, however, Gray began expressing reservations about publishing the work. In an August 18 letter he asked Berman to "tone down the emotionally charged phrases and locutions."[87] Berman refused, arguing that he would rather see the book go unpublished than for it to become a "mish-mash of compromises." "Will ALA print *what* I write the *way* I write it?" he asked brashly on August 30. "And is ALA *ready* to issue a radical, muck-racking tract even though it may not wholly accord in form or philoso phy with your usual editorial policy and predilections, nor perhaps with the current sentiments and sensibilities of a majority of the profession?"[88]

Gray responded on October 6. It was normal procedure that highly argumentative works proceed slowly through the publishing process, he said, and because ALA was an academic publisher, it required "thorough scholarly documentation," especially because Berman's work was "severely critical of an old and venerable institution." The Association could publish a "temperately reasoned critique" of Library of Congress subject headings, he said, but it could not, "by its imprint, endorse a book which often partakes of the nature of a diatribe." Gray ended by saying Berman was free to confer with other publishers and that the Memorandum of Agreement between them was terminated.[89] Although it seemed to Berman that Gray was bluffing, he and his RTSRL cohorts sensed the rebuff did not bode well for RTSRL, for ACONDA/ANACONDA, nor for new directions in ALA.

While Berman and Gray battled by letter behind the scenes, ACONDA and ANACONDA met together October 17–19, 1970, at ALA's Chicago headquarters. There they agreed that "the purpose of Council's actions would be best served" if: (1) ACONDA confined itself to further consideration of problems in the democratization and possible reorganization of ALA"; and (2) ANACONDA restricted itself to a review of ACONDA's final report items not acted on at Detroit, and any recommendations made in the two-day meeting.[90]

While ACONDA/ANACONDA prepared for ALA's 1971 midwinter conference in Los Angeles, ALA's Intellectual Freedom Committee chair David K. Berninghausen worried about ACONDA's connection to RTSRL. In "Defending the Defenders of Intellectual Freedom," an article he published in the January issue of *American Libraries*, he asserted that if ACONDA's recommendations "to dispense with neutrality on substantive issues is acceptable to librarians in large numbers, the Library Bill of Rights can no longer be a basis for defending intellectual freedom." "Neither the strength of a librarians' conviction nor the urgency of a currently critical issue," he argued, is justification for ACONDA's proposal to "support one side of an issue."[91]

On January 4, 1971, Berman asked Eric Moon (who had become president of Scarecrow Press in 1968) if he was interested in publishing *Prejudices and Antipathies*.[92] Moon did not hesitate. After reading only part, he wrote Berman that it was a landmark book and enclosed a publishing contract. Berman quickly signed it, and Moon turned the manuscript into what Berman called "an honest-to-God book within nine months, static-free."[93]

Jackie Eubanks, who watched all this from the sidelines, was pleased that Scarecrow had picked up *Prejudices and Antipathies* and furious that ALA had rejected it. She recognized in the Berman-ALA brouhaha a common Association practice, i.e., ALA said it supported the idea of collecting material on all sides of issues, but it did not practice what it preached. She later asked ALA Editorial Committee chairman Donald E. Wright if he had seen the correspondence between ALA and Berman, and informed him that the Task Force on Alternatives in Print would not submit *Alternatives in Print* to ALA for publishing—first because it was so slow, but more importantly because of the kind of "pre-censorship" efforts Berman experienced with his manuscript. Did not ALA Publishing Services, she asked, support intellectual freedom?[94]

The issue of ALA's purpose, a focal point of the Chicago midwinter conference, persisted throughout the summer conference in Detroit and into the fall. At the heart of the debate was the issue of intellectual freedom. The Freedom to Read Foundation announced in the October issue of *Wilson Library Bulletin* that its Board of Trustees had established the LeRoy Merritt Humanitarian Fund in recognition of "individuals' need for subsistence and support when their positions are jeopardized or lost as a result of defending intellectual freedom."[95] The Fund was designed to offer immediate financial response by the Freedom to Read Foundation, prior to establishment of all pertinent facts in an alleged violation of intellectual freedom, and regardless of whether or not legal action was launched. Also the Foundation announced that it had awarded grants to Joan Bodger ($500), T. Ellis Hodgin ($500), and the Marshall E. Woodruff Legal Defense Fund ($250), to aid "the young newsdealer who was convicted and fined for distributing the *Washington Free Press*."[96] The ALA handling of ACONDA /ANACONDA in the following year, however, resulted in inaction where intellectual freedom and the Association were concerned.

Notes

1. Robert Sheridan, "A Membership Dilemma," *American Libraries* 1, no. 1 (January 1970): 52, 54.

2. *American Library Association Proceedings of the Midwinter Meeting Chicago January 18-24, 1970 and the 89th Annual Conference Detroit June 28–July 4, 1970* (Chicago: ALA, 1970), 5.

3. *Ibid.*, 27-28.

4. "The Month in Review," *Wilson Library Bulletin* 44, no. 7 (March 1970): 687.

5. *Ibid.*, 687, 690.

6. *Proceedings*, 1970, 28.

7. Bundy and Stielow, *Activism*, 116.

8. Bill DeJohn, Affiliates, including newsletters, 1968–71, ALA's SRRT Papers, Box 1.

9. Forsman, "Up Against the Stacks," 10–11.

10. "The Month in Review," March 1970, 688–689.

11. *Ibid.*

12. *Ibid.*, 691.

13. *Proceedings*, 1970, 27.

14. *Ibid.*, 6.

15. *SRRT Newsletter* 1, rev., (22 June 1969): 5.

16. Bundy and Stielow, *Activism*, 7.

17. *Ibid.*, 7, x.

18. "Subcommittee Report: Social Responsibilities," DeJohn Correspondence, 1969–70, ALA's SRRT Papers, Box 1.

19. *Ibid.*

20. "New Directions," *American Libraries* 1, no. 8 (September 1970): 747.

21. "The Month in Review," May 1970, 901, 903.

22. John Berry, "Electing an ALA Council," *Library Journal* 95, no. 9 (1 May 1970): 1683.

23. Gordon McShean, Sidney Jackson, Eric Moon, Richard D. Galloway, Oliver Kirkpatrick, Leo Fichtelberg, Bruce Najema, Junius Morris, and Nina Ladof.

24. Librarians for Peace was not a national organized group. Instead a variety of activities were organized under the banner, such as the librarians' marches in November, 1969. Washington, D.C., San Francisco, New Jersey, New York, and California had Librarians for Peace groups as well.

25. Forsman, "Up Against the Stacks," 6.

26. Mary McKenney to Sanford Berman, 1970, Mary McKenney, 1970–72, ALA's Sanford Berman Papers.

27. James O. Lehman, "*Choice* as a Selection Tool," *Wilson Library Bulletin* 44, no. 9 (May 1970): 960.

28. Arthur Curley, "ALA Identity Crisis: Dilemma or Delaying Device," *Library Journal* 95, no. 11 (1 June 1970): 2089–2090.

29. *Ibid.*

30. *SRRT Newsletter* 5 (1 June 1970): 4.

31. ALA Meetings, 1969–70, ALA's SRRT Papers, Box 8.

32. John Berry, "Part of the Solution," *Library Journal* 95, no. 12 (15 June 1970): 2205.

33. Ervin J. Gaines, "Faddism," *Library Journal* 95, no. 12 (15 June 1970): 2235.

34. "ALA Was the Subject," *Library Journal* 95, no. 14 (August 1970): 2613.

35. "Another Opening, Another Show: Detroit 1970," *American Libraries* 1, no. 7 (July-August 1970): 668.

36. "In Search of Soul," *Library Journal* 95, no. 14 (August 1970): 2634.

37. Forsman, "Up Against the Stacks," 10.

38. "Another Opening," 668.

39. "ALA 1970: Notes and Comments," *Wilson Library Bulletin* 45, no. 1 (September 1970): 14, 16.

40. "Another Opening," 660–661.

41. Reprint within: Geoffrey Dunbar, "Librarian and/or Citizen," *Library Journal* 97, no. 1 (1 January 1972): 42.

42. "Another Opening," 670–671.

43. *Ibid.*, 670-672.

44. "ALA was the Subject," 2615.

45. "Another Opening," 672–673.

46. *Ibid.*, 673-675.

47. *Ibid.*, 675.

48. "ALA 1970: Notes & Comments," 26.

49. "Another Opening," 675.

50. Ismail Abdullahi, ed. *E.J. Josey: An Activist Librarian* (Metuchen, NJ: Scarecrow Press, 1992), vii–viii.

51. "Another Opening," 676.

52. "ALA was the Subject," 2623.

53. "ACONDA Revised Recommendations on Democratization and Reorganization: A report presented for consideration of Council and Membership, Midwinter Meeting, January 1971," *American Libraries* 2, no. 1 (January 1971): 81–92.

54. "Another Opening, 677.

55. Paul Bixler, "On Taking a Stand," *American Libraries* 1, no. 4 (April 1970): 329.

56. "The Month in Review," March 1970, 689–690.

57. *Ibid.*, 681.

58. "ALA 1970," 19, 22.

59. George, F. Heise, "Status in the 80s," *American Libraries* 1, no. 6 (June 1970): 522–524.

60. "New Directions," 745–747.

61. John M. Carter, "Lovebites & Loobies," *Library Journal* 95, no. 20 (15 November 1970): 3885.

62. Richard B. Moses, "Detroit as Drama or is the Process the Only Payoff?" *American Libraries* 1, no. 9 (October 1970): 841–842.

63. "ALA 1970," 16–17.

64. ALA Meetings, 1969-70, SRRT-ALA General Meeting Proposal for an Alternative "BIP" National Task Force, ALA's SRRT Papers, Box 8.

65. "ALA was the Subject," 2614.

66. Lillian M. Bradshaw, "Library Response to a Restive World," *American Libraries* 1, no. 7 (July-August 1970): 690.

67. "ALA 1970," 18.

68. Pat Schuman to William DeJohn, 4 August 1969, ALA's SRRT Papers, Box 7.

69. Hoyt R. Galvin, "Mixed Bag Debate," *American Libraries* 1, no. 8 (September 1970): 745.

70. Celeste West, "The Body Politic," *Synergy* 29 (October 1970): 3–5.

71. West, "Stop!," 3.

72. Peattie, *A Passage for Dissent*, 138.

73. Jackie Eubanks to Martha Ann Kollmorgan, 25 March 1974, ALA's SRRT Papers, Box 7.

74. "Librarians in Action," *Workforce* (March-April 1973): 20–23.

75. "SRRT-ified Action — A Task Force Report for SLJ," 734–735.

76. *Sipapu* 7, no. 2 (July 1976): 1–5.

77. Jackie Eubanks to Martha Ann Kollmorgan, 25 March 1974, ALA's SRRT Papers, Box 7.

78. Betty-Carol Sellen (1970-87), Getting Library Attention, ALA's SRRT Papers, Box 11.

79. Mary McKenney to Sanford Berman, 23 January 1971, Mary McKenney, 1970–72, ALA's Sanford Berman Papers.

80. Michael F. Winter, *The Culture and Control of Expertise: Toward a Sociological Understanding of Librarianship* (New York: Greenwood Press, 1988), 99.

81. Jeffrey R. Luttrell, review of *Prejudices and Antipathies: A Tract on the LC Subject Heads Concerning People,* by Sanford Berman, in *The Journal of Academic Librarianship* 19, no. 4 (September 1993): 246.

82. Sanford Berman, "Chauvinistic Headings," *Library Journal* 94, no. 4 (February 15 1969): 695.

83. Richard A. Gray, Senior Editor (ALA) to Sanford Berman, 12 May 1970, SRRT Correspondence, 1969–75, ALA's Sanford Berman Papers.

84. Sanford Berman to Patricia Schuman, Joan Marshall, and Sandy Goin, 17 June 1970, SRRT Correspondence, 1969–75, ALA's Sanford Berman Papers.

85. Sanford Berman, *Prejudices and Antipathies: A Tract on the LC Subject Heads Concerning People* (Metuchen, N.J.: Scarecrow Press, 1971), ix–xiv.

86. Richard A. Gray to Jackie Eubanks, 13 August 1970, SRRT Correspondence, 1969–75, ALA's SRRT Papers, Box 11.

87. Richard A. Gray to Sanford Berman, 18 August 1970, ALA's SRRT Papers, Box 11.

88. Sanford Berman to Richard A. Gray, 30 August 1970, ALA's SRRT Papers, Box 11.

89. Richard A. Gray to Sanford Berman, 6 October 1970, ALA's SRRT Papers, Box 11.

90. "ACONDA Revised Recommendations on Democratization and Reorganization," 81.

91. David K. Berninghausen, "Intellectual Freedom," *American Libraries* 2, no. 1 (January 1971): 20.

92. Sanford Berman to Eric Moon, 4 January 1971, ALA's SRRT Papers, Box 11.

93. Sanford Berman to Gerald R. Shields, 18 February 1972, ALA's SRRT Papers, Box 11. Note: In 1993 McFarland & Company, Inc., Publishers reprinted

the work with corrections, a foreword by Eric Moon, a new preface by Sanford Berman, a revamped index, and a cover photo. In 1994, the reprint won the Carey McWilliams Award, presented by *Multicultural Review*.

94. Jackie Eubanks to Donald E. Wright, 22 February 1971, ALA's SRRT Papers, Box 11.

95. *Intellectual Freedom Manual*, 1996, xxxvi.

96. "Emergency Fund Within Freedom Foundation." *Wilson Library Bulletin* 45, no. 2 (October 1970): 122.

Chapter 5

The Changing of the Guard, 1971–1972

The temperature was 95 degrees "in the shade" when the American Library Association midwinter conference got under way in Los Angeles on January 18, 1971. Members took shelter from the sun inside the "aged" and "homey" Biltmore Hotel ("showplace of legendary big bands of the thirties") and congregated in its "cavernous bar" to exchange views on the study of ALA.[1] Members of the Round Table on Social Responsibilities of Libraries "jammed" into the hotel's sixth floor RTSRL suite and waved around copies of the ALA Ad Hoc Council Committee on ACONDA report — both out of passion and to keep the air circulating.[2] Membership and Council meetings were held in the Biltmore Bowl which some conference-goers dubbed the "Stupor-Bowl" because they believed ACONDA /ANACONDA was being used as an excuse to "*do nothing.*" "Establishment Turks" and the "established nabobs," they argued, were "locked in" a "sterile courtship dance."[3] In the Bowl, for example, two microphones were set up for Membership; eight for Council. Skeptics believed it "was a subtle way of telling you which way the wind was going to blow."[4]

At the Membership meeting on January 18, Katherine Laich sought feedback on ACONDA's revised recommendations on democratization and reorganization, but Al Trezza (Illinois State Library) moved to resubmit ACONDA's recommendations, still left over from Detroit. The 2,000 members in attendance, however, defeated his motion two to one.[5] In basic terms, ACONDA Revised offered four recommendations that rehashed previous ACONDA discussions. The ACONDA Recommendation 1 — that "ALA staff develop and carry out an elaborate and *systematic* communications program" — passed, even though no one knew how much the program would cost, and "not before some debate and considerable concern" for *American Libraries* — ALA's journal. "No one," for example, "wanted

Gerald Shields" (*American Libraries* editor) or ALA's "excellent" publication "to be subsumed by some new bureaucracy."[6] Recommendation 2 — that a "management firm study ALA organization"— passed after it was amended to read "skilled consultant or consultants" instead of "management firm."[7] Finally, Membership passed ACONDA's Recommendation 3 — that Council change to a 100-member body, "elected at large, from nominations based on geographical districts"— as well as Recommendation 4 — that "divisions and sections weed out all non-essential committees."[8]

At the subsequent Council meeting, Kenneth Duhac delivered an informal presentation on recommendations from ANACONDA. That body's job was merely to study and comment upon ACONDA's recommendations. Thus, ANACONDA's recommendations were drawn primarily from sections of the Detroit ACONDA report, which had not been discussed by membership. For the most part, these recommendations supported existing ALA programs, but after two Executive Board members — Marietta Shepard (Pan American Union, Washington, D.C.) and Robert McClarren — "sang the song of the snail," the *ALA Proceedings* reported, the "majority of Council members looked out from under their rock" and, except for three non-controversial ANACONDA recommendations, "sluggishly" voted 87 to 57 (of the 216-member council, many were absent) to postpone action on ACONDA/ANACONDA reports until the summer conference.[9] These three recommendations reaffirmed ALA's commitment to activities and programs in the area of international relations, provided sufficient budgetary support to ALA's Washington Office and Legislation Committee, and established a permanent Committee on Planning. At the same time, Council voted to defer ANACONDA's recommendation to create a Library Manpower Office, which was to deal with "salaries, status, welfare, employment practices, job definition, organization of personnel, administration, tenure, and ethics." Thus, "one more time," *Library Journal* noted, ALA Council "took all kinds of verbal action in support of what exists, but when the specter of change reared its ugly head, they voted to postpone."[10]

Because Council deferred most of ACONDA's recommendations to the summer conference in Dallas, ALA action on democratization and reorganization was effectively postponed another six months. "All this frustration, this delay and lack of action," *Library Journal* surmised, angered RTSRL and "other dissident bodies," who looked for alternatives to ALA's complex structure," which was "so easily able to offer up consultants and committees, instead of reform." Although ALA's membership had declined 18 percent since 1970, most dissidents did not want to abandon ALA for a union or a new organization, but many members stopped attending ALA's "fray" to work for local, regional, and state associations.[11] The 25 local affiliates of RTSRL (spread out all over the country), for example, were developing telephone reference services, reforming state associations, organizing neighborhoods and communities to demand better library services, providing assistance to minority groups, and gaining bibliographic control over alternative press materials.[12] Affiliate members usually issued their own newsletters and cooperated with RTSRL task forces through mailings and the telephone. Also, many affiliates used the national library press for issuing progress statements on their actions.

Despite Council inaction, however, RTSRL moved forward on the issue of intellectual freedom. For example, the Task Force on Intellectual Freedom declared its primary responsibility to be investigating alleged intellectual freedom violations. Previously, the Task Force deferred to state or local committees before taking action; now victims had one central place to register complaints.[13] Also, after the RTSRL Action Council declared any kind of political repression an intellectual freedom issue and therefore part of librarianship's professional jurisdiction, RTSRL voted a $200 donation to the National United Commission to Free Angela Davis Defense Fund to protect her rights in court. Davis, a young University of California philosopher, had been fired by the University Regents on September, 1969, after she admitted to being a Communist. Although she was soon reinstated to her position by the courts, she found herself teaching in an "atmosphere of increasing conflict" until June, 1970, when she was again dismissed — this time for giving "inflammatory speeches" in defense of activists. Davis was subsequently imprisoned in October, 1970, on kidnapping, murder and conspiracy charges relating to a courthouse bombing.[14] The RTSRL also called for President Nixon's impeachment for violating intellectual freedom and freedom of information, urged Congress to hold open committee meetings on the CIA, and asked ALA to formulate an editorial policy for *American Libraries* so the editor had independence in news gathering and reporting.

The Round Table also resolved to solicit financial support for Zoia Horn (Bucknell University), who had been subpoenaed by a federal grand jury as a witness in a Pennsylvania conspiracy case, in which Father Daniel Berrigan and other anti–Vietnam War activists were indicted. But Horn had refused to testify on several grounds: that "government-sponsored spying" violated the principle of intellectual freedom, that government intimidation of anti–Vietnam War activists was wrong, that the Conspiracy Act of 1968 worked as "a weapon" against citizens seeking justice, that the "professional relationships of librarians to the people they served" be respected as confidential, and that "no librarian would lend himself to a role as informant by voluntarily revealing circulation records or identifying patrons and their reading habits."[15]

Council also took action on intellectual freedom issues. It passed strong statements on the confidentiality of library records, loyalty oaths (as a requirement for library employment) and loyalty investigations, and "sanctions against parties violating ALA policies on intellectual freedom."[16] But Council actions lacked meaning; ALA already had an existing action program for matters related to intellectual freedom, including mechanisms for investigation and sanction. The Association also had a link to the Freedom to Read Foundation's program to support individuals in trouble. In other areas of concern, such as "fair employment both in libraries and with their suppliers, in the composition of library boards, even in minority recruitment," ALA lacked the "built-in-backup." Thus, resolutions on these particular issues represented "only words on paper."[17]

Since 1968, the RTSRL Action Council served as a clearinghouse to identify membership's interests and to support affiliates and task forces. Thus, in Los Angeles, RTSRL's Task Force on the Status of Women met to discuss substantive issues like, Why were there so few women in leadership positions in the feminized profession? Why did the women who held top positions earn less than their male counterparts? What role did women play in these issues? The Round Table also created several new task forces, including those for improving library and information services for American Indians, migrant workers, and prisoners.[18]

Although RTSRL leadership reaffirmed principles of participatory democracy, "petty squabbles" broke out in the Action Council meeting that revealed cracks in the social responsibilities community. While some RTSRL members pointed out that being attached to ALA gave activist librarians a voice at policy meetings and in conference displays, meetings and workshops, others questioned the RTSRL Action Council's ability to effect ALA reforms. Carolyn Forsman (a member of the Action Council), for example, argued that the Action Council's responsibilities did not allow RTSRL to have an "identifiable position in ALA activities or to exercise a position of leadership in the Association." And Joan Marshall's report on the Freedom to Read Foundation and Arthur Curley's update on ACONDA's progress since Detroit, reflected frustration and doubt about RTSRL's ability to continue working with ALA's establishment.[19]

In the months leading up to the midwinter conference, many RTSRL members had felt free to criticize current RTSRL officers, but only two candidates had volunteered for the five vacancies on the Action Council and no one at all had volunteered for three Clearinghouse vacancies — small numbers compared to RTSRL's total membership of 1,300. The Round Table leadership (Patricia Schuman, Action Council coordinator; Jackie Eubanks, Action Council affiliate coordinator; Ellen Gay Detlefsen, Action Council task force coordinator; and George Hathaway, Clearinghouse coordinator) seemed somewhat out of touch with the membership, who had grown more inclined to serve their local affiliates than RTSRL's troubled national network. In the meantime, "quietly powerful" local affiliates had emerged as "the sleeping giants in librarianship."[20] Thus, a "general philosophical difference" existed between the Action Council and some RTSRL members present. The Round Table left Los Angeles with this problem unresolved.[21]

The ALA midwinter meeting in Los Angeles "was a bum trip!," *Library Journal* concluded. "There were *groovy* speeches and resolutions, lots of words — but by the time you got home, it all boiled down to a fundamental inaction, and defeat or retreat for the forces that wanted reform in the old association." Ultimately, the old guard had "waited out" the "more impatient" activists, and had "ganged up to choke the microphones."[22]

That RTSRL leaders were concerned about their status in the social responsibilities community was obvious. In March, 1971, William DeJohn published an article in *American Libraries* titled "Social Responsibilities: What It's All About." In it he argued that because RTSRL had become an official ALA round table it now walked "the tight wire between being somewhat independent and becoming part of the ALA establishment," that it was "not dominated by any one person or group of persons," and that it was an "amorphous group of concerned librarians" who wanted "to serve as more than passive collectors of books and materials."[23] He also argued that RTSRL members were "committed to the concept of libraries and librarians having a broad social responsibility in our society," but did not wish "as some will have you believe, to impose any beliefs on the library community." Rather, RTSRL wished to "discuss social issues out in the open in the library world and to discuss with members of the library profession how librarians and libraries fit into our concept of the library profession." Although DeJohn intended the article to give *American Libraries* readers a clearer picture of RTSRL's role in ALA, it failed to do so.

That same month RTSRL member Tyron D. Emerick addressed the issue of the Round Table's status in more concrete terms. On March 15 he wrote Round Table members that it was time RTSRL redirected its attention to the Round Table's positive qualities. The group was the "vanguard for new ideas and responses," he said, the impetus for ALA to change and restructure, the Association's "main link to the changing society," and the "timepiece" that would keep the library profession current and "outward looking."[24] Emerick's strong words were timely. The ALA Committee on Organization had just asked RTSRL for a progress report and an evaluation of the round table's structure and activities. The RTSRL Action Council quickly recognized this as an opportunity for the Round Table to illustrate its accomplishments and potential.[25]

During March, Jackie Eubanks, Patricia Schuman, and David Weill collaborated on the *Report to the SRRT Membership and the Committee on Organization.* The first section showed how RTSRL functioned as a forum for discussing libraries' social responsibilities, organizing conference program meetings and program and work meetings for 19 task forces and local, regional and national affiliate groups, establishing a communications Clearinghouse, starting a newsletter, and sponsoring general membership resolutions — most particularly the 1969 resolution to end the Vietnam war.

Other sections addressed RTSRL's efforts to foster and promote the exchange of information on current social problems among all ALA units, and to stimulate ALA and its units to respond to the problems associated with social change. To this end, RTSRL reported that it planned or completed guidelines on the structure of task forces and on the development of affiliate groups. Most task forces (e.g., the Task Force on Reprinting of Negro Literature) contributed to the work of existing ALA committees and then dissolved. This reinforced the perception of RTSRL as an action-oriented rather than a bureaucratic operation.

The report's final section addressed current programs, exhibits, and other activities. First, authors noted, RTSRL served as a stimulus to ALA by providing alternative methods for membership involvement and by showing how an issue-oriented round table could accomplish projects like *Alternatives in Print.* This type of activity had largely been excluded from Association activities because of ALA's cumbersome and parochial "type-of-library" or "type-of-service" partitions. The RTSRL, the report further indicated, was made up of volunteers who came to work with commitment. In contrast, ALA appointees often came to their positions through organizational or personal ties and on a basis of past actions. Second, RTSRL passed a resolution calling political repression a matter of intellectual freedom, and donated money to the National United Commission to Free Angela Davis Defense Fund. Together the resolution and donation reminded ALA to take the issue of intellectual freedom seriously. Finally, RTSRL had stimulated new projects, including the National Freedom Fund for Librarians, which led to the formation of the Freedom to Read Foundation and the creation of the LeRoy Merritt Humanitarian Fund. And with a RTSRL loan, Librarians for 321.8 started an alternative slate to ALA Council nominations. The RTSRL also assisted groups like Librarians for Peace, the Congress for Change, and the National Call for Library Reform.

The document concluded that as the largest round table in ALA, RTSRL had, at minimum, created an arena for moral and financial support and a structure for discussion and change in the profession. Round Table speakers addressed many non–RTSRL sponsored functions, ranging from regional, state, and local meetings to community and library school forums. The RTSRL conference suite provided space for exhibits and idea exchange, a practice that was copied by several ALA groups. The Round Table also sponsored *Alternatives in Print*, which reflected its commitment to alternative reference works for the profession. Finally, RTSRL sponsored programs, exhibits, and other activities to groups outside ALA who sought librarians' expertise. Over 20 librarians, the document stated, were clipping and copying news items that related to the defense in trials involving political repression.

While Eubanks, Schuman, and Weill finalized the *Report to the SRRT Membership and the Committee on Organization*, ALA's Library Administration Division, Association of College and Research Libraries, Intellectual Freedom Committee, and Office for Intellectual Freedom were working on a proposed modified version of a Program of Action in Support of the Library Bill of Rights through a rather laboriously titled joint committee called Program of Action for Mediation, Arbitration, and Inquiry. These ALA units wanted ALA to create "a central investigatory body, with responsibility for dealing with violations concerning matters such as tenure, status, fair employment practices, due process, ethical practices, and intellectual freedom."[26]

The perceived need for the Program of Action for Mediation, Arbitration, and Inquiry followed several incidents. First, the Intellectual Freedom Committee failed to act on a Black Caucus resolution regarding "censure of libraries giving aid from public funds to educational institutions established to circumvent desegregation laws.[27] Although ALA had resolved to do so in Chicago, when the matter was referred to the Intellectual Freedom Committee, it disappeared, even though E.J. Josey had supplied evidence of library support of segregated schools to the Committee.[28] Second, on March 18, ALA's Executive Board decided Zoia Horn's case was not worthy of ALA support or financial aid because she had acted as "a private citizen." Third, J. Michael McConnell was refused employment at the University of Minnesota Library in July, 1970, following publicity concerning his application for a marriage license with another male — University of Minnesota law student Jack Baker. As a result, McConnell charged the University with discrimination.

Other incidents drew librarians' attention in the spring and summer. For example, on March 8 in a closed meeting, the Groton, Connecticut,

Public Library succumbed to public pressure and reversed an earlier decision by voting six to three to remove *Evergreen Review* from open shelves, and to place all "future issues on a restricted basis." Contacted by *Library Journal* soon after the board's backdown, librarian John T. Carey said he would not let the decision impact his acquisition policies. He noted he was "bitter about the lack of active support forthcoming from either the state library agency or from fellow librarians." "Statements of disapproval of censorship are all right," he observed, "but they are forgotten in a month."[29]

In April, RTSRL's San Francisco–Bay Area chapter developed a position paper on library materials selection based on its study of "existing policy statements." In May, *American Libraries* published the position paper on "Selection of Library Materials" that concluded libraries historically neglected right and left alternative political views, foreign language publications, tabloid or pulp periodicals, and materials on legal, medical, intellectual freedom, and religious issues. It also cited the RTSRL Bay Area chapter's belief that "the selection of materials for libraries, especially public libraries has not always been representative of the total community, but rather tends to emphasize that vocal segment of the community which now uses its public library." Again and again, the article stated, "the concept of balance comes up in our discussions" and "many of us felt that this concept was the loophole which allowed librarians to subtly censor materials from the public."[30] The issue of professional "neutrality" was at the heart of the matter.

In the May issue of *American Libraries*, Homer Fletcher argued that ALA "should be able to take a position on any matter that the membership desires." He said David K. Berninghausen was wrong to assume that once ALA had taken a stand on an issue librarians would "bend their collections" in the direction of that position. "Certainly any librarian following the Library Bill of Rights," Fletcher said, "will not allow this to occur." Taking positions on issues should not make the policy document "no longer a basis for intellectual freedom." Besides, he argued, "most libraries do not now observe strict neutrality in the forum for the combat of ideas."[31]

The ALA executive director, David Clift, learned that RTSRL's Action Council had sent a check bearing the Association's name to the National United Commission to Free Angela Davis Defense Fund, *Library Journal* reported on May 1, and that he refused to reimburse the Round Table from the ALA general fund. Payment to the Fund, Clift argued, would be in conflict with a bylaw that said round tables could not commit ALA to declared policies or incur expenses on behalf of ALA unless authorized.[32] Clift asked Patricia Schuman (RTSRL's coordinator) to remove RTSRL from the National United Commission to Free Angela Davis Defense Fund's list of contributors.

As the Round Table prepared for ALA's summer conference in Dallas (June 20–26), *Wilson Library Bulletin* reported a case of "SRRT Blues." In general, RTSRL suffered from the same "general slump" in 1971 that had affected "activist and reformist spirit throughout many organizations, institutions, and the country at large," the *Bulletin* noted.[33] In specific, RTSRL was bothered by its perception that ALA had a hypocritical attitude towards the Library Bill of Rights, as expressed in its handling (or mishandling) of the alternative press — a vanguard issue for the Round Table.[34] Members of the RTSRL were upset by the *Evergreen* incident at the Groton Public Library as well as rumors about the recent publication of *The Underground Press Syndicate–Bell & Howell Microfilm of Underground Papers, 1965-1969.*

In 1970, Bell & Howell had decided to prepare a subject index for *The Underground Press Syndicate–Bell & Howell Microfilm of Underground Papers, 1965-1969* with the assistance of the Radical Research Center. Disagreement between them, however, blocked progress. For example, the publications Bell & Howell microfilmed were not publications the Radical Research Center indexed. As a solution, Bell & Howell suggested the Center provide copies of the materials it indexed, let Bell & Howell microfilm them, and then "give away" the index with the microfilm package. The Center would get good publicity, Bell & Howell noted, and a free copy of the microfilm. But the Center saw no advantage to the offer; making extra index copies available to Bell & Howell added costs to their operation.

After hearing about the Radical Research Center's experience with Bell & Howell, Joan Marshall decided that ALA in particular, and libraries in general, needed to meet their own publishing needs. With RTSRL's support, in January, 1971, she formed RTSRL's Task Force to Index the Underground Press Microfilm Collection.[35] Its goal was to identify underground newspaper titles, address questions of binding and the problems of physical preservation, and develop subject access to the newspapers in the collection before the *Alternative Press Index* picked up coverage.[36] Along with fellow RTSRL alternative press advocates, including Jackie Eubanks and Mimi Penchansky, Marshall also planned a preconference workshop on indexing the underground press to be held June 17–19. In a notice announcing the workshop, Marshall stated "We're librarians, we're indexers, we're needed!" The preconference was intended to solicit volunteer indexers for RTSRL's Task Force to Index the Underground Press Microfilm Collection, for RTSRL's Task Force on Alternative Books in Print, and for the Radical Research Center. Although perhaps intended to alleviate "SRRT Blues," the original purpose of the workshop got lost in a "tug of war for power" within ALA at the Dallas conference.[37]

Amidst the "marquees everywhere and signs in shop windows" welcoming 8,000 librarians to town, for six days the Dallas Memorial Arena became home to Membership and Council meetings that "cast a mood of bigness and importance" to the conference.[38] Those who wanted ALA to represent the nation's libraries (i.e., the establishment) and those who wanted ALA to represent all librarians (i.e., RTSRL and ACONDA supporters) came to realize, *Library Journal* said, that "the power to change and govern ALA lies not in the members, not in the ALA Council, but rather with those who have the final decision over that all-important budget." *Library Journal* referred to the 30-member Committee on Program Evaluation and Support (COPES) that determined ALA's budget priorities, the Executive Board, and "a few heavies from the ALA Headquarters Staff."[39] Thus, what had largely been an ideological battle of opposing morals, or a war of words, had boiled down to a competition for financial resources.

The budget recommendations of COPES — to reduce funding rather than eliminate activity — did not bode well for new programs or for ALA's priorities. To be fair, COPES had to deal with "a national near-depression, library austerity, a surplus of trained librarians, a shrinking ALA membership ... burgeoning demands for association money, and its own decision to keep all existing programs at reduced funding." But Vince J. Aceto, professor at SUNY–Albany's School of Library Science and chairman of ALA's Coordinating Committee on Library Service to the Disadvantaged, had to fight with COPES to get $13,000 for ALA's Office for Library Service to the Disadvantaged — an office ALA named as a top priority the year before.[40] "Similar disregard for Council and Membership sentiment" was manifest in COPES's final decision not to fund a proposal for employing a minority recruitment specialist on ALA's staff, even though ALA had set aside $50,000 at midwinter in Chicago to fund its priority goals and despite the fact that $31,700 of the allocated fund was still unspent. Because of the perception that COPES refused to fund programs given highest priority by ACONDA/ANACONDA, John Carter moved that "ALA not let a penny from its budget until the ACONDA/ANACONDA priorities were set in motion." The "only way to effect change," he argued, "was for membership to declare that it intends to get its hands on the purse strings." Membership voted 331 to 203 to freeze the budget.[41] Obviously not everyone shared Carter's commitment to change. Approximately 8,000 people attended the conference; only 534 voted.

In response, Council voted to reorganize, to authorize a study of ALA, to defer an ACONDA recommendation for a communications program until the proposed study was completed, to endorse the recommendation to create a Library Manpower Office, but on the most important matter — the budget — Council tabled the Membership's motion to freeze. "So ACONDA/ANACONDA came to an end," *Wilson Library Bulletin* reported.[42] After the three years of debate, ACONDA/ANACONDA had failed to resolve a number of questions: Should ALA address general questions of social responsibility or only those directly affecting librarianship? Should ALA defend all challenges to free speech, or just those pertaining to the freedom to read? Should ALA actively work to improve the conditions of minorities in the nation, or simply remain on record as favoring equal opportunity? Should ALA concern itself with improving salaries and working conditions of librarians, or maintain its traditional focus on promoting libraries?[43]

Council also resolved that "ALA recognizes oppressed minorities not ethnic" ones urged "libraries to combat discrimination," voted to rescind the outdated Policy on Sanctions and the Program in Support of the Library Bill of Rights, and to create a staff committee on Mediation, Arbitration, and Inquiry (consisting of the executive secretaries of the Library Administration Division and the Association of College and Research Libraries, the director of the Office of Intellectual Freedom, one staff member at-large, and ALA's executive director), and then charged the Committee with "determining appropriate action on all complaints of violations" and authorizing it to appoint a fact-finding subcommittee to conduct a review by peers.[44] Council also gave the committee responsibility for interpreting all ALA policies, but gave it no policy-making function. Thus, the Council took several significant actions in its overall response to ACONDA/ANACONDA. It pledged to reorganize itself into a new and more directly elected body, promised to set up a Library Manpower Office to coordinate actions on behalf of librarians, went on record against discrimination toward homosexuals within libraries, and created a Staff Committee on Mediation, Arbitration, and Inquiry.[45]

At the conference, the Intellectual Freedom Committee presented a series of interpretations that elaborated specific points in the Library Bill of Rights. Council adopted three of these interpretations on June 25. The first "affirmed general principles on availability of materials of diverse views, opposition to labeling, challenging laws restricting the publication of or access to certain materials, resistance to censorship, etc." The second updated the Statement on Labeling by removing "some of its archaic verbiage" and "expanding its applicability to a wide range of labeling problems." The third, a direct response to Groton Public Library's case, offered "protection for librarians who refused to remove library materials that have never been judged obscene or unprotected."[46] Finally, on June 29 the Intellectual Freedom Committee adopted a statement backing Zoia Horn's refusal to testify in the Harrisburg 8 conspiracy case. Council echoed Intellectual Freedom Committee action. Within a few days, it resolved that ALA "sees the danger of government spying, opposes intimidation by grand jury procedure and the use of the Conspiracy Act of 1968 to intimidate, asserts professional-patron confidentiality, and asserts that no librarian would be [an] informant."[47]

Because by its action the Intellectual Freedom Committee now appeared ready to defend librarians and libraries against attacks by censors, RTSRL's Task Force on Intellectual Freedom voluntarily disbanded at the conference. In its place, RTSRL groups planned to organize around specific task forces and resolutions. All new RTSRL task forces were expected to operate closely with other ALA groups working in related areas. The RTSRL also formed some new task forces, including those on the role of media services in free schools, service to political prisoners, and government publications. Furthermore, RTSRL passed a variety of resolutions in Dallas in support of the Library Bill of Rights, including resolutions on the freedom of the press, minority recruitment, government intimidation, the Southeast Asia conflict, gay liberation, and library service to the disadvantaged. Finally, the *Report to the SRRT Membership and the Committee on Organization* received special (perhaps disingenuous) commendation by COO as the best report submitted at the conference.

The RTSRL *Newsletter* reported, that according to COO, the Round Table "provided some thought to COO for future recommendations for ALA reorganization," and approved a change in its name from Round Table on Social Responsibilities of Libraries to Social Responsibilities Round Table (SRRT). The *Newsletter* also noted that while ALA membership was dropping, SRRT's membership was growing.[48] But at the subsequent Action Council meeting, Eubanks urged SRRT to push harder. She moved that the Round Table change its name to "ALA Provisional Revolutionary Government" so that it would more closely associate with movement, Third World, and other similar groups and emphasize a people, rather than an institution, oriented philosophy. Members generally responded that this action might be divisive and alienate a large portion of SRRT membership. A better course of action, some suggested, was for the Action Council to write a policy statement outlining SRRT goals and directions. Disagreement over SRRT's name showed that a minority was much more "radical" than the rest of the Round Table.

Other issues also occupied conference centerstage. The Gay Liberation Task Force members of SRRT staged a sit-in protest before the Intellectual Freedom Committee and demanded "an end to discrimination to homosexuals." J. Michael McConnell and Jack Baker charged the Intellectual Freedom Committee with inaction. Members of the Intellectual Freedom Committee responded by saying "jurisdictional problems" in ALA prevented the committee from acting. For example, the Association of College and Research Libraries and the Library Administration Division had claimed the case was in their jurisdiction and that under the existing Program of Action in Support of the Library Bill of Rights, the Intellectual Freedom Committee's authority was limited to evaluating violations of the Library Bill of Rights.[49]

At one point in the discussion, Intellectual Freedom Committee chair Berninghausen was heavily criticized by the gay Task Force members. His role in the McConnell case was complicated by his affiliation with both the Intellectual Freedom Committee and the University of Minnesota — where he sat on the University Senate, the Senate Library Committee, and the Senate Judicial Committee. Berninghausen told Task Force members he had supported McConnell at Minnesota by helping draft a favorable resolution by the Senate Library Committee. But Task Force members were not persuaded. They continued their sit-in, making the McConnell case the cause célèbre of the week — the incident, *Library Journal* said, "effectively dramatized the jurisdictional morass in which ALA floundered, weighed down by conflicting authority and meaningless policies."[50]

Israel Fishman, librarian at Upsala College, coordinated the gay group that some later argued shattered the Association's customary etiquette by sponsoring a Hug-a-Homosexual booth in the exhibit hall. For an entire afternoon, SRRT gay and lesbian members offered free hugs and kisses to anyone passing by. Two Dallas television channels showed same sex kisses and hugs that night; *Life* ran photos in its next issue. At its business meeting, the Task Force on Gay Liberation presented the first annual Gay Book Award to Isabel Miller for her first novel *A Place for Us* (1969). Because no commercial publisher would handle her book, Miller had established her own firm (Bleecker Street).

"Although different observers came away from Dallas with different scorecards," *Library Journal* noted, "there was some agreement on the kind of ball game that was being played, with a three-way tug-of-war going on for power." First, there were the "federation types whose unit of loyalty" was the type of library they worked in and who were "allied to a type of library division in ALA." Second, there were the "populists," who were "loosely clustered around SRRT" and who demanded "a larger representation in the governance of ALA based on the principle of one-man-one-vote." By the end of the conference in Dallas, the federationists "had the numbers, but not the power to influence change." Indeed, there was a third group—the "elitist triangle composed of the Executive Board, the ALA Headquarters staff and COPES," who controlled the budget and designed the structure in which it was spent.[51]

But SRRT had its own battles to fight. Schuman, for example, had presented the case for SRRT's National United Commission to Free Angela Davis Defense Fund donation to ALA's Executive Board in Dallas. She had noted that because Davis had been denied library materials while in prison, and because passages contained in both the Library Bill of Rights and the Freedom to Read Statement were clear examples of existing ALA policies on intellectual freedom, the donation to the Davis Commission was justified.[52] After the conference, ALA's Executive Board voted to reimburse SRRT Action Council for its $200 contribution to the National United Commission to Free Angela Davis Defense Fund.[53] And because ALA's Intellectual Freedom Committee had voted that McConnell's rights were violated, on October 19, trustees of the LeRoy Merritt Humanitarian Fund awarded $500 to J. Michael McConnell for legal expenses. These actions helped refine ALA's definition of intellectual freedom and constituted an accomplishment for library activists.

But some ALA members were angered by the Davis fund reimbursement. Joan L. Newberry (Columbus, Georgia) wrote in *American Libraries* that ALA's social responsibility did not "compel us to become a political body."[54] Rudolph Bold (Ridgewood, New York) urged "a return to true independence where our association would concentrate only on library matters and avoid partisan politics unless library service seems threatened."[55] Katherine Hubbard (Detroit) said SRRT had gone "too far."[56] Martha Boaz (dean, University of Southern California School of Library Service) argued that "librarians have library work to do," that "our personal, social and political, and sexual interests should be pursued personally," and that "library business is a librarian's first responsibility."[57] *American Libraries* later published six letters supporting Boaz.[58]

Meanwhile, the Radical Research Center was searching for new quarters. Center members wanted to be able to operate with autonomy and without harassment. Late in the year, the Center decided to move its offices to a free-university called Rochdale College in downtown Toronto because it appeared to be a place where the collective could operate on an independent, non-profit educational basis. But there were problems. Higher printing costs, a general lack of funds, and difficulties getting the center legally situated in Canada delayed the Center's relocation. (Immigration officials seemed to think that the Center members were "weatherpeople going up to Canada to set up a base from which to overthrow the U.S. gov't.").[59] Production of the *Alternative Press Index* was caught in a limbo between Carleton and Rochdale. Ultimately, the unexpected delay in crossing the United States–Canadian border resulted in a three-month "stopover" in Detroit, where the Center published Volume II, number 4 of the index in January, 1972.[60]

With the Radical Research Center temporarily in flux, Jackie Eubanks sought more publicity for *Alternatives in Print*. She drew on her connections with the alternative press community and sent a flyer about the publication to non–ALA groups such as the Committee of Small Magazines and Publishers (COSMEP). On October 18, 1971, Richard Morris (COS-MEP editor) offered to run a note about *Alternatives in Print* in his newsletter. Morris also commented about the lack of small press reviews in library publications, and suggested that SRRT and COSMEP "apply pressure to correct" the situation. The best tactic, he suggested, might be to get reviews of small press publications printed in the core journals. *Publishers Weekly*, he remarked, regularly discriminated against small movement publishers as well as publishers of poetry chapbooks by not including pamphlets of less than 40 pages in its listing of forthcoming books.[61]

Sanford Berman maintained contact with the Radical Research Center.[62] He, like many activist librarians, recognized the importance of the Center and the ongoing need for reference tools like *Alternative Press Index*. On October 20, he told Mary McKenney that the library could function as a change agent "merely on the basis of the old-time public service/all points of view ethic/philosophy," but he also noted that the "BIG hurdle was still to build truly full-spectrum collections" and to eradicate those "unbalanced" toward the right and middle. Finally, he argued, libraries did not service all groups in society, a clear violation of the meaning of the Library Bill of Rights.[63] These factors, Berman believed, indicated the need for a more socially responsible library in which citizens could get the information they wanted, no matter who they were. Yet, for most librarians, the alternative press was not important.

But librarians also subverted the potential influence of the *Alternative Press Index* in more direct ways. Many failed to shelve it with key sources like the *Reader's Guide to Periodical Literature*; and, instead placed the index in "some obscure place."[64] "It'll be a while," Mary McKenney had observed in January, 1970, "before you start seeing the radical represented VISIBLY in most libraries."[65] A year later, nothing had changed. Whether by ignorance or design, librarians' failure to educate themselves about and provide access to alternative press materials had serious implications for library users. It reflected a truth about librarianship's view of its professional responsibilities to the Library Bill of Rights and intellectual freedom.

In his January 15, 1972, *Library Journal* editorial, John Berry reported that the Fund for Librarians was "dead," that it had turned its "meager treasury" over to the LeRoy Merritt Humanitarian Fund of the Freedom to Read Foundation, and that while the National Freedom Fund for Librarians had been formed spontaneously to provide aid to "embattled librarian" Ellis Hodgin (and had been "a motivating force" in the creation of the Freedom to Read Foundation)—"we always felt that all of this should have taken place within [ALA] as the legitimate business of a professional society, and we still do." Joan Marshall was also upset that ALA had passed the fund to a sister organization. "ALA can do anything that the Freedom to Read Foundation can do," she said, "since both have the same kind of tax-exempt status."[66]

"The Palmer House Hotel, meeting site, was in the mid-nineties, as if to atone for the frigid, flu-bearing drafts" of the Sherman House in 1970. And "as if to make up for the cold-shoulder turned on ALA by some 7,000 members over the last three years," members "whooshed into Palmer House for preliminary meetings and pre-preliminary meetings days before the official registration at 2 pm" on January 23. Approximately 2,000 delegates and 100 exhibitors registered for the Chicago midwinter conference (January 22–23). The 1,000 meetings took place in dozens of meeting rooms on several levels of the Palmer House, "causing participants to spend so many hours going up and down on the speedy elevators that their sense of balance would probably never be the same." *Wilson Library Bulletin* said, the conference mood swung from up to down, from hot to cold.[67] On the up-side, Council voted to force ALA to retroactively pay the salary of Peter Doiron, fired editor of the ALA Association of College and Research Libraries professional review journal *Choice,* "for the nine months during which he failed, allegedly, to receive due process, and until he does receive such process." Doiron was "abruptly" dismissed on July 29, 1971, after ALA sued him for "causing the removal from the CHOICE offices of a file listing CHOICE reviewers."[68] And "for those who place human values above institutional structure," *The Report of the Library of Congress Inquiry Team* (chaired by David Kaser) found "a pattern of actions for which it could conceive no other motivation than racial discrimination." Many rejoiced with Joslyn N. Williams (a Library of Congress employee), who had been "charging discrimination in personnel practices" for almost a year. "I can [now] go back to my colleagues ... and say to them in all sincerity—I have found equity," Williams said.[69]

On the down-side, Freedom to Read Foundation chair Alex Allain tried to exclude all observers from the board meeting, except the press. Only after Katherine Laich and Ervin J. Gaines challenged Allain's decision did the board open the meeting. Judith Krug announced that, following a campaign, membership had grown to 648 (78 of whom were new), but Joan Marshall criticized the campaign for failing to highlight the LeRoy Merritt Humanitarian Fund. "Professional fund raisers had advised" against mentioning it, the Board responded limply.[70]

Also on the down-side, Executive Board members rejected a request to support Zoia Horn at a special meeting. And while the Board instructed the ALA executive director to ask the Intellectual Freedom Committee to continue gathering all available facts in the Horn case and to keep the Board updated, it failed to mention it had been warned by legal counsel against support. Horn later responded that she always felt the library profession was as strong in action as in words, but that the Executive Board contradicted that belief.[71] The Social Responsibilities Round Table also experienced "bad vibrations." Several Action Council members quit and to "ease the strain" Robert Wedgeworth chaired the last SRRT session. "Once a united front for association reform," the Round Table had by "all appearances lost its momentum and its very meaning as a single coherent group," *Wilson Library Bulletin* reported. Instead, it had splintered its efforts among a variety of task forces — women's liberation forces, gay liberation forces, and others.[72]

When the conference closed on January 23, the librarians who had traveled to Chicago in the hopes of seeing demonstrated changes in ALA left with mixed emotions. The conference's ups and downs had left them uncertain. But just a few months later, the ALA scene looked brighter. In March, ALA announced Robert Wedgeworth had been appointed executive director to assume office in September. Wedgeworth had worked in libraries since 1961, and for a while was the editor of *Library Resources and Technical Services.* He was a doctoral candidate and assistant professor at Rutgers Graduate School of Library Service, and most recently had been part of the committee investigating the Library of Congress for alleged discriminatory employment practices. *American Libraries* editor Gerald Shields wrote that Wedgeworth was "welcome not only for his youth, his education and his easy and articulate understanding of his role in the profession," but also for his "quick wit, his sense of justice, and his dedication to the importance of the individual and the library."[73] John Berry wrote in *Library Journal* that the "honeymoon is on" because "everyone sees in Bob an ally or an advocate." For example, Wedgeworth's "credential with ALA's rebel wing" was in "good order." He was a member of the Black Caucus, but the "technical processes and library education people" also viewed him as "the first leader with some real experience and understanding regarding their problems." And the establishment felt that he took a "considerably less than militant stand on social and racial issues." But Berry also pointed out that "Wedgeworth's ability to be everyone's advocate fit the bill" and was perhaps "the key reason for his appointment."[74]

In April Zoia Horn was released on bail after spending three days in a Pennsylvania jail for refusing to testify at the trial of Philip Berrigan. Although Judith Krug (director, ALA's Office for Intellectual Freedom) had offered to ask the LeRoy Merritt Humanitarian Fund for bail money, trustees decided Horn was "not eligible for aid because her case did not clearly involve intellectual freedom issues." In response, SRRT set up a "Harrisburg Fund" for Horn and pledged $500. Embarrassed Fund trustees reversed themselves and offered $500 "after all."[75] The ALA Executive Board held its ground, however. Horn would get no financial support from the world's largest library association. In contrast, SRRT, the New Jersey Library Association's Executive Board, and many ALA members felt that because her case involved intellectual freedom and because at the Dallas conference the Council protested "government intimidation of citizens and government interference in library affairs," Horn deserved ALA's support.[76] The issue threatened to disrupt the forthcoming summer conference.

That same month *American Libraries* published a lengthy article by Eric Moon titled "Association Agonies: Life with ALA." In it, Moon urged "the young, the dissident, the radical, the change-seekers to keep up the pressure" and to "resist despondency about the temporary losses." The Social Responsibilities Round Table, he said, had "done much to upset the equilibrium of the upper Establishment" and it had "changed the climate of ALA." "There is nervousness, even fear, among those who were merely complacent before," said Moon, "and some of the inertia has been translated into an unwilling receptivity." But for SRRT to accomplish more, Moon predicted, it would have to learn "the machinery — the Bylaws and the Constitution — and the election procedures."[77]

Moon also wrote about what he called the "morality gap" between those who grew up during the Depression and World War II — they seemed to have an "understandable survival complex and a deliberate (i.e. slow) rate of change"— and the younger librarians and "a goodly number of oldies too" ("who do not get so hung up on principle that expediency can appear downright immoral"). He explained, for example, that as the "pressures against dissent in the U.S." had mounted in recent years, "librarians themselves (not just books and magazines on their shelves)" fell "victim to repression and attack" for "supporting the very principles which ALA has long espoused." As the "casualty list" grew, the gap between ALA's "promise and performance in the intellectual freedom arena" had intensified. But while "impatience with the continued parade of statements" grew "more vocal, and the demands for action, not just words," grew "more insistent," he said, the "dollar has been ALA's paramount interest." When, for example, librarians made demands on ALA for a defense fund, Moon argued, they were told that "it cannot be done because it might injure ALA's tax-exempt status." Thus, he called the Freedom to Read Foundation ALA's "master-ploy," because it allowed the Association to preserve "its precious tax-exempt status" and at the same time give "the appearance of action." Moon's second example of how ALA's "morality gap" led to a preoccupation with finances pertained to the Dallas ALA conference. Here, the membership "vented its spleen on the ALA budget committee (COPES) for making no attempt in its 1971-72 budget to reflect the priorities of the association which had been voted in by the membership" and adopted by Council — ALA's "supposed policy-making body."[78]

Moon's article also addressed what he called ALA's "attitude gap." This he illustrated by referring to "a little internal document circulated among members of the ALA Nominating Committee for 1972-73," which "spelled out some of the proposed criteria for president-elect and treasurer." The Committee, Moon said, wanted candidates who had "some evidence of having accomplished good for the association, or evidence of cultural refinement"; who had "presence;" and who were of a "desirable" age — between 45 and 55 years old. Moon wrote, the establishment "picks carefully" and "seems to know its own kind very well, even when they are in the embryo stage." It was also interesting, he noted, how "establishment like some of the young malcontents of only a year or two ago look and sound, after just a short period of close contact with the establishment bosom." However, Moon argued, a variety of social issues were still most important, including "race, sex, and war, to name three potent elements."[79] Two months later, the following comments were published in *American Libraries*: (1) "I'm afraid that women, blacks, and homosexuals will be better advised to join a labor union or the AAUP," (2) "How far must tolerance go when what is tolerated is making a laughing stock of the profession?" (3) "The spectacles presented by the minority groups at the Dallas convention jeopardized continued public support for libraries," (4) "I want Angela Davis to have a fair trial ... it is my opinion that it is not within the province of a library association to make this decision for me," and (5) "Where are the nationally shown television spots focusing on how libraries serve the nation?"[80]

But that was not the only item promising controversy. In its June 1 issue, *Library Journal* mentioned that it looked as though "a strong bid is shaping up for curbing [SRRT] movement which has been so much a part of the yeasty ferment whence have sprung the volatile ethers of change in recent ALA history." Proposals aimed at SRRT included "taking control" of its money and restricting its ability "to affiliate with other groups outside ALA." The article also stated that ALA's legal counsel had warned ALA "in a lengthy report that its tax status can be seriously jeopardized by the present permissive arrangement for member round tables." But *Library Journal* did not despair. In SRRT's favor, "many forces" were "arrayed on the side of round table freedom, including ALA's academic and school library divisions (which were wary of centralized authority), two new round tables for federal librarians and government librarians (who wanted to pursue their own interests), and a "broad new pattern" emerging in ALA to form "mission-oriented action units" as opposed to the "highly centralized organization of the past." Over the last three to four years, *Library Journal* noted, "changebound members" had challenged "well-entrenched people" by forming SRRT, the Office for Intellectual Freedom, and ACONDA/ANACONDA. And as a result of these new directions, Council had "committed hari-kari while arranging for its reincarnation as a smaller more representative body — and one with key powers successfully wrestled from ALA Executive Board." Furthermore, new faces like Robert Wedgeworth now appeared "in the upper echelons." Indeed, *Library Journal* concluded, some power had already changed hands.[81] And *Library Journal* was right.

Approximately 9,700 members turned out for ALA's annual conference in Chicago (June 25–July 1), *Wilson Library Bulletin* reported, and with a Council "streamlined" from 222 members to 168, a "committee on committees to aid the president-elect in choosing members for key committees, a number of high-level appointments to be made, and a vigorous new executive director," it looked "like a bright new day at the end of a long tunnel — not just another tunnel."[82] At the conference, Robert Wedgeworth posed with crossed arms for *Library Journal* in front of a white background with red lettering that spelled out "ALA." Below the Association banner were the words "Changing of the Guard." Indeed, *Library Journal* later wrote, at Chicago, the activism that emerged in Kansas City and peaked in Atlantic City, "insinuated itself into the organizational structure and after that, was finally part and parcel of the Conference, if not of the ALA organization itself." Those library activists "who had been out on the floor shouting in Atlantic City were now sitting in some of the seats of power, either on the Council, on ALA committees, or in their own highly structured groups" like SRRT, JMRT, or the Black Caucus. "Membership meetings, once the only open forum for activist concern, were quiet, even dull affairs in Chicago." The Council and the Executive Board, "once frightened to inaction by proposals with external social or political ramifications, took strong positions on a number of questions without any real conservative dissent." And the "internal, organizational reforms that traditionally would produce so much heat and rhetoric about ALA priorities and reform, became pretty much matters of ratification." Thus, ALA-Chicago was a mild mannered meeting" — "all the issues that had been brewing since Dallas were settled or postponed with little debate."[83]

The Executive Board approved the "toughest" ALA budget in years with very little discussion, while "planned resolutions favoring restorations of many of the cuts were either dropped before presentation or tabled by the Council."[84] The Executive Board rescinded its March 18 statement about Zoia Horn, and the Intellectual Freedom Committee resolved to support her by stating that ALA "recognizes factual grounds for Mrs. Horn's actions which were a protest against infringement of academic and intellectual freedom." It also referred to the Library Bill of Rights and concluded that ALA commended "Mrs. Horn's commitment and courage in defense of the principles of intellectual freedom." Other resolutions by Council passed. One read "ALA shall have no affiliation with, memberships in, nor formal relationships with organizations which violate its principles and commitments to human rights and social justice," another said ALA staff should "take care to schedule conferences only at hotels which practice equal employment or agree to institute affirmative action," and a third called upon ALA "to work harder to recruit and aid in the profes sional education of Chicano librarians."[85]

Among the new faces in the ALA hierarchy were Executive Director Robert Wedgeworth, who "seen in action [unofficially] for the first time in Chicago," *Library Journal* said, "looks like a tough negotiator and a willing problem solver" and first "ACONDA president" Katherine Laich, whose ACONDA/ANACONDA service had "set the stage for the reformed Association." The new Council, "possibly the most representative in ALA history," noted *Library Journal*, represented a "new order in ALA internal politics." For example, 73 of the 100 new Councilors elected at large, were new to ALA Council; many were new to ALA activity in general. There were also rumors that established icons Deputy Executive Director Ruth Warncke and Comptroller LeRoy Gaertner might leave their posts. The "quietness" of Chicago might have reflected the fact that members were willing "to see how the new ALA team responds to old issues."[86]

The Social Responsibilities Round Table had a memorable week. A new Action Council coordinated by Tyron D. Emerick re-oriented SRRT "to be less involved in the internal politics of ALA and more in the neglected areas of library service." The group also sponsored a speech by the Rev. Jesse Jackson, which was considered the "most outstanding" and "well-attended" conference event. As *Library Journal* reported it, Jackson spoke to a "packed and overflowing" audience; his "enthralling," library-oriented, "electric" talk, was "a stirring call to advocacy through library services," while the content of his speech, which related the librarian and society, "was one of the clarion refutations of the library neutrality positions yet on record."[87] Conference-goers left Chicago relieved that the turmoil of the previous four years was beginning to subside.

After the conference, debate concerning ALA's priorities and professional jurisdiction shifted from free-for-all discussions to more carefully crafted entries in the professional literature. For example, in an article written for the July-August issue of *American Libraries,* Dan Lacy (senior vice-president of McGraw-Hill) compared the state of the nation in 1952 — when "an embittered and internally divided country under an unpopular president comes to the end of a frustrating and unsuccessful Asian war and everyone is seeking scapegoats"— to 1972, which reflected many of the same problems. The atmosphere, he said, "invites another McCarthy era." Here Lacy referred to Vice President Spiro Agnew's assault on the mass media; the use of "federal investigative power" to "pressure or intimidate news correspondents critical of the administration," the use of conspiracy charges to link vigorous opposition spokesmen to distant acts "of which they may have been entirely unaware," forcing news "correspondents to turn over their research notes, etc. to the government," and preventing the publication of information "classified by a government agency" like the *Pentagon Papers.* "Every resource of freedom will need to be devoted to its defense," asserted Lacy. "On this front," he added, libraries need "to stand together shoulder-to-shoulder with their colleagues in writing, publishing, film, and broadcasting."[88]

At the time, David K. Berninghausen (director of the University of Minnesota library school) was also working on a paper. Over the course of the summer he circulated it to members of ALA's Council and to ALA officers. In a cover letter, he expressed a concern that "intellectual freedom as defined in the Library Bill of Rights has been put in jeopardy recently by a minority of librarians who seem to be intent, as one of my correspondents puts it, upon ruling or ruining the ALA."[89] *Library Journal* printed the paper in its November 15, 1972, issue with the title "Antithesis in Librarianship: Social Responsibility vs. The Library Bill of Rights."[90] It ushered in a germinal debate concerning professional "neutrality" that significantly affected librarianship for the rest of the century.

Notes

1. *American Library Association Proceedings 1971 of the Midwinter Meeting Los Angeles January 18–22, 1971, and the Annual Conference Dallas June 20–26, 1971* (American Library Association: Chicago, 1971), 638, 628.

2. "Midwinter Night's Summer Dream," *American Libraries* 2, no. 1 (January 1971): 23.

3. *ALA Proceedings*, 1971, 628; "Headin' for the Last Roundup," *American Libraries* 2, no. 3 (March 1971): 273.

4. "Midwinter Night's Summer Dream," 23.

5. "ALA Midwinter — Post-Analytic Depression," *Wilson Library Bulletin* 45, no. 7 (March 1971): 628.

6. "Council Cop-Out," *Library Journal* 96, no. 6 (15 March 1971): 923.

7. ACONDA members were "audibly relieved" when membership defeated an amendment that would have made them the consultants. *ALA Proceedings*, 1971, 628.

8. *Ibid.*

9. *ALA Proceedings*, 1971, 628.

10. "Council Cop-Out," 924.

11. Many attributed the drop in membership to dues. See "ALA Membership Slides 6,471," *Wilson Library Bulletin* 45, no. 6 (February 1971): 525; "Social Responsibility: The Neighborhood Alternative," *Library Journal* 96, no. 6 (15 March 1971): 930.

12. Affiliates of SRRT included Black Caucus of ALA, Concerned Librarians of University Training (CLOUT), Congress for Change, Librarians for Peace, Librarians for 321.8, Concerned Library Students, National Call for Library Reform, Librarians' Tribe, People's Librarians, National Women's Liberation Front for Librarians, Pittsburgh Group, No Chicago Group, Freedom to Read Foundation, Liberated Librarians, as well as numerous local social responsibilities library groups such as the Colorado Librarians in Transition (COLT), who published the *Silver Bullet;* the New Jersey Social Responsibilities Group, who published their own *Newsletter* c/o Martha Williams, Princeton Public Library; and NYSRRT, who published *Response.* ALA Meetings, 1969–70, ALA's SRRT Papers, Box 8.

13. Gordon McShean, "SRRT-IF Task Force," *American Libraries* 2, no. 4 (April 1971): 342.

14. Davis was acquitted of all of these charges in the spring of 1972. Regina Nadelson, *Who Is Angela Davis: The Biography of a Revolutionary* (New York: Peter H. Wyden, Inc., 1972), xi–xii. See also J.A. Parker, *Angela Davis: The Making of a Revolutionary* (New Rochelle, NY: Arlington House, 1973); Angela Davis, *Angela Davis: An Autobiography* (New York: Random House, 1974).

15. "Government Intimidation," *American Libraries* 2, no. 8 (September 1971): 804.

16. "Intellectual Freedom and the Jurisdictional Jungle," *Library Journal* 96, no. 6 (15 March 1971): 925; *ALA Proceedings*, 1971, 634.

17. "Council Cop-Out," 919.

18. *Workforce* (March-April 1973): 20–23.

19. "ALA Midwinter: Post-Analytic Depression," 624.

20. "Social Responsibility: The Neighborhood Alternative," 929. For example, the Los Angeles Committee on Social Responsibilities sponsored programs on ethnic groups, community information centers, and correctional facilities at the annual California Library Association conference; the Finger Lakes group served prisoners and worked with Cornell students on a bus tour to rural communities with community service information; the Missouri group compiled a list of outreach programs and services to the disadvantaged which were offered by Missouri libraries; the Maryland group produced a feminist reading list titled "Women: A Selected Bibliography"; the Philadelphia group introduced a resolution concerning invasion of privacy by governmental searches of library records at the Pennsylvania Library Association's annual conference; the Detroit group worked with the League of Black Workers to help them compile a collection on labor; and the Washington group was active in the areas of status of women in librarianship, library service to Chicanos, and participatory management. For more information see the 1971 issues of the *SRRT Newsletter.*

21. *SRRT Newsletter* 12 (February 1971): 7.

22. "Council Cop-Out," 918.

23. Bill DeJohn, "Social Responsibilities: What It's All About," *American Libraries* 2, no. 3 (March 1971): 300–302.

24. SRRT Elections, January 1971–June 1973, SRRT and the Structure of ALA, March 15, 1971, Candidate for Action Council, Tyron D. Emerick, ALA's SRRT Papers, Box 4.

25. Publicity Pamphlet, 1973, Report to the SRRT Membership and the Committee on Organization, March 1971, ALA's SRRT Papers, Box 11.

26. "Intellectual Freedom at Dallas," *Library Journal* 96, no. 14 (August 1971): 2447.

27. *Ibid.*

28. "Action/Resolutions: Midwinter," *Library Journal* 96, no. 6 (15 March 1971): 905.

29. "Censors Fell Evergreen in Groton," 45, no. 8 *Wilson Library Bulletin* (April 1971): 717; "Groton Censors Win: Trustees Back Down," *Library Journal* 96, no. 8 (15 April 1971): 1318.

30. "Selection of Library Materials," *American Libraries* 2, no. 5 (May 1971): 452. See also "Historically Neglected Materials," *Wilson Library Bulletin* 45, no. 8 (April 1971): 733.

31. Homer L. Fletcher, "How Pure Is Neutrality?" *American Libraries* 2, no. 5 (May 1971): 449.

32. "Clift Balks at Davis Gift Voted by SRRT Council," *Library Journal* 96, no. 9 (May 1971): 1553.

33. "SRRT Blues," *Wilson Library Bulletin* 45, no. 8 (April 1971): 737.

34. *SRRT Newsletter* 12 (February 1971): 5.

35. Joan K. Marshall, "Bawl & Howl," *Booklegger Magazine* 5 (July/August 1974): 22–25.

36. "The SRRT & the SRRT Concept, 1968 through 1975," ALA's SRRT Papers, Box 9.

37. "Shadows of the Future," *Library Journal* 96, no. 14 (August 1971): 2431.

38. "ALA-1971: Notes & Comments," *Wilson Library Bulletin* 46, no. 1 (September 1971): 8, 10.

39. "Shadows of the Future," 2433.

40. *Ibid.*

41. "ALA-1971: Notes & Comments," 16.

42. *Ibid.*, 20.

43. Raymond, "ACONDA and ANACONDA," 356.

44. "ALA-1971: Notes & Comments," 21.

45. Raymond, "ACONDA and ANACONDA," 356.

46. "Shadows of the Future," 2448.

47. "ALA-1971: Notes & Comments," 21.

48. *SRRT Newsletter* 15 (1 August 1971): 4.

49. "Shadows of the Future," 2447.

50. *Ibid.*, 2447-2448.

51. *Ibid.*, 2431.

52. "SRRT $200 for Angela Davis Approved by ALA Executive Board," *Library Journal* 96, no. 1 (1 July 1971): 1913.

53. Tyron D. Emerick, "One More Wedge," *Library Journal* 96, no. 13 (July 1971): 2239.

54. Joan L. Newberry, "Social or Political," *American Libraries* 2, no, 8 (September 1971): 791.

55. Rudolph Bold, "Usurped Sympathy," *American Libraries* 2, no. 9 (October 1971): 929.

56. Katherine Hubbard, "Protest Indecency," *American Libraries* 2, no. 10 (November 1971): 1039.

57. Martha Boaz, "The First Responsibility," *American Libraries* 2, no. 10 (November 1971): 1035.

58. "Commentary," *American Libraries* 3, no. 3 (March 1972): 220–221.

59. Kathy Martin to *WIN*, 20 October 1971, RRC Papers, Box 7.

60. History of the Radical Research Center/Alternative Press Center, RRC Papers, Box 7.

61. Richard Morris to Jackie Eubanks, 18 October 1971, Jackie Eubanks Correspondence, May–October, 1971, ALA's SRRT Papers, Box 7.

62. Art Plotnik, "The Berman File," *Wilson Library Bulletin* 47, no. 10 (June 1973): 861.

63. Sanford Berman to Mary McKenney, 20 October 1971, Mary McKenney, 1970–72, ALA's Sanford Berman Papers.

64. Kathy Martin to Albert Bofman, 9 December 1971, RRC Papers, Box 1.

65. Mary McKenney to Sanford Berman, 30 January 1970, Mary McKenney, 1970–72, ALA's Sanford Berman Papers.

66. John Berry, "Death and Taxes," *Library Journal* 97, no. 2 (15 January 1972): 137.

67. "ALA Midwinter: Hot Winds, Cold Winds, Ups and Downs," *Wilson Library Bulletin* 46, no. 7 (March 1972): 638.

68. "A Hearing for Doiron," *Library Journal* 96, no. 21 (1 December 1971): 3931. See also "Peter Doiron Seeks Appeal," *Wilson Library Bulletin* 46, no. 2 (October 1971): 124.

69. *Ibid.*, 638–641.

70. *Ibid.*, 646, 640.

71. *SRRT Newsletter* 20 (June 1972): 2.

72. "ALA Midwinter: Hot Winds," 647.

73. "Editors' Choice: Robert Wedgeworth," *American Libraries* 3, no. 6 (June 1972): 591.

74. John Berry, "Happy Honeymoon," *Library Journal* 97, no. 8 (15 April 1972): 1465.

75. "Zoia Horn Released on Bail During Berrigan Trial," *Library Journal* 97, no. 8 (15 April 1972): 1367.

76. "Support for Zoia Horn: Issue Splitting ALA," *Library Journal* 97, no. 19 (15 May 1972): 1760–1761.

77. Eric Moon, "Association Agonies: Life with ALA," *American Libraries* 3, no. 4 (April 1972): 398–400.

78. *Ibid.*, 396-398.

79. *Ibid.*, 396-399.

80. "Commentary," *American Libraries* 3, no. 6 (June 1972): 579-581.

81. "Through a Crystal Ball—Dimly: The Coming ALA Annual Convention," *Library Journal* 97, no. 11 (1 June 1972): 2053.

82. "ALA Chicago 1972," *Wilson Library Bulletin* 47, no. 1 (September 1972): 62.

83. "The Changing Guard: The 1972 ALA Conference," *Library Journal* 97, no. 14 (August 1972): 2523.

84. *Ibid.*

85. "ALA Chicago 1972," 64.

86. "The Changing Guard," 2530, 2524.

87. *Ibid.*, 2528-2529. Simultaneously, on June 20, 1972, the Supreme Court refused to hear the case of Ellis Hodgin and "all judicial recourse was exhausted." "Supreme Court Refuses to Hear Hodgin Case," *Wilson Library Bulletin* 47, no. 1 (September 1972): 8.

88. Dan Lacy, "Suppression and Intellectual Freedom: Two Decisive Decades," *American Libraries* 3, no. 7 (July-August 1972): 809–810.

89. "Berninghausen Charges Minority Wants to Rule or Ruin ALA," *American Libraries* 4, no. 1 (January 1971): 9.

90. Berninghausen, "Antithesis in Librarianship," 3675–3681.

Epilogue

Reaffirming Professional "Neutrality," 1973–1974

On the otherwise all-black cover of the *Library Journal* issue carrying Berninghausen's article, editors placed a quote in bright yellow lettering that read "Attempts to make this organization into a political organization for the promotion of specific causes unrelated to librarianship could destroy the viability of the ALA. They have already weakened it."[1] Inside, the article made two main points about social responsibility. First, Berninghausen drew a distinction between the librarian's personal and professional life. As a citizen, it was legitimate for a librarian to get involved in non-library problems, but not as a professional. Second, he suggested that the American Library Association was considerably disarmed by involvement in controversies that, in his opinion, were outside the scope of librarianship. Both points pertained to the issue of library "neutrality."

Berninghausen argued that since ALA adopted the Library's Bill of Rights and established a Committee on Intellectual Freedom to Safeguard the Rights of Library Users in 1939, the Association had appropriately concerned itself with maintaining intellectual freedom for library users and recognizing "its responsibility to provide information without censorious limitations." Thus, Berninghausen asserted that the Library Bill of Rights served to codify and standardize a moral stance on intellectual freedom by which impartiality and "neutrality" on non-library issues functioned as core values for the profession. But Berninghausen also noted that since 1940, ALA's jurisdiction —"maintaining and preserving intellectual freedom for the user of libraries"— was in danger of being extended far beyond the "original, logical limits" when the Committee shortened its name to Committee on Intellectual Freedom. Thus, he tracked the "first direct attempt to discard" the principle of intellectual freedom to the 1970 conference in Detroit when the Activities Committee for New Directions for ALA (ACONDA) Subcommittee on Social Responsibility called on the Association to guide and support "members on current critical issues and to create means for libraries to become more effective instruments of social change."[2]

Although Berninghausen believed that many social, scientific and political issues were vital, he felt that librarians, in their professional activities, had to view them as subordinate to the principle of intellectual freedom in a pluralistic society, because an organization like ALA was necessary to counter the censoring activities of organized pressure groups. He thought a "neutral" account of intellectual freedom required librarians to make accessible library materials presenting all sides on controversial issues, while the concept of social responsibility promoted the selection and dissemination of specific materials, i.e., the practice of censorship. Berninghausen conceded, however, that libraries with limited book budgets could not purchase everything. He also admitted that librarians "do not claim that they have omniscience, infallibility of judgment, or a foolproof test which can meet all arguments and pressures as to which books or other media are of sound, factual authority."[3]

Berninghausen also expressed his dismay that the social responsibility concept had undermined traditional library discourse. In recent years, he argued, key publications like *Library Journal*, *Wilson Library Bulletin*, and *American Libraries* were fast becoming "viewsletters" because they used advocacy journalism, included personal value judgments in library news reporting, and gave extensive coverage to the social responsibility movement.[4] These journalistic devices, he asserted, distorted the library news and deviated from the ethic of "neutrality." Thus Berninghausen suggested that press articles and editorials advocating social responsibility for the library themselves violated the principle of intellectual freedom for library users.

Berninghausen's article was a damning critique on the role that social responsibility played in 1960s librarianship and he anticipated that his analysis would be unpopular with activist librarians as well as the library press. And it was. Because Berninghausen's article had appeared in *Library Journal*, most of the reaction to it filtered through *Library Journal* offices. In particular, an enormous amount of mail poured into the *Library Journal* bureau in November and December. In response, *Library Journal* devoted its January 1, 1973, issue to what its staff dubbed the "Berninghausen Debate." The issue's cover looked the opposite of the November 15 issue — bright yellow with contrasting black lettering that read "Social Responsibility and the Library Bill of Rights: The Berninghausen Debate." It included a selection of letters to the editor that replied to Berninghausen, a prickly editorial by John Berry, and a feature article titled "Social Responsibility and the Library Bill of Rights: The Berninghausen Debate" that included comment by 19 ALA members who had written responses to Berninghausen at *Library Journal*'s request.[5]

In the letters to the editor section, Richard H. Rosichan from Miami, Florida, accused Berninghausen of excluding "from ALA's *raison d'être* ... the eradication of racial injustice and the preservation of the separation of church and state. Yet racial injustice has had and still is having the most profound effects upon library policies and services in terms of discriminatory hiring, inadequate representation in terms of materials, and discriminatory service patterns. The church and state issue rears its head in matters pertaining to open hours, unjust personnel practices (remember why Ellis Hodgin was fired?)." Rosichan concluded that "a continuing narrow-scope ALA policy such as has prevailed to date will either fossilize the organization or tear it asunder." Philip G. Becker of the New Milford, New Jersey, Public Library wrote that intellectual freedom "is important, Mr. Berninghausen, but human freedom and the *right to be free*—that is, not to be discriminated against ... is more important. Without the second principle, the first is sterile, a testament in a test tube.... Librarians' failure ... to be advocates of what they believe to be morally right ... accounts in part for their extraordinary lack of influence and general low esteem in the mainstream American life."[6]

Library Journal also included a few letters that supported Berninghausen. Verna Nistendirk's of Leon County–Tallahassee Public Library typified several. "Three cheers for the David Berninghausen article!" wrote Nistendirk. "Most of us are tired and some of us are astounded at the waste of time and money at national meetings when crucial library matters are not discussed because of political, moral, or sexual opinions of a few members or non-members. In ALA I'm a librarian; in League of Women Voters I'm working for good government; and in ACLU I'm looking after citizens' rights."[7]

John Berry's editorial was a pointed response to Berninghausen's attack on the library press and the social responsibility movement in U.S. librarianship. Berry accused Berninghausen of being "as slanted in favor" of his own views as "anything ever printed in *Library Journal*." But "where we really part company with you," Berry asserted, "is on the proper position of libraries, journals, and organizations. You seem to think that all three are required to be neutral on social questions. We disagree." *Library Journal*, Berry argued, "is not a library ... ALA is not a library either. It is an organization that has taken stands on social questions for decades." Here Berry cited race, copyright, and social legislation as examples of past library stands. The library, he added, "came out against the Axis in World

War II and has damned Totalitarianism many times over since. That is proper. We hope ALA won't be scared off or turned away from its social responsibilities because some members mistake the Library Bill of Rights for the ALA By-Laws."[8]

But the feature section of the January 1 issue was a sample of essays by selected ALA members. Berry admitted the sample was not "balanced … it is consciously skewed in favor of those we expected to oppose Berninghausen, since their position was not represented in the issue of *Library Journal* in which his article appeared." He wrote, "it is our opinion that this debate, confronting as it does, the basic foundations of our profession and its organization, is vitally important, both in terms of theoretical and ideological definition of librarianship, and the translation of that theory into library practice."[9] The contributors included Robert F. Wedgeworth, F. William Summers (University of South Carolina College of Librarianship), Betty-Carol Sellen (Brooklyn College Library), Patricia Glass Schuman (newly associate editor, *School Library Journal*), Jane Robbins (University of Pittsburgh Graduate School of Library and Information Sciences), Eli Oboler (Idaho State University), Allie Beth Martin (Tulsa City-County Library System), Katherine Laich (ALA President), E.J. Josey (New York State Library), Clara S. Jones (Detroit Public Library), John P. Immroth (University of Pittsburgh Graduate School of Library and Information Sciences), James M. Hillard (the Citadel, Charleston, South Carolina), Ervin J. Gaines (Minneapolis Public Library), Peter M. Doiron (former editor of *Choice*), William DeJohn (Missouri State Library), Arthur Curley (Montclair, New Jersey, Public Library), Milton S. Byam (District of Columbia Public Library), Dorothy Bendix (Drexel University Graduate School of Library Science), and Andrew Armitage (Owen Sound, Ontario, Public Library).

Authors accused Berninghausen of "smear tactics" and of pitting librarians against one another. They railed at Berninghausen for proposing that social responsibility depended on an anti-intellectual freedom rationale, for misinterpreting the social responsibility movement, for assuming social responsibility led to censorship, and for suggesting that intellectual freedom was the only ethic of the profession. "You frighten me, David Berninghausen," wrote Patricia Schuman. "You promulgate your thesis by setting up a dangerous and insidious syllogism that says: intellectual freedom is the guiding ethic of our profession: therefore, all other ethics are incompatible with it." Clara S. Jones accused Berninghausen of turning "back the clock." E.J. Josey stated: "If Berninghausen's proposals are what intellectual freedom is like, I for one want no part of it. As a black man who was born and grew up in the South, I have experienced this kind of intellectual freedom and I reject it as inimical to my freedom as a human being.[10]

Authors also criticized Berninghausen's portrayal of library "neutrality" and his idealization of balance in library collections in a number of ways. First, they pointed to flaws in his thesis that the concepts of social responsibility and intellectual freedom were antithetical. Josey, for example, rejected the distinction Berninghausen drew between the librarian's personal and professional life; librarians were not mere technicians or human computers, he argued, but whole persons whose social responsibilities as citizens had to carry over to their professional practice.[11] And "viewing librarians and libraries in the political process," Robert Wedgeworth noted, "it seems somewhat more difficult to separate the non-library issues from the library issues than Berninghausen implies."

Second, they argued that library practice did not represent all points of view. "Where were you, David Berninghausen," Patricia Schuman asked, "when movement groups publications were not being purchased by libraries?" Furthermore, libraries "repeatedly accommodated its policies to the prevailing moral and political attitudes of its constituents," Robert Wedgeworth asserted. "Analysis of employment practices and book selection practices clearly revealed this," he wrote.[12]

Third, the essayists claimed that collection building based on social responsibility was more, rather than less inclusive, and that although librarians who believed in social responsibility wanted "to add the underground press to their collections," they did not want to "toss out the traditional press." Fourth, they asserted that collection building based on social responsibility did not lead to censorship. In 1970, they reminded *Library Journal* readers, SRRT had created a Task Force on Alternative Books in Print which, with its publication *Alternatives in Print*, directly addressed the issue of balance in library collections. No one in SRRT advocated "the burning of BIP [*Books in Print*]."[13] Ultimately, the essayists argued Berninghausen may believe that social responsibility led to removal or labeling of materials and that the involvement in social issues compromised libraries' "neutral" stance, but his definition of intellectual freedom masked a "neutrality" which supported the status quo.[14] Again Schuman asked Berninghausen: "Do you really believe that our society is controlled by individuals acting as individuals? That there are not 'special interest' groups like General Motors? The National Rifle Association? The American Library Association? which attempt — and often do— influence the progress (and regression) of society?"[15]

After *Library Journal* printed Berninghausen's article "Antithesis in Librarianship: Social Responsibility vs. The Library Bill of Rights" in

November, 1972, the germinal debate concerning professional "neutrality" shifted ground from the ALA conference arena to the broader context of library discourse. The January, 1973, Berninghausen debate, for example, generated widespread interest in professional issues, theories, and practices. Even ALA's Council recognized problems associated with library selection. At its midwinter conference in Washington, D.C. (January 28–February 3), Council opposed "the *silent censorship* practiced under the old term *weeding*." A new interpretation of the Library Bill of Rights stated that weeding "is sometimes used as a convenient means to remove materials thought to be too controversial or disapproved by segments of the community. Such abuse of the reevaluation function," it read, "is in opposition to Articles I and II of the Library Bill of Rights." The Council also approved a second interpretation that "restricted access to library materials whether it be via the locked case, closed shelf, or *adults only* collection, is in violation of the Library Bill of Rights."[16] But these Council actions at ALA's midwinter conference, the February, 1973, *SRRT Newsletter* noted, were accompanied by frustrations.

Midwinter meetings were long, tempers short when SRRT membership discussed the Round Table's viability. "Much, maybe too much, of the discussion involved *in house* matters," the *Newsletter* opened; "SRRT seemed to be going through a reevaluation or rebuilding period. This has probably been brought about because the leadership is mostly new to the organization; the background and understanding of how SRRT developed in its early years is not there," wrote Tyron D. Emerick.[17] By spring, the situation had not improved and the April *Newsletter* reported that the election of Round Table leaders was impaired because so few volunteered for administrative roles.[18] Librarianship's continued neglect of the alternative press worsened the mood in the post-conference months.

By spring, 1973, *Alternatives in Print* was going into its third edition, which covered publications by 800 groups and small presses — only 100 of which had appeared in *Books in Print* and only 50 of which were cited in the *Small Press Record of Non-periodical Publications*.[19] But Noel Peattie and Sanford Berman discovered that most librarians used and reviewed *Alternatives in Print* as a bibliography rather than a buying tool and, and as a result, the publication landed on reference shelves, not in acquisitions offices as intended. To counter this practice, SRRT's Task Force on Alternative Books in Print planned to include an article about the distribution of alternative publications in the upcoming edition, because many librarians still seemed unaware of how to order and acquire alternative materials. Meanwhile, other evidences of unbalanced collections and favorable treatment continued to surface. For example, when the Philadelphia-area

SRRT Intellectual Freedom Committee surveyed materials in neighborhood libraries, it found that (1) "relatively favorable book budgets are no guarantee that the library's collection will include controversial materials in any significant quantities," (2) the "values of the institution and the librarian inevitably come into play," and (3) "some librarians with modest budgets and a sense of social and artistic adventure are building more contemporary and provocative collections than others, who have more money at their disposal but suspect or dislike the unorthodox or feel compelled to ignore it because of institutional policy."[20] While these other signs of unbalanced collections and favorable treatment came to light, the larger library social responsibility suffered visibly as well.

At the annual ALA conference in Las Vegas in June, 1973, ALA established its first Intellectual Freedom Round Table. Noel Peattie commented that "many saw it as an attempt to co-opt the dissidents from ALA's intellectual freedom 'club,' and certainly later experience has shown that headquarters control of this supposedly grass roots group is as strong as it is with any intellectual freedom activity in ALA."[21] It was during this organizational change that, despite its influence on the profession, the social responsibility movement began to dissipate. Ultimately, the library counterculture mirrored the larger world—where the 1960s counterculture became institutionalized or incorporated into the "slick-surfaced, mass-produced" cultural scene of the 1970s."[22] Many small presses joined organizations like COSMEP, the Alternative Press Syndicate, and the Coordinating Council of Literary Magazines. And "for many of the underground poets," for example, "even COSMEP" became too "efficient," too much an "institution" or "computer," noted Abe Peck. Alternative publishing had clearly shifted course. Fewer underground papers existed and they tended to be more topical—feminist, environmental, Third World, and so on.[23]

By 1973, the nation's mood for activism had waned. Gitlin notes that as the war subsided, so too did "the urgency of politics." The "vision of One Big Movement," he said, "dissolved."[24] Not unexpectedly, the impetus for change in librarianship lessened as well. The Social Responsibilities Round Table had also alienated many mainstream librarians by its inability to define social responsibility in a way which appealed to the majority in ALA. On September 30, 1973, for example, alternative library publisher Samuel Goldstein wrote Sanford Berman that he feared too many activist librarians were "stuffy about how un-stuffy" they were and lamented the fact that the social responsibility library movement only addressed itself to a relatively small portion of ALA's membership. In his view, if the movement wanted to effect change it would have to learn to compromise rather than simply "turn off the faucet of the larger library constituency."[25] Goldstein believed that the social responsibility library movement depended upon its usefulness to library practitioners, not its rhetoric. His comment pointed to another problem — idealism.

Another blow to the struggling social responsibility library movement came in August, 1973, when the *SRRT Newsletter* announced that California State librarian Ethel Crockett was terminating federal funding for *Synergy*— the journal that jump-started the library social responsibility movement in 1967. Crockett maintained that Title I of the Library Services and Construction Act funded demonstration projects for not more than two years and because *Synergy* had already received five, she told it to seek financial assistance elsewhere.[26] But while Crockett initially claimed she notified the Bay Area Reference Center (BARC) of the funding cut on April 26 and followed it up with a May 4 memorandum to "Persons Interested in the Future of *Synergy*," she later admitted that somehow the "information was not given to the *Synergy* staff, so that the announcement that funds would, indeed, be cut off after this June 30 came as a shock." Celeste West maintained that the abrupt notice left little time to save *Synergy* and, disgusted with the funding flap and tired of hassles, she resigned. In her resignation letter, West asked, "WHAT DOES THE STATE LIBRARY HAVE IN ITS CROCK O'RELEVANCE?" She believed *Synergy*'s many bibliographies or reviews on topics such as feminism, Native Americans, unions, children's liberation, occultism, head comix, radicals in the professions, free schools, and independent publishing were very "relevant" to the contemporary library world.[27]

The San Francisco Public Library talked publicly of taking over the magazine, but BARC feared censorship. Its members recognized the library press was not free. In general, it was monopolized by a blend of associations and institutions and was controlled by particular publishing interests. Even the vanguard alternative library title *Synergy*, for example, was not only financially dependent on a federal grant, but each issue required San Francisco Public Library's approval before publication. The library had previously "bollixed five different reprint offers which might have brought in money," West argued, "choked creativity on the bone of prior censorship," and suppressed "protesting editorials." West maintained she had to kidnap the final *Synergy* issue from the printer just to get it published. Other staff members complained of "odd military-school-like reprimands" and threats that they would be denied legal salary increases.[28]

Ironically, in its last year of existence *Synergy* received its second H.W. Wilson Periodical Award (a highly regarded library press prize) and sold 2,000 copies per month. In hindsight, West argued (without providing evidence) that Crockett's real objection to the high-impact periodical was not a question of money. Instead, she asserted, California governor Ronald Reagan had appointed Crockett state librarian, and in West's view, directed Crockett "to kill" *Synergy*— the flagship alternative library publication that fostered an attitude for change in the profession, gave rise to a wave of alternative library literature, provided a ground for library activists to express their opinions and make connections, and "upped the ante on library periodicals" at a time when most librarians remained the "purveyors of Reader's Digested Status Quo print."[29]

Sanford Berman once noted that although some of the "most committed and influential library-cats nationwide" produced core alternative library literature, they were often "heavily shit upon" by the establishment. He believed that alternative library publishers were targeted precisely because the literature they produced tightened connections between the alternative library movement and other movement groups and had the potential to make libraries "more like the social catalysts they should be — rather than the Establishment ass-lickers that most of them [were]."[30] In late, 1973, he supported West's venture to publish a new library journal free of institutional restrictions under the Booklegger Press banner, the independent publishing house which West had founded in 1972.[31] The first book that came off the new press was titled *Revolting Librarians* (1972), an anthology of provocative essays edited by West and Valerie Wheat that took the field by storm with its savvy coverage of such topics as the librarians' image, the library press, library schools, and professionalism. *Revolting Librarians* was reviewed in numerous library publications ranging from *Library Journal, College & Research Libraries,* and *Library Resources & Technical Services* to *Library Union Caucus Newsletter* to *School Media Quarterly.* Eugene Darling's *Library Union Caucus Newsletter* review said "we have in this book some very vivid and accurate pictures of what's wrong with libraries." Charles W. Conaway's *Library Resources & Technical Services* review said the book deserved "at least selective reading by all librarians and particularly by administrators and library educators, the groups with whom the revolting librarians have the most difficulty in communicating." Georgia Mulligan's *College & Research Libraries* review recommended that "you at least *look*" at *Revolting Librarians*. And in *Library Journal* John Berry wrote, "Get the little red book!"[32]

West called the new journal *Booklegger Magazine* and, like *Revolting Librarians*, intended it to take on the library establishment and assist librarians in taking power over their working lives. Soon after *Booklegger Magazine*'s first issue, a bimonthly Toronto journal called *Emergency Librarian* appeared as a sister publication. Edited by Canadian librarians

Sherrill Cheda and Phyllis Yaffe, *Emergency Librarian* emerged from a surge of feminist interest at the 1972 Canadian Library Association conference. Together the two journals became the first "women-owned and published library magazines ... in a profession run by women but still ruled by men."[33] And as the mouthpieces for some of the profession's leading feminist voices, *Booklegger Magazine* and *Emergency Librarian* blended the 1960s women's, alternative press, and library movements.

From its outset, the new *Booklegger* staff offered to help SRRT plan a Task Force on Women preconference to generate discussion on the 1974 ALA conference theme, "The Woman Librarian: Her Job Situation." Librarians involved were excited by the conference banner, hoping it signified the Association's willingness to address women's issues. The ALA Executive Board approved the preconference, provided the Office of Library Personnel Resources was co-sponsor. Soon afterwards, however, SRRT and *Booklegger* learned that the Office of Library Personnel questioned the wisdom of co-sponsoring the event. Some of the controversial language contained in the Office of Library Personnel's internal memos was printed by SRRT in its November, 1973 *Newsletter*. The Round Table "has the connotation of being entirely composed of radicals, be they homosexual or communist," one memorandum read. "Obviously this is not true. The connotation, though, will operate to the detriment of the preconference. It may attract the radical librarian ... it may repel the conservative and middle-of-the-road librarian."[34] Simultaneously, in a November, 1973, oral history of SRRT, "a quiet unobtrusive elder" was quoted as saying, "To strengthen our socially responsible fabric we [the Council] want to co-sponsor every SRRT activity." "What for?" someone asked — "So serious librarians will not think that SRRT is a haven for radicals ... lesbians ... uh, homosexuals ... and Communists...."[35] Although the accuracy of this quote is unknown, it is fair to say that library activists remained under establishment scrutiny.

Despite the controversy the preconference (July 3–6) went ahead. Thus, ALA's July 7–13 conference in New York was preceded by a gathering of women interested in discussing ALA and librarianship in general. Approximately 115 of these librarians met at Douglass College in New Brunswick, New Jersey, to talk about their role in a feminized profession. Patricia Schuman, Joan Marshall, Sue Critchfield, Elizabeth Futas (Queens College), Joyceanne Kent (Seattle Public Library), and Margaret Myers (Rutgers Graduate School of Library Service) led panels on self-image, discrimination, library education, age, and salaries.[36] The central issue, *Library Journal* said, was whether libraries "should be changed to achieve equity for their women employees" or should women "devise tactics for getting ahead in libraries the way they are."

The impact of the women's preconference was evident in a number of resolutions put forth for action by ALA membership and Council during their official conference meetings. For example, the Committee on Accreditation decided that, in future, it would include affirmative action criteria in its evaluation of library school programs. The Office for Library Personnel Resources resolved to upgrade service jobs in libraries so that they shared salary equity with administrative positions. The Association also went on record endorsing the ratification of the Equal Rights Amendment. But the women did not win every battle. Several of their motions were defeated, including those to eradicate sexist terminology from ALA publications, to press libraries to provide child care services for employees, and to have ALA initiate regular staff evaluations of library administrators.[37]

With the exception of the women's preconference, the annual meeting proved dull. Indeed, most of the 14,000 librarians present "seemed to have given up much interest in the internal politics and procedure of ALA in favor of more participation in the professional concerns of the unit to which they belong." And although a record breaking number of attendees "hustled and bustled" through more than 1,100 sessions housed in "New York's midtown tourist traps," *Library Journal* had little to report.[38] For library activists at least, the highlight in New York was not the ALA conference, rather the coincident (July 7–9) New York Book Fair at Lincoln Center.

The New York Book Fair was organized by Jackie Eubanks and SRRT's Task Force on Alternative Books in Print, SRRT's Task Force on Minority Publishing, the ALA Black Caucus, and other movement groups, literary presses, and Third World and feminist publishers. Over 300 publishers participated. The attending crowd, *Sipapu* reported, was a mix of literary types and movement group workers. Eubanks noted that it was her aim to mesh the two groups because they stood together in the "benign neglect" of the alternative press through libraries and books stores. Unfortunately, although the book fair was free of charge at Eubanks' insistence, few ALA librarians bothered to attend. Booklegger and SRRT later heard rumors that discussion at an ALA Exhibits Round Table meeting had turned to putting the New York Book Fair out of business.

The Library Bill of Rights directed librarians to make accessible material on all sides of issues and to ensure that no issues be regarded as taboo, and yet the long standing neglect of the alternative press indicated that this rhetoric was consistently compromised in practice. As library activists had pointed out numerous times between 1967 and 1974, mainstream library collections reinforced and perpetuated mainstream thought and culture and publicly funded libraries catered to the middle of the road patron. Thus, library collections not only preserved certain cultural records, they also reflected certain ideologies. And these reflections extended beyond the library's walls into the realm of ideas. As Stanley Fish asserted in *There's No Such Thing as Free Speech*, "the canon is the repository, the ark of principles, not only containing them but extending them in the effects it has on its readers."[39]

In *The Freedom to Lie: A Debate About Democracy*, John Swan explains why selection procedures for alternative press products could not be developed in the same way as establishment press products. "The products of the commercial and academic marketplace are given preference over those works which are outside of that relatively normalizing sphere." With little effort, he adds, "this point can be extended to include all of our standard indexes and other access tools, inevitably given preference over the few counter-cultural reference works."[40] Although Swan states that librarians shape library collections and reference sources in an effort to increase the availability of some materials at the expense of others, he is careful to emphasize that "selection and collection development which favor one community's world view over all others is not *ipso facto* censorship."[41] There are many positive and negative reasons, he suggests, for choosing and rejecting and weeding that have nothing to do with repressing views. Evelyn Geller observes, for example, that all libraries are constrained both by budgets and values "to exclude some books."[42] She identifies three sets of conflicting values that are inherent in censorship activity: the tension between the elite tastes of library selectors and the popular tastes of user groups; the library's "neutral" role in the community and some librarians' desires to effect community change; and ideas that support the status quo and those that threaten it. Clearly, all of these factors contributed to ALA's response to the New York Book Fair.

The profession's neglect of the alternative press was symptomatic of ALA's broader status quo politics and by the summer of 1974 the library social responsibility movement showed damaging signs of its effect. Few people had attended SRRT meetings in New York. Afterwards, members griped that few librarians got together to strategize courses of action to turn the situation around and complained that while the Round Table was set up as a group organization, a few individuals seemed to do all the work. Tyron D. Emerick acknowledged in SRRT's post-conference *Newsletter* that the Round Table suffered from lack of leadership, loss of membership, communications breakdowns, and members who abused their positions. But he also added that while some argued SRRT ought to disband because it had outlived its usefulness, those who made the complaint had done nothing to improve the situation. Though still an ALA Round Table, SRRT had lost some of the insight and spark of its early years.[43]

Conclusion

ALA exercised moral, intellectual, and organizational dominance over its membership. But because ALA's development and expansion depended upon a dynamic relationship with other groups, the establishment made compromises when faced with minor calls for reform. Concessions, however, were made only up to a point. Whenever calls for social responsibility challenged ALA's vital interests, such as preservation of the traditional role and privileges of the profession or of the entrenched interests of the elite, ALA not only exercised its moral, intellectual, and political leadership prerogatives, but also flexed its organizational muscle to overcome the challenge. Berninghausen's November, 1972, article, for example, shows the establishment as less interested in the value of the Library Bill of Rights than in its own professional well-being. Thus, the status quo—hardly a "neutral" site in the early 1970s—secured the profession's ethical jurisdiction.

In his work on the 1960s, Gitlin noted that "the system is absorptive, so it's always taking account of where the push is."[44] Despite the social responsibility movement's counter-establishment tactics, for example, ALA seemed to create room to absorb the agitation, then incorporate and contain it within its institutional focus, bureaucracy, and organizational structure.[45] Thus, despite the strength of the essayists' rebuttal in "Social Responsibility and The Library Bill of Rights: The Berninghausen Debate," many librarians found Berninghausen's perspective on intellectual freedom compelling because so much of the social responsibility activity resulted from ideological stands, because of their traditional reluctance to abandon a "neutral" position, and because of their fear of potential social, financial and legal consequences of ALA involvement in non-library matters.[46]

The institutional focus of ALA had serious implications for SRRT, which had raised the question of whether the Association should focus on libraries or librarians and called upon ALA to improve the profession's service orientation. In its effort to make ALA more responsive to the needs of librarians, SRRT organized task forces to find and create jobs for librarians, to support librarians in intellectual freedom disputes, and to back jeopardized librarians such as union organizers, open homosexuals, peace workers, and political activists. Despite these efforts, however, ALA seemed incapable of shifting its focus to the individual librarian. Feminist library scholar Roma Harris noted that while legal and medical associations are comprised of personal memberships, library associations have been made up of institutional ones; while other associations act almost as white-collar unions, library associations have not traditionally dealt with workers' issues.[47] This matter dated back to the 1930s, when progressives in the profession lobbied ALA to pay attention to the needs of the librarian, not just the institution.

The bureaucratic nature of ALA was also a concern for library activists. SRRT certainly found its horizons limited within ALA. As early as 1969, Patricia Schuman had asserted that "it seems unfortunate that we have been able to function almost completely on our own for almost a year and must now be so dependent on ALA's approval.... The question is," she wrote, "Do we operate as any other cog in the vast ALA machinery, or can we be vital, effective, free from red tape?"[48] At the alternative press movement's Liberation News Service, Ray Mungo had also noted that ideals were often "lost altogether in the clamor of daily ped-xing." It was possible," he said, "to spend an entire day typing and transcribing and telephoning the words of Eldridge Cleaver without once considering their meaning, or feeling their strength."[49] Indeed, SRRT affiliates had risen in popularity among Round Table members precisely because of the perception that they were less a part of ALA's infrastructure than of the national SRRT Action Council.

Then there was the problem of ALA's overwhelming organizational structure. It was SRRT that brought the issue of social responsibility to librarianship's attention, but once the battle was engaged in the open, the Round Table itself faded into the background. Although it started in 1968 as a "think tank" and an agent to usher in change, five years later the focus of its agenda diffused as it passed through the various layers of organizational bureaucracy. The Round Table's energy gradually waned and finally it lost its momentum, and probably also some of its relevance. The Association, whether intentionally or not, delivered the *coup de grâce* by smothering SRRT out with a plethora of overlapping round tables, e.g., a round table for intellectual freedom, a round table for women, a round table for international relations, a round table for government documents, and a round table for exhibits, among many others.

An examination of the research material collected and referred to in this book suggests that while the library was positioned in the 1960s to play a role in social change, the conservative tradition and structure of the institution prevented it from realizing such a transformation.[50] Accustomed to serving middle class patrons, many librarians were conditioned by ALA and library schools to preserve the status quo.[51] Historically, ALA had been run by the "successful and on the whole conservative" top administrators of large university and public library systems. The nature of these administrative positions was to maintain a narrow focus on the professional jurisdiction and "promote library service and librarianship" (Article II, Section I of the ALA Constitution).[52] Given these limited parameters, it was unlikely that members would broaden their professional mandate simply because a minority called for the library to become an instrument of social change, a call that threatened the "largest and most conservatively respectable power base" which the profession favored.[53]

Arthur Curley believed that library activists' failure to define what the term "social responsibility" meant was a blessing because the term's "very vagueness enabled it to serve as a vehicle for a multiplicity of important causes," i.e., "library service to the disadvantaged, minorities recruitment, moral stands on social and political issues, cooperation with other social agencies, reordering of priorities, meaningful defense of intellectual freedom and its practitioners, spring-cleaning for many a cobweb-infested library, [and] the bum's rush for limitations on access to libraries." But Curley also viewed the social responsibility effort as a "field day for idealism" that "didn't last of course." "Many a wrong turn has been taken in the pursuit" of social responsibility, he said "even causing some to abandon the search." For others, it is "the passing of youth," the "tiring of causes," or other "causes coming along" that lead to abandonment. But most of all, Curley asserted, "the reaction always sets in ... the wave of idealism was itself a reaction, in the first place."[54] And Berninghausen's article was a reaction to the reaction of the idealists. Each reaction left its mark on ALA, which absorbed some of the essential change and thus survived, sustained itself, and matured to retain its relevance.

By depicting the library profession in general, and ALA in particular, as an instrument of power and illustrating how its development and expansion included an ongoing relationship with dissenting librarians, the present work has explored how ALA made compromises regarding its professional interests, while ultimately maintaining its professional jurisdiction. Both the creation of this collective will and the exercise of political leadership drew on the profession's intellectual, moral, and ideological leadership, as manifest in its interpretation of the Library Bill of Rights and the pressure it exerted upon dissenting librarians to conform to "neutral" behavior. Thus Berninghausen, supported by the establishment, steered many librarians away from the topic of social responsibility by playing upon ALA's deep concern for what Betty-Carol Sellen once called ALA's "action-crippling fear" about its "extremely favorable tax-status."[55]

The issue of ALA's tax-exempt status had first surfaced during the 1968 discussions about whether SRRT should be accepted as a round table. In June, 1969, John Berry reported that in the opinion of its attorneys, ALA was "in danger of losing its tax-exempt status if its objectives are changed from the classic stance of serving libraries to that of serving its personal professional members."[56] That concern threaded its way through ACONDA meetings and peaked in June, 1974, when the ALA attorney reported that "the IRS was concerned about *certain activities* undertaken by *certain units.*" The Social Responsibilities Round Table deemed the tax-exempt status issue its worst enemy, but thought the threat bogus. Zoia Horn, for example, criticized "the climate of fear, intimidation, and defensiveness" created by the tax status issue. She argued that ALA members should run the Association and not the Internal Revenue Service.[57] But Berninghausen argued vociferously and gave much emphasis in publications and speeches towards one conclusion: as an educational association, ALA was tax-exempt and "thus not permitted by law to actively support work for or against positions on issues that do not involve professional interests." At the same time, he admitted quietly: "it is sometimes difficult to draw the line sharply."[58] Thus, Berninghausen warned librarians against taking positions on social issues, but did not demonstrate how to avoid them.

It was difficult to pinpoint when the discussion of "neutrality" first appeared in the discourse of librarianship in the 1960s. In 1964, Eric Moon, then editor of *Library Journal*, endorsed President Johnson and Senator Humphrey in the presidential election in his October 15 editorial entitled "A Clear Choice."[59] Senator Goldwater, he added, was less likely to provide support and aid for libraries. Two years later, Moon brought the Library Bill of Rights into discussion of social responsibility in a keynote speech to the Ohio Library Association. In the speech, Moon complained that most libraries still clung "tenaciously to the middle of the rainbow," and that, in doing so, they compromised the Library Bill of Rights. How many libraries, he asked the audience, gave "even minimal representation to the views and philosophies of Mao Tse-Tung, the Black Muslims, the [John] Birch Society, or beat poets and novelists?"[60] In an October 15, 1967, *Library Journal* editorial entitled "Voices on Vietnam," Moon invited librarians to lend their names and donate their dollars to finance a full-page *New York Times* statement calling for cessation of the bombing of North Vietnam. Moon later indicated that the piece was a conscious effort to get librarians involved in the social issue of war and peace.[61] Six years later ALA reaffirmed library "neutrality" in a deeply coded interpretation of the Library Bill of Rights.

The historical force of a chain of action-reaction helps to account for the events of 1960s American librarianship. Like broader social movements in the United States in the 1960s the social responsibility library movement was a reaction to the inertia of the status quo. In turn, the establishment reacted to the social responsibility movement. In addition to showing "the process of change through the conflict of opposing forces," the struggle for power inside ALA (with its implications for the cultural role of the library in 1960s society) is also in keeping with the idea that hegemony or effective control of power is the result of a complex interplay of diverse forces that include political, economic, and other social forces.

"Neutral institutions perpetuate such social ills as racism and sexism," the Radical Research Center's Mary McKenney stated in 1971. "They don't go around advocating that blacks and women be denied equal rights, and libraries don't brag that their collections contain nothing but the story of John Q. WASP ... but burying one's prejudices in a bureaucracy does not qualify one as neutral."[62] Her strong words evoke the struggles of 1960s library activists, serve as a reminder that the library can be a powerful purveyor of ideology, and caution contemporary library administrators, library scholars, library educators, and library users that their own practices have consequences. In a memoir published in a 1996 issue of *American Libraries*, Noel Peattie stated that after 26 years of alternative library publishing he saw little transformation in the library institution. Much as in the 1960s, large publishers, distributors, and producers of databases were still the primary exhibitors at library conferences and primary advertisers in library periodicals. Because librarians were so familiar with these products, because they seldom asked for alternatives, Peattie argued that the library system continued to be self-reinforcing, a kind of "closed circuit."[63]

At the beginning of a new millennium, as ALA tackles enduring problems such as censorship and challenges to the freedom to read as well as newer social problems such as opposition to Internet access policies, the ethos of librarianship and the responsibility of librarians to society deserve continuing attention. As media scholar Allan Rachlin notes, "information is not simply collected." Rather, "selected information is organized" by librarians "with the lens provided by his/her culture."[64] The question for the future is: Whose culture is library culture?

Epilogue Notes

1. Berninghausen, "Antithesis in Librarianship," 3675–3681.
2. *Ibid.*, 3675–3676, 3681.
3. *Ibid.*, 3675–3676, 3679.
4. *Ibid.*, 3676.
5. Wedgeworth et al., "Social Responsibility," 25–41.

6. "Replies to Berninghausen," *Library Journal* 98, no. 1 (1 January 1973): 6–7.

7. *Ibid.*, p. 6.

8. John Berry, "Dear Dean Berninghausen," *Library Journal* 98, no. 1 (1 January 1973): 11.

9. Wedgeworth et al., "Social Responsibility," 25.

10. *Ibid.*, 28, 33.

11. Geoffrey Dunbar, "Librarian and/or Citizen?" *Library Journal* 97, no. 1 (1 January 1972): 42–43.

12. Wedgeworth et al., "Social Responsibility," 25, 28.

13. *Ibid.*, p. 28.

14. Mary McKenney, 1970–72, Notes from the Other Side by Mary McKenney & Edith Ericson-Sonntag, ALA's Sanford Berman Papers.

15. Wedgeworth et al., "Social Responsibility," 28-29.

16. "A New Management Mood," *Library Journal* 98, no. 6 (15 March 1973): 828.

17. *SRRT Newsletter* 24 (February 1973): 1.

18. *SRRT Newsletter* 25 (April 1973): 2.

19. *Books in Print* (New York: R.R. Bowker, 1948–); Len Fulton, *Small Press Record of Non-periodical Publications* (Paradise, CA: Dustbooks, 1969–1975). In 1975, *Small Press Record of Non-periodical Publications* became *Small Press Record of Books*.

20. S. J. Leon, "Book Selection in Philadelphia," *Library Journal* 98, no. 7 (1 April 1973): 1089.

21. Bundy and Stielow, *Activism*, 50-51.

22. Hugh Fox, *The Living Underground: A Critical Overview* (Troy, NY: Whitson, 1970): 11.

23. *Sipapu* 5, no. 1 (January 1974): 16.

24. Gitlin, *The Sixties*, 421–422.

25. Samuel Goldstein to Sanford Berman, 30 Sept. 1973, CALL/Sam Goldstein, 1973–74, 1977, ALA's Sanford Berman Papers.

26. *Synergy* (1973), ALA's Sanford Berman Papers. See also Edward Swanson, "*Synergy* Protest," *American Libraries* 4, no. 7 (July/August 1973): 408; Noel Peattie, "The Fortunes of *Synergy*," *Sipapu* 4, no. 2 (July 1973): 8–10.

27. "*Synergy* Editor Resigns," *American Libraries* 7, no. 4 (July/August 1973): 412.

28. "Celeste West on Synergy," *Sipapu* 4, no. 2 (July 1973): 71.

29. "A Conversation with Celeste West," 3–6.

30. Sanford Berman to Mr. Brian Kirby, March 1971, Libraries to the People, 1971–1973, ALA's Sanford Berman Papers.

31. Celeste West, Elizabeth Katz, eds., *Revolting Librarians* (San Francisco: Booklegger Press, 1972), iii.

32. Eugene Darling, "Are Librarians Revolting?," *Library Union Caucus Newsletter* 2, no. 1 (January 1973): 5; John Berry, "Little Red Book," *Library Journal* 98, no. 4 (15 February 1973): 515; Georgia Mulligan, *College & Research Libraries* 34, no. 2 (March 1973): 165–166; Charles W. Conaway, *Library Resources and Technical Services* 18, no. 3 (Summer 1974): 294–295; and *School Media Quarterly* 1,

no. 3 (1974): 227 [reviews of *Revolting Librarians*, eds. Celeste West and Elizabeth Katz].

33. "A Conversation with Celeste West," 3–6.

34. "Women: Preconference Hassles, But Otherwise Good Vibes," *SRRT Newsletter* 28 (November 1973): 4.

35. "VIEWPOINT: Oral history," *Library Journal* 98, no. 20 (15 November 1973): 3355.

36. "Women: Preconference Hassles," 4.

37. "Strategy, Structure, and Specialization," *Library Journal* 99, no. 14 (August 1974): 1901–1902.

38. *Ibid.*, 1902.

39. Fish, *There's No Such Thing*, 40.

40. Swan and Peattie, *The Freedom to Lie*, 31.

41. *Ibid.*

42. Geller, *Forbidden Books*, xviii–xix.

43. *SRRT Newsletter* 27 (August 1973): 2–3.

44. "After the Revolution: Who Are they Now?," chapter in *Uncovering the Sixties: The Life and Times of the Underground Press*, Abe Peck, (New York: Pantheon Books, 1985), 308.

45. William DeJohn to Kay Cassell, 14 July 1969, ALA's SRRT Papers, Box 1.

46. "Subcommittee Report — Social Responsibilities," prepared by George J. Alfred, A.P. Marshall and Shirley Olofson, [n.d.], ALA's SRRT Papers, Box 1.

47. *Ibid.*

48. Pat Schuman to Bill DeJohn, 8 April 1969, ALA's SRRT Papers, Box 1.

49. Ray Mungo, *Famous Long Ago: My Life and Hard Times with Liberation News Service* (Boston: Beacon Press, 1970), 70.

50. Dennis Carbonneau, Action Council, 1972/73, ALA's SRRT Papers, Box 2.

51. Wedgeworth et al., "Social Responsibility," 27.

52. Action Council Business, 1972–1973, ALA's SRRT Papers, Box 11.

53. Wedgeworth et al., "Social Responsibility," 27.

54. Arthur Curley, "Ideals," *Library Journal* 97, no. 22 (15 December 1972): 3973.

55. Betty-Carol Sellen (1970–1987), Beginning of the ALA Social Responsibilities Round Table, ALA's SRRT Papers, Box 11.

56. "The New Constituency," *Library Journal* 94, no. 14 (August 1969): 2728.

57. *SRRT Newsletter* 29 (January 1974): 6.

58. ALA Meetings, 1969–1970, Should ALA Take a Stand, ALA's SRRT Papers, Box 8.

59. Eric Moon, "A Clear Choice," *Library Journal* 89, no. 18 (15 October 1964): 3927.

60. Eric Moon, "Hungry and Not Very Scrupulous," Speech presented at the meeting of the Ohio Library Association, 13 October 1966, *Ohio Library Association Bulletin* 37, no. 5 (January 1967): 6, 8–14.

61. Eric Moon, "Voices on Vietnam," *Library Journal* 92, no. 18 (15 October 1967): 3577.

62. Mary McKenney, "Neutrality Is Partisan," *Library Journal* 96, no. 6 (15 March 1971): 902.

63. Noel Peattie, "On My Mind: Reflections on the *Sipapu* Years," *American Libraries* 27, no. 5 (May 1996): 39.

64. Allan Rachlin, *News as Hegemonic Reality: American Political Culture and the Framing of News Accounts* (New York: Praeger, 1988), 127.

Appendix

Library's Bill of Rights—1938

Now when indications in many parts of the world point to growing intolerance, suppression of free speech, and censorship, affecting the rights of minorities and individuals, the Board of Trustees of the Des Moines Public Library reaffirms these basic policies governing a free public library to serve the best interests of Des Moines and its citizens.

1. Books and other reading matter selected for purchase from public funds shall be chosen from the standpoint of value and interest of the people of Des Moines, and in no case shall selection be based on the race or nationality, political, or religious views of the writers

2. As far as available material permits, all sides of controversial ques tions shall be represented equally in the selection of books on subjects about which differences of opinion exist.

3. Official publications and/or propaganda of organized religious, political, fraternal, class, or religious sects, societies, or similar groups, and of institutions controlled by such, are solicited as gifts and will be made available to library users without discrimination. This policy is made necessary because of the meager funds available for the purchase of books and reading matter. It is obviously impossible to purchase the publications of all such groups and it would be unjust discrimination to purchase those of some and not of others.

4. Library meeting rooms shall be available on equal terms to all organized nonprofit groups for open meetings to which no admission fee is charged and from which no one is excluded.

Intellectual Freedom Manual, 5th ed. (Chicago: American Library Association, Office for Intellectual Freedom, 1996), 5–6.

Library's Bill of Rights—1939

Today indications in many parts of the world point to growing intolerance, suppression of free speech, and censorship affecting the rights of minorities and individuals. Mindful of this, the Council of the American Library Association publicly affirms its belief in the following basic policies which should govern the services of free public libraries.

1. Books and other reading matter selected for purchase from public funds should be chosen because of value and interest to people of the community, and in no case should the selection be influenced by the race or nationality or the political or religious views of the writers.

2. As far as available material permits, all sides of questions on which differences of opinion exist should be represented fairly and adequately in the books and other reading matter purchased for public use.

3. The library as an institution to educate for democratic living should especially welcome the use of its meeting rooms for socially useful and cultural activities and the discussion of current public questions. Library meeting rooms should be available on equal terms to all groups in the community regardless of their beliefs or affiliations.

Intellectual Freedom Manual, 5th ed. (Chicago: American Library Association, Office for Intellectual Freedom, 1996), 6–7.

Library Bill of Rights—1948

The Council of the American Library Association reaffirms its belief in the following basic policies which should govern the services of all libraries.

1. As a responsibility of library service, books and other reading matter selected should be chosen for values of interest, information and enlightenment of all the people of the community. In no case should any material be excluded because of the race or nationality, or the political or religious views of the writer.

2. There should be the fullest practicable provision of material presenting all points of view concerning the problems and issues of our times, international, national, and local; and books or other reading matter

of sound factual authority should not be proscribed or removed from library shelves because of partisan or doctrinal disapproval.

3. Censorship of books, urged or practiced by volunteer arbiters of morals or political opinion or by organizations that would establish a coercive concept of Americanism, must be challenged by libraries in maintenance of their responsibility to provide public information and enlightenment through the printed word.

4. Libraries should enlist the cooperation of allied groups in the fields of science, of education, and of book publishing in resisting all abridgment of the free access to ideas and full freedom of expression that are the tradition and heritage of Americans.

5. As an institution of education for democratic living, the library should welcome the use of its meeting rooms for socially useful and cultural activities and discussion of current public questions. Such meeting places should be available on equal terms to all groups in the community regardless of the beliefs and affiliations of their members.

Intellectual Freedom Manual, 5th ed. (Chicago: American Library Association, Office for Intellectual Freedom, 1996), 9–10.

Library Bill of Rights — 1961

The Council of the American Library Association reaffirms its belief in the following basic policies which should govern the services of all libraries.

1. As a responsibility of library service, books and other reading matter selected should be chosen for values of interest, information and enlightenment of all the people of the community. In no case should any book be excluded because of the race or nationality or the political or religious views of the writer.

2. There should be the fullest practicable provision of material presenting all points of view concerning the problems and issues of our times, international, national, and local; and books or other reading matter of sound factual authority should not be proscribed or removed from library shelves because of partisan or doctrinal disapproval.

3. Censorship of books, urged or practiced by volunteer arbiters of morals or political opinion or by organizations that would establish a coercive concept of Americanism, must be challenged by libraries in maintenance of their responsibility to provide public information and enlightenment through the printed word.

4. Libraries should enlist the cooperation of allied groups in the fields of science, of education, and of book publishing in resisting all abridgment of the free access to ideas and full freedom of expression that are the tradition and heritage of Americans.

5. The rights of an individual to the use of a library should not be denied or abridged because of his race, religion, national origins or political views.

6. As an institution of education for democratic living, the library should welcome the use of its meeting rooms for socially useful and cultural activities and discussion of current public questions. Such meeting places should be available on equal terms to all groups in the community regardless of the beliefs and affiliations of their members.

By official action of the Council on February 3, 1951, the "Library Bill of Rights" shall be interpreted to apply to all materials and media of communication used or collected by libraries.

Intellectual Freedom Manual, 5th ed. (Chicago: American Library Association, Office for Intellectual Freedom, 1996), 11.

Library Bill of Rights—1967

The Council of the American Library Association reaffirms its belief in the following basic policies which should govern the services of all libraries.

1. As a responsibility of library service, books and other library materials selected should be chosen for values of interest, information and enlightenment of all the people of the community. In no case should any library materials be excluded because of the race or nationality or the social, political, or religious views of the authors.

2. Libraries should provide books and other materials presenting all points of view concerning the problems and issues of our times; no library materials should be proscribed or removed from libraries because of partisan or doctrinal disapproval.

3. Censorship should be challenged by libraries in the maintenance of their responsibility to provide public information and enlightenment.

4. Libraries should cooperate with all persons and groups concerned with resisting abridgment of free expression and free access to ideas.

5. The rights of an individual to the use of a library should not be denied or abridged because of his age, race, religion, national origins or social or political views.

6. As an institution of education for democratic living, the library should welcome the use of its meeting rooms for socially useful and cultural activities and discussion of current public questions. Such meeting places should be available on equal terms to all groups in the community regardless of the beliefs and affiliations of their members, provided that the meetings be open to the public.

Intellectual Freedom Manual, 5th ed. (Chicago: American Library Association, Office for Intellectual Freedom, 1996), 13–14.

Bibliography

Monographs

Abbott, Andrew. *The System of Professions: An Essay on the Division of Expert Labor.* Chicago: University of Chicago Press, 1988.

Adamson, Walter L. *Hegemony and Revolution: A Study of Antonio Gramsci's Political and Cultural Theory.* Berkeley: University of California Press, 1980.

Allen, Robert Clyde, ed. *Channels of Discourse: Television and Contemporary Criticism.* Chapel Hill: University of North Carolina, 1987.

Alternative Papers: Selections from the Alternative Press, 1979–1980. Philadelphia: Temple University Press, 1982.

American Library Association. *Proceedings 1969 of the Midwinter Meeting, Washington, D.C., January 26–February 1, 1969, and the 88th Annual Conference Atlantic City, June 22–28, 1969* Chicago: American Library Association, 1969

_____. *Proceedings of the Midwinter Meeting, Chicago, January 18–24, 1970, and the 89th Annual Conference, Detroit, June 28–July 4, 1970.* Chicago: American Library Association, 1970.

_____. *Proceedings 1971 of the Midwinter Meeting, Los Angeles, January 18–22, 1971, and the Annual Conference, Dallas, June 20–26, 1971.* Chicago: American Library Association, 1971.

_____. Office for Intellectual Freedom. *Intellectual Freedom Manual.* 4th ed. Chicago: American Library Association, 1992.

_____. _____. *Intellectual Freedom Manual.* 5th ed. Chicago: American Library Association, 1996.

Apple, Michael W. *Cultural Politics and Education.* New York: Teachers College Press, 1996.

_____. *Education and Power,* 2nd ed. New York: Routledge, 1995.

_____. *Ideology and Curriculum,* 2nd ed. London: Routledge, 1990.

Armstrong, David. *A Trumpet to Arms: Alternative Media in America.* Los Angeles: J.P. Tarcher, 1981.

Aronowitz, Stanley. *The Politics of Identity: Class, Culture, Social Movements.* New York: Routledge, 1992.

Baughman, James L. *The Republic of Mass Culture: Journalism, Filmmaking, and Broadcasting in America Since 1941.* Baltimore: Johns Hopkins University Press, 1992.

153

Beechey, Veronica. *Unequal Work*. London: Verso, 1987.

Bell, Daniel. *The End of Ideology*. Glencoe, IL: The Free Press, 1960.

Berelson, Bernard. *The Library's Public: A Report of the Public Library Inquiry*. New York: Columbia University Press, 1949.

Berman, Ronald. *America in the Sixties: An Intellectual History*. New York: The Free Press, 1968.

Berman, Sanford. *Prejudices and Antipathies: A Tract on the LC Subject Heads Concerning People*. Metuchen, NJ: Scarecrow Press, 1971.

_____. *Prejudices and Antipathies: A Tract on the LC Subject Heads Concerning People*, corrected edition, with a foreword by Eric Moon, and a new preface. Jefferson, NC: McFarland, 1993.

_____, and James P. Danky, eds. *Alternative Library Literature, 1982/1983: A Biennial Anthology*. Phoenix: Oryx, 1984.

Berninghausen, David K. *The Flight from Reason: Essays on Intellectual Freedom in the Academy, the Press, and the Library*. Chicago: American Library Association, 1975.

Bloom, Allan. *The Closing of the American Mind: How Higher Education Has Failed Democracy and Impoverished the Souls of Today's Students*. New York: Simon and Schuster, 1987.

Blum, John Morton. *Years of Discord: American Politics and Society, 1961–1974*. New York: W. W. Norton, 1991.

Books in Print. New York: Bowker, 1948–.

The Bounds of Race: Perspectives on Hegemony and Resistance. Ithaca, NY: Cornell University Press, 1991.

Bourdieu, Pierre. *Distinction: A Social Critique of the Judgment of Taste*. Cambridge, MA: Harvard University Press, 1984.

Boyer, William W., ed. *Issues 1968*. Lawrence, KS: The University of Kansas Press, 1968.

Brichford, Maynard, and Anne Gilliland. *Guide to the American Library Association Archives*, 2nd. ed. [microform]. Chicago: American Library Association, 1987.

Bryan, Alice Isabel. *The Public Librarian: A Report of the Public Library Inquiry*. New York: Columbia University Press, 1952.

Bundy, Mary Lee, and Frederick J. Stielow, eds. *Activism in American Librarianship, 1962–1973*. New York: Greenwood Press, 1987.

Busha, Charles H., ed. *An Intellectual Freedom Primer*. Littleton, CO: Libraries Unlimited, 1977.

Carroll, Peter N. *It Seemed Like Nothing Happened: The Tragedy and Promise of America in the 1970s*. New York: Holt, Rinehart and Winston, 1982.

Casey, Kathleen. *I Answer with My Life: Life Histories of Women Teachers Working for Social Change*. New York: Routledge, 1993.

Chevigny, Paul. *More Speech: Dialogue Rights and Modern Liberty*. Philadelphia: Temple University Press, 1988.

Collier, David, and David Horowitz. *Destructive Generation: Second Thoughts About the Sixties*. New York: Summit Books, 1989.

Danky, James P., and Elliott Shore, eds. *Alternative Materials in Libraries*. Metuchen, NJ: Scarecrow Press, 1982.

Davidson, Alastair. *Antonio Gramsci: Towards an Intellectual Biography*. London: Merlin Press, 1977.

Davis, Angela. *Angela Davis: An Autobiography*. New York: Random House, 1974.

Davis, Donald G., and John Mark Tucker. *American Library History: A Comprehensive Guide to the Literature*. Santa Barbara, CA: ABC-CLIO, 1989.

Ditzion, Sidney Herbert. *Arsenals of a Democratic Culture: A Social History of the American Public Library Movement in New England and the Middle Class States from 1850 to 1900*. Chicago: American Library Association, 1947.

Downs, Robert B. *Perspectives on the Past: An Autobiography*. Metuchen, NJ: Scarecrow Press, 1984.

_____, and Ralph E. McCoy, eds. *The First Freedom: Critical Issues Relating to Censorship and to Intellectual Freedom*. Chicago: American Library Association: 1984.

Echols, Alice. *Daring to Be Bad: Radical Feminism in America, 1967–1975*. Minneapolis: University of Minnesota Press, 1989.

Ennis, Phillip H. *Seven Questions About the Profession of Librarianship*. Chicago: University of Chicago Press, 1962.

Eshenaur, Ruth Marie. *Censorship of the Alternative Press: A Descriptive Study of the Social and Political Control of Radical Periodicals (1964–1973)*. Carbondale, IL: [s.n.], 1975.

Evans, Sara. *Personal Politics: The Root of the Women's Liberation in the Civil Rights Movement and the New Left*. New York: Alfred Knopf, 1979.

Farber, David., ed. *The Sixties: From Memory to History*. Chapel Hill, NC: University of North Carolina Press, 1994.

Fidell, Linda S., and John DeLamater. *Women in the Professions: What's All the Fuss About?* Beverly Hills, CA. Sage Publications, 1971.

Fish, Stanley. *Is There a Text in This Class? The Authority of Interpretive Communities*. Cambridge, MA: Harvard University Press, 1980.

_____. *There's No Such Thing as Free Speech, and It's a Good Thing Too*. New York: Oxford University Press, 1994.

Fiske, John. *Reading the Popular*. London: Routledge, 1989.

_____ *Understanding Popular Culture*. London: Routledge, 1989.

Foskett, D. J. *The Creed of a Librarian — No Politics, No Religion, No Morals*. London: The Library Association, 1962.

Foucault, Michel. *The Archaeology of Knowledge and the Discourse on Language*. New York: Pantheon Books, 1972.

Franklin, Bob, and David Murphy. *What News? The Market, Politics and the Local Press*. London: Routledge, 1991.

Fulton, Len. *Small Press Record of Non-periodical Publications*. Paradise, CA: Dustbooks, 1969–1975.

Galbraith, John Kenneth. *The Affluent Society*, 4th ed. Boston: Houghton Mifflin Company, 1984.

Garceau, Oliver. *The Public Library in the Political Process: A Report of the Public Library Inquiry*. New York: Columbia University Press, 1949.

Garrison, Dee. *Apostles of Culture: The Public Librarian and American Society, 1876–1920*. New York: Free Press, 1979.

Geller, Evelyn. *Forbidden Books in American Public Libraries, 1876–1939: A Study in Cultural Change*. Westport, CT: Greenwood Press, 1984.

Gitlin, Todd. *The Sixties: Years of Hope, Days of Rage.* Toronto: Bantam Books, 1987.

Gless, Darryl J., and Barbara Hernstein-Smith, eds. *The Politics of a Liberal Education.* Durham, NC: Duke University Press, 1992.

Glessing, Robert J. *The Underground Press in America.* Bloomington: Indiana University Press, 1970.

Goines, David Lance. *The Free Speech Movement: Coming of Age in the 1960s.* Berkeley: Ten Speed Press, 1993.

Goodman, Mitchell. *The Movement Toward a New America: The Beginning of a Long Revolution (A College)— A What? ...* Philadelphia: Pilgrim Press, 1970.

Goodwin, Richard N. *Remembering America: A Voice from the Sixties.* Boston: Little, Brown, 1988.

Gramsci, Antonio. *An Antonio Gramsci Reader: Selected Writings, 1916–1935.* New York: Schocken Books, 1988.

_____. *Letters from Prison.* Volumes I & II, ed. by Frank Rosengarten. Translated by Raymond Rosenthal. New York: Columbia University Press, 1994.

_____. *Selections from Political Writings (1910–1920).* Selected and edited by Quintin Hoare and G. Nowell Smith. Translated by John Matthews. London: Lawrence and Wishart, 1977.

_____. *Selections from the Prison Notebooks.* Translated and edited by Quintin Hoare and G. Nowell Smith. New York: International Publishers, 1971.

Habermas, Jurgen. *Communication and the Evolution of Society.* Boston: Beacon Press, 1979.

_____. *Jurgen Habermas on Society and Politics: A Reader.* Boston: Beacon Press, 1989.

_____. *The Structural Transformation of the Public Sphere: An Inquiry Into a Category of Bourgeois Society.* Cambridge, MA: MIT Press, 1989.

Hafner, Arthur W., ed. *Democracy and the Public Library: Essays on Fundamental Issues.* Wesport, CT: Greenwood Press, 1993.

Haiman, Franklyn S. *Speech and Law in a Free Society.* Chicago: University of Chicago Press, 1981.

Harrington, Michael. *The Other America: Poverty in the United States,* rev. ed. Baltimore: Penguin Books, 1971.

Harris, Michael H., and Davis Donald G. *American Library History: A Bibliography.* Austin: University of Texas Press, 1978.

Harris, Roma. *Librarianship: The Erosion of a Woman's Profession.* Norwood, NJ: Ablex, 1992.

Hauptman, Robert. *Ethical Challenges in Librarianship.* Phoenix, AZ: Oryx Press, 1988.

Hayden, Tom. *Rebellion and Repression: Testimony by Tom Hayden Before the National Commission on the Causes and Prevention of Violence, and the House Un-American Activities Committee.* New York: World Publishing, 1969.

Hennepin County Library Collection Maintenance Manual. Rev. Material Selection Section, Collection and Special Services Division. Minnetonka, MN: The Library, 1988.

Hentoff, Nat. *The First Freedom: The Tumultuous History of Free Speech in America.* New York: Delacorte Press, 1980.

Herman, Edward S., and Noam Chomsky. *Manufacturing Consent: Changes in the Labor Process Under Monopoly Capitalism.* Chicago: University of Chicago Press, 1982.

_____. *Manufacturing Consent: The Political Economy of the Mass Media.* New York: Pantheon Books, 1988.

Hernstein-Smith, Barbara. *Contingencies of Value: Alternative Perspectives for Critical Theory.* Cambridge, MA: Harvard University Press, 1988.

Hoffman, Frank. *Intellectual Freedom and Censorship: An Annotated Bibliography.* Metuchen, NJ: Scarecrow Press, 1989.

Horn, Zoia. *Zoia! Memoirs of Zoia Horn, Battler for the People's Right to Know.* Jefferson, NC: McFarland, 1995.

Ingham, John N. *Sex 'N' Drugs 'N' Rock 'N' Roll: American Popular Culture Since 1945.* Toronto: Canadian Scholars' Press, 1989.

ITP Nelson Canadian Dictionary of the English Language. Toronto: ITP Nelson, 1997.

Jackson, Rebecca. *The 1960's: An Annotated Bibliography of Social and Political Movements in the United States.* Westport, CT: Greenwood Press, 1992.

Jaffe, Harold, and John Tytell, eds. *The American Experience: A Radical Reader.* New York: Harper and Row Publishers, 1970.

Javorski, Susanne, et al., comp. *Alternative Press in Wisconsin.* Madison: Memorial Library, University of Wisconsin–Madison, 1980.

Jenkins, Christine A. "The Strength of the Inconspicuous: Youth Services Librarians, the American Library Association, and Intellectual Freedom for the Young, 1939–1955." Ph.D. diss., University of Wisconsin–Madison, 1995.

Jezer, Marty. *The Dark Ages: Life in the United States, 1945–1960.* Boston: South End Press, 1982.

Josey, E.J. *The Black Librarian in America.* Metuchen, NJ: Scarecrow Press, 1970.

_____, and Marva L. DeLoach, eds. *Ethnic Collections in Libraries.* New York: Neal-Schuman, 1983.

_____, and Ann Allen Shockley, eds. *Handbook of Black Librarianship.* Littleton, CO: Libraries Unlimited, 1977.

Karkhanis, Sharad, and Betty-Carol Sellen, eds. *A New College Student: The Challenge to City University Libraries.* Rockaway, NY: Scientific Book Service, 1969.

Kauffman, Linda, ed. *Feminism & Institutions: Dialogues on Feminist Theory.* Cambridge, MA: Basil Blackwell, 1989.

Kliebard, Herbert M. *Forging the American Curriculum: Essays in Curriculum History and Theory.* New York: Routledge, 1992.

Krassner, Paul. *Confessions of a Raving, Unconfined Nut: Misadventures in the Counter-Culture.* New York: Simon and Schuster, 1993.

_____. *How a Satirical Editor Became a Yippie Conspirator in Ten Easy Years.* New York: Putnam, 1971.

Kruchkow, Diane, and Curt Johnson, eds. *Green Isle in the Sea: An Informal History of the Alternative Press, 1960–85.* Highland Park, IL: December Press, 1986.

LaCapra, Dominick. *History & Criticism.* Ithaca, NY: Cornell University Press, 1985.

Larrabee, Mary Jeanne, ed. *An Ethic of Care: Feminist Interdisciplinary Perspectives.* New York: Routledge, 1993.

Larson, Magali Sarfatti. *The Rise of Professionalism: A Sociological Analysis.* Berkeley: University of California Press, 1977.

Leamer, Laurence. *The Paper Revolutionaries: The Rise of the Underground Press.* New York: Simon and Schuster, 1972.

Learned, William Setchel. *The American Public Library and the Diffusion of Knowledge.* New York: Harcourt, Brace, 1924.

Lewis, Roger. *Outlaws of America: The Underground Press and Its Context.* Harmondsworth, England: Penguin, 1972.

Lowenthal, Marjorie Fiske. *Book Selection and Censorship: A Study of School and Public Libraries in California.* Berkeley: University of California Press, 1959.

Lukes, Steven. *Power: A Radical View.* London: Macmillan, 1974.

Marcuse, Herbert. *One Dimensional Man.* London: ABACUS, Sphere Books, 1972.

Marshall, Joan K., comp. *On Equal Terms: A Thesaurus for Nonsexist Indexing and Cataloging.* New York: Neal-Schuman, 1977.

McAuliffe. Kevin. *The Great American Newspaper: The Rise and Fall of the Village Voice.* New York: Scribner, 1978.

Mill, John Stuart. *On Liberty and Considerations on Representative Government.* Oxford: B. Blackwell, 1946.

Milton, John. *Areopagitica, and Of Education.* Oxford: Clarendon Press, 1973.

Moon, Eric. *Book Selection and Censorship in the Sixties.* New York: R. R. Bowker, 1969.

_____, and Karl Nyren, eds. *Library Issues: The Sixties.* New York: R. R. Bowker, 1970.

Morgan, Edward P. *The Sixties Experience: Hard Lessons About Modern America.* Philadelphia: Temple University Press, 1991.

Mouffe, Chantal, ed. *Gramsci and Marxist Theory.* London: Routledge, 1979.

Mungo, Raymond. *Between Two Moons: A Technicolor Travelogue.* Boston: Beacon Press, 1972.

_____. *Famous Long Ago: My Life and Hard Times with Liberation News Service.* Boston: Beacon Press, [1970].

Munthe, Wilhelm. *American Librarianship from a European Angle: An Attempt at an Evaluation of Policies and Activities.* Hamden, Conn.: Shoe String Press, 1964.

Nadelson, Regina. *Who Is Angela Davis?: The Biography of a Revolutionary.* New York: Peter H. Wyden, 1972.

National Catalog of Sources for the History of Librarianship. Chicago: ALA, 1982.

Nemeth, Thomas. *Gramsci's Philosophy: A Critical Study.* Sussex: Harvester Press, 1980.

Oboler, Eli M. *Defending Intellectual Freedom: The Library and the Censor.* Westport, CT: Greenwood Press, 1980.

Parker, J. A. *Angela Davis: The Making of a Revolutionary.* New Rochelle, NY: Arlington House, 1973.

Peattie, Noel. *The Living Z: A Guide to the Literature of the Counter-Culture, the Alternative Press, and Little Magazines.* Milwaukee: Margins, 1975.

_____. *A Passage for Dissent: The Best of Sipapu, 1970–1988.* Jefferson, NC: McFarland, 1989.

Peck, Abe. *Uncovering the Sixties: The Life and Times of the Underground Press.* New York: Pantheon Books, 1985.

Poster, Mark. *The Mode of Information: Poststructuralism and Social Context.* Chicago: University of Chicago Press, 1990.

Postlewait, Thomas, and Bruce A. McConachie, eds. *Interpreting the Theatrical Past: Essays in the Historiography of Performance.* Iowa City: University of Iowa Press, 1989.

Preconference on the Status of Women in Librarianship (1974: Douglass College). *Women in a Woman's Profession: Strategies of the Preconference on the Status of Women in Librarianship, Sponsored by the American Library Association Social Responsibilities Round Table Task Force on the Status of Women.* Douglass College, Rutgers University, July 1974, edited by Betty-Carol Sellen and Joan K. Marhall. [s.l. : s.n., 1974].

Proceedings of the 87th Annual Conference 1968 American Library Association Kansas City, Missouri June 23–29, 1968. Chicago: American Library Association, 1968.

Raboy, Marc, and Bernard Dagenais, eds. *Media, Crisis and Democracy: Mass Communication and the Disruption of Social Order.* London: Sage Publications, 1992.

Rachlin, Allan. *News as Hegemonic Reality: American Political Culture and the Framing of News Accounts.* New York: Praeger, 1988.

Reich, Charles A. *The Greening of America: How the Youth Revolution Is Trying to Make America Liveable.* New York: Random House, 1970.

Rips, Geoffrey. *The Campaign Against the Underground Press.* San Francisco: City Lights Books, 1981.

_____. *Unamerican Activities: The Campaign Against the Underground.* San Francisco: City Lights Books, 1981.

Robins, Natalie. *Alien Ink: The FBI's War on Freedom of Expression.* New Brunswick, NJ: Rutgers University Press, 1992.

Robbins, Louise S. *Censorship and the American Library: The American Library Association's Response to Threats to Intellectual Freedom, 1939–1969.* Westport, CT: Greenwood Press, 1996.

Rosenstein, Allen B. *A Study of a Profession and Professional Education: The Final Publication Recommendations of the UCLA Educational Development Program.* Los Angeles: University of California, School of Engineering and Applied Science, 1969.

Ruddick, Sara, and Pamela Daniels, eds. *Working It Out: 23 Women Writers, Artists, Scientists, and Scholars Talk About Their Lives and Work.* New York: Pantheon Books, 1977.

Salamini, Leonardo. *The Sociology of Political Praxis: An Introduction to Gramsci's Theory.* London: Routledge and Kegan Paul, 1981.

Sassoon, Anne Showstack, ed. *Approaches to Gramsci.* London: Writers and Readers Publishing Cooperative Society, 1982.

Schuman, Patricia Glass., comp. and ed. *Social Responsibilities and Libraries: A Library Journal/School Library Journal Selection.* New York: R.R. Bowker, 1976.

Sharpe, David. *Rochdale: The Runaway College.* Toronto: Anansi, 1987.

Shera, Jesse Hauk. *Foundations of the Public Library: The Origins of the Public Library Movement in New England, 1629–1855.* Chicago: University of Chicago Press, 1949.

Simon, Roger. *Gramsci's Political Thought: An Introduction.* London: Lawrence and Wishart, 1982.

Skolnick, Jerome H. *The Politics of Protest: A Report.* New York: Simon & Schuster, 1969.

Stone, I. F. *The Haunted Fifties.* London: Merlin Press, 1963.

Swan, John, and Noel Peattie. *The Freedom to Lie: A Debate About Democracy.* Jefferson, NC: McFarland, 1989.

Thompson, John B. *Critical Hermeneutics: A Study in the Thought of Paul Ricoeur and Jurgen Habermas.* Cambridge, MA: Cambridge University Press, 1981.

Tipton, Steven M. *Getting Saved from the Sixties: Moral Meaning in Conversion and Cultural Change.* Berkeley: University of California Press, 1982.

Wachsberger, Ken, ed. *Voices From the Underground — Volume 2: A Directory of Sources and Resources on the Vietnam Era Underground Press.* Tempe, AZ: MICA Press, 1993.

Wasserman, Harvey. *Harvey Wasserman's History of the United States.* New York: Harper & Row, 1972.

West, Celeste. *The Passionate Perils of Publishing.* San Francisco: Booklegger Press, 1978.

_____, and Elizabeth Katz, eds. *Revolting Librarians.* San Francisco: Booklegger Press, 1972.

Whitaker, Cathy Seitz, ed. *Alternative Publications: A Guide to Directories, Indexes, Bibliographies, and Other Sources.* Jefferson, NC: McFarland, 1990.

Wiegand, Wayne A. *An Active Instrument for Propaganda: The American Public Library During World War I.* New York: Greenwood Press, 1989.

_____. *Leaders in American Academic Librarianship: 1925–1975.* New York: Greenwood Press, 1983.

_____. *The Politics of an Emerging Profession: The American Library Association, 1876–1917.* Westport, CT: Greenwood Press, 1986.

Winter, Michael. *The Culture and Control of Expertise: Toward a Sociological Understanding of Librarianship.* Westport, CT: Greenwood Press, 1988.

Zinn, Howard. *A People's History of the United States.* New York: Harper & Row, 1990.

_____. *Postwar America 1945–1971.* Indianapolis: Bobbs-Merrill, 1973.

_____. *You Can't Be Neutral on a Moving Train: A Personal History of Our TImes.* Boston: Beacon Press, 1994.

Periodical Literature

"ACONDA Revised Recommendations on Democratization and Reorganization: A report presented for consideration of Council and Membership, Midwinter Meeting, January 1971." *American Libraries* 2, no. 1 (January 1971): 81–92.

"Actions/Resolutions: Midwinter." *Library Journal* 96, no. 6 (15 March 1971): 905.

"Activities Committee on New Directions for ALA." *ALA Bulletin* 63, no. 10 (November 1969): 1383.

Adams, Charles J. "A Checklist of the Dissident Press." *RQ* 6, no. 2 (Winter 1966): 54–61.

"ALA 1970: Notes & Comments." *Wilson Library Bulletin* 45, no. 1 (September 1970): 14–31.

"ALA 1971: Notes & Comments." *Wilson Library Bulletin* 46, no. 1 (September 1971): 8–28.

"ALA Asked to Act on Bodger Case in Missouri." *Wilson Library Bulletin* 44, no. 2 (October 1969): 136.

"ALA Chicago 1972." *Wilson Library Bulletin* 47, no. 1 (September 1972): 62–76.

"ALA Interim Report." *American Libraries* 1, no. 3 (March 1970): 238–241.

"ALA Membership Slides 6,471." *Wilson Library Bulletin* 45, no. 6 (February 1971): 525.

"ALA Midwinter: Hot Winds, Cold Winds, Ups and Downs." *Wilson Library Bulletin* 46, no. 7 (March 1972): 638–647.

"ALA Midwinter: Post-Analytic Depression." *Wilson Library Bulletin* 45, no. 7 (March 1971): 622–638.

"The ALAiad, or, A Tale of Two Conferences." *Wilson Library Bulletin* 44, no. 1 (September 1969): 80–91.

Altbach, Phillip G. "Publishing and the Intellectual System." *Annals of the American Academy of Political and Social Science.* 42, no. 1 (1975): 1–13.

"Alternative Press Index." *SRRT Newsletter* 64 (July 1982): 6–7.

"American Library Association." *ALA Bulletin* 61, no. 10 (November 1967): 1155.

"Another Opening, Another Show: Detroit 1970." *American Libraries* 1, no. 7 (July–August 1970): 660–684.

"Anti-Chicago Resolution Aired at AALS." *Library Journal* 94, no.5 (1 March 1969): 927.

Asheim, Lester. "Not Censorship, But Selection." *Wilson Library Bulletin* 28, no. 1 (1953): 63–67.

_____. "Selection and Censorship: A Reappraisal." *Wilson Library Bulletin* 58, no. 3 (November 1983): 180–184.

Baldwin, Gordon. "The Library Bill of Rights — A Critique." *Library Trends* 45, no. 1 (Summer 1996): 7–27.

Barber, Peggy. "Ladies in Waiting." *Synergy* 24 (December 1969): 22–25.

Bass, Doris. "Can This Marriage Be Saved?" *Library Journal* 94, no. 16 (15 September 1969): 3023–3025.

Benediktsson, Daniel. "Hermeneutics: Dimensions Toward LIS Thinking." *Library and Information Science Research* 11, no. 3 (1989): 201–234.

Berelson, Bernard. "The Myth of Library Impartiality: An Interpretation for Democracy." *Wilson Bulletin for Librarians* 13, no. 2 (October 1938): 87–90.

Berman, Sanford. "Chauvinistic Headings." *Library Journal* 94, no. 4 (15 February 1969): 695.

_____. "Where It's At: Advice on How to Enliven, Enrich, Un-barnacle and Controversialize Library Collections." *Library Journal* 93, no. 22 (15 December 1968): 4615–4618.

"Berninghausen Charges Minority Wants to Rule or Ruin ALA." *American Libraries* 4, no. 1 (January 1971): 9.

Berninghausen, David K. "Antithesis in Librarianship: Social Responsibility vs. The Library Bill of Rights." *Library Journal* 97, no. 20 (15 November 1972): 3675–3681.

_____. "Intellectual Freedom in Librarianship: Advances and Retreats." *Advances in Librarianship* 9 (1979): 1–29.

_____. "The Librarian's Commitment to the Library Bill of Rights." *Library Trends* 19, no. 1 (July 1970): 19–38.

_____. "Toward an Intellectual Freedom Theory for Users of Libraries." *Drexel Library Quarterly* 18, no. 1 (1982): 57–81.

Berry, John. "The Best Defense." *Library Journal* 94, no. 7 (1 April 1969): 1401.

_____. "Channels for Change." *Library Journal* 95, no. 4 (15 February 1970): 611.

_____. "Dear Dean Berninghausen," *Library Journal* 98 no. 1 (1 January 1973): 11.

_____. "Death and Taxes." *Library Journal* 97, no. 2 (15 January 1972): 137.

_____. "Electing an ALA Council." *Library Journal* 95, no. 9 (1 May 1970): 1683.

_____. "Happy Honeymoon." *Library Journal* 97, no. 8 (15 April 1972): 1365.

_____. "Help for Hodgin." *Library Journal* 94, no. 15 (1 September 1969): 2853.

_____. "Little Red Book." Review of *Revolting Librarians,* eds. Celeste West and Elizabeth Katz, In *Library Journal* 98, no. 4 (15 February 1973): 515.

_____. "The New Constituency." *Library Journal* 94, no. 14 (August 1969): 2725–2739.

_____. "No Answers Yet." *Library Journal* 94, no. 14 (August 1969): 2709.

_____. "Part of the Solution." *Library Journal* 95, no. 12 (15 June 1970): 2205.

_____. "Programming the ALA Program." *Library Journal* 94, no. 12 (15 June 1969): 2379.

_____. "Service: Social or Reference?" *Library Journal* 94, no. 8 (15 April 1969): 1563.

Bewley, Lois M. "Censorship and Librarians." *Canadian Library Journal* 40, no. 6 (December 1983): 353–357.

Billings, Dwight B. "Religion as Opposition: A Gramscian Analysis." *American Journal of Sociology* 96, no.1 (July 1990): 1–31.

Bixler, Paul. "On Taking a Stand." *American Libraries* 1, no. 4 (April 1970): 329–330.

Blake, Fay M. "Ammo for Yahoos." *Library Journal* 94, no. 11 (1 June 1969): 2175–2176.

Blanke, Henry. "Libraries and the Commercialization of Information." *Progressive Librarian* 2 (Winter 1990/91): 9–13.

Boaz, Martha. "The First Responsibility." *American Libraries* 2, no. 10 (November 1971): 1035.

Bold, Rudolph. "Usurped Sympathy." *American Libraries* 2, no. 9 (October 1971): 929.

Booklegger Magazine 5 (July/August 1974).

Borden, Arnold K. "The Sociological Beginnings of the Library Movement." *Library Quarterly* 1 (July 1931): 278–282.

Bradshaw, Lillian M. "Library Response to a Restive World." *American Libraries* 1, no. 7 (July-August 1970): 688–690.

Bundy, Mary Lee. "Factors Influencing Public Library Use." *Wilson Library Bulletin* 42, no. 4 (December 1967): 371–382.

_____, Amy Bridgman, and Laura Keltie. "Public Library Reference Service: Myth and Reality." *Public Library Quarterly* 3, no. 3 (Fall 1982): 11–22.

_____, and the Rev. Michael V. Thornton. "Who Runs the American Library Association: Implications for Professional Development." In *Social and Political Aspects of Librarianship: Student Contributions to Library Science,* eds. Mary

Lee Bundy and Ruth Aronson, 23–30. New York: School of Library Science, State University of New York at Albany, 1965.

_____, and Teresa Stakem. "Librarians and Intellectual Freedom: Are Opinions Changing?" *Wilson Library Bulletin* 56, no. 8 (April 1982): 584–589.

Buschman, John, and Michael Carbone. "A Critical Inquiry into Librarianship Applications of the *New Sociology of Education*." *Library Quarterly* 61, no. 1 (1991): 15–40.

"Business Not Quite as Usual." *Library Journal* 93, no. 14 (August 1968): 2797–2810.

Carnovsky, Leon. "The Obligations and Responsibilities of the Librarian Concerning Censorship." *Library Quarterly* 20, no. 1 (January 1950): 21–32.

Carter, John M. "Lovebites & Loobies." *Library Journal* 95, no. 20 (15 November 1970): 3885.

"Celeste West on *Synergy*." *Sipapu* 4, no. 2 (July 1973): 71.

"Censors Fell Evergreen in Groton." *Wilson Library Bulletin* 45, no. 8 (April 1971): 717.

"Change: 1969–1979: A State-of-the-Art Review 10 Years After the Library 'Revolution.'" *American Libraries* 10, no. 6 (June 1979): 301–373.

"The Changing Guard: The 1972 ALA Conference." *Library Journal* 97, no. 14 (August 1972): 2523–2530.

"Charge Nation's Professions Lacking in Responsibility." *Library Journal* 94, no. 14 (August 1969): 2714.

Christianson, Elin B. "Mergers in the Publishing Industry, 1958–1970." *Journal of Library History* 7, no. 1 (January 1972): 5–32.

"Clift Balks at Davis Gift Voted by SRRT Council." *Library Journal* 96, no. 9 (May 1971): 1553.

Comedia. "The Alternative Press: The Development of Underdevelopment." *Media, Culture and Society* 6, no. 2 (April 1984): 95–102.

"Commentary." *American Libraries* 3, no. 3 (March 1972): 220–228.

"Commentary." *American Libraries* 3, no. 6 (June 1972): 579–589.

"Congress for Change Issues New Manifesto." *Library Journal* 94, no. 18 (15 October 1969): 3596.

"Congress for Change Set for June 20–21." *Library Journal* 94, no. 12 (15 June 1969): 2384.

"A Conversation with Celeste West." *Technicalities* 2, no. 4 (April 1982): 3–6.

Conway, Charles. Review of *Revolting Librarians*, eds. Celeste West and Elizabeth Katz. In *Library Resources and Technical Services* 18, no. 3 (Summer 1974): 294–295.

"Council Cop-Out." *Library Journal* 96, no. 6 (15 March 1971): 918–924.

Crickman, Robin D. "The Emerging Information Professional." *Library Trends* 28, no. 2 (Fall 1979): 311–327.

Cronenberg, Richard. "SYNERGIZING Reference Service in the San Francisco Bay Region." *ALA Bulletin* 62, no. 11(December 1968): 1379–1384.

Crosby, Charles W. "Mirror to Social Issues?" *Library Journal* 93, no. 20 (15 November 1968): 4219–4220.

Curley, Arthur. "ALA Identity Crisis: Dilemma or Delaying Device." *Library Journal* 95, no. 11 (1 June 1970): 2089–2090.

_____. "Ideals." *Library Journal* 97, no. 22 (15 December 1972): 3973.

Cyzyk, Mark. "Canon Formation, Library Collections, and the Dilemma of Collection Development." *College and Research Libraries* 54 no. 1 (1993): 58–65.

Darling, Eugene. "Are Librarians Revolting?" Review of *Revolting Librarians,* eds. Celeste West and Elizabeth Katz, In *Library Union Caucus Newsletter* 2, no. 1 (January 1973): 5.

Dawson, Don. "Educational Hegemony and the Phenomenology of Community Participation." *Journal of Educational Thought* 16, no. 3 (1982): 150–160.

DeJohn, Bill. "Social Responsibilities: What It's All About." *American Libraries* 2, no. 3 (March 1971): 300–302.

Ditzion, Sidney H. "The Research and Writing of Library History." In *Toward a Theory of Librarianship: Papers in Honor of Jesse Hauk Shera*. Metuchen, NJ: Scarecrow Press, 1973.

Dix, William S. "Status Quo or Quo Vadis?" *Library Journal* 94, no. 19 (1 November 1969): 3941–3942.

"Dix-Mix Committee Meets on ALA Changes." *Library Journal* 94, no. 20 (15 November 1969): 4081.

Downs, Robert B. "Freedom of Speech and Press: Development of Concept." *Library Trends* 19, no. 1 (July 1970): 8–18.

Duhac, Kenneth. "A Plea for Social Responsibility." *Library Journal* 93, no. 14 (August 1968): 2798–2799.

Dunbar, Geoffrey. "Librarian and/or Citizen." *Library Journal* 97, no. 1 (1 January 1972): 42–43.

Durkin, Henry P. "Berman vs. Durkin, Again." *Library Journal* 94, no. 18 (15 October 1969): 3585.

_____. "Where It's Also At." *Library Journal* 94, no. 9 (1 May 1969): 1839.

"Editors' Choice: Robert Wedgeworth." *American Libraries* 3, no. 6 (June 1972): 591.

"Emergency Fund Within Freedom Foundation." *Wilson Library Bulletin* 45, no. 2 (October 1970): 122.

Emerick, Tyron D. "One More Wedge." *Library Journal* 96, no. 13 (July 1971): 2239.

Ferrero, David. "Antonio Gramsci and His Relevance for American Public Education." *Research and Society* 7 (1994): 41–68.

Fiske, John. "British Cultural Studies and Television." In *Channels of Discourse: Television and Contemporary Criticism,* ed. Robert Clyde Allen, 254– 289. Chapel Hill: University of North Carolina, 1987.

Fletcher, Homer L. "How Pure Is Neutrality? *American Libraries* 2, no. 5 (May 1971): 449.

Forsman, Carolyn. "Up Against the Stacks: The Liberated Librarian's Guide to Activism." *Synergy* 28 (July-August 1970): 6–12.

Freedman, Janet Lois. "The Liberated Librarian? A Look at the Second Sex in the Library Profession." *Library Journal* 95, no. 9 (1 May 1970): 1709–1711.

Freedman, Maurice. "Cataloging Systems: 1973 Applications Status." In *Library Automation: State of the Art II*, eds. Susan K. Martin and Brett Butler, 56–86. Chicago: American Library Association, 1975.

Freiser, Leonard H. "The Bendix-Duhac Establishment," *Library Journal* 93, no. 16 (15 September 1968): 3105.

Gaines, Ervin J. "Faddism." *Library Journal* 95, no. 12 (15 June 1970): 2235.

Galvin, Hoyt R. "Mixed Bag Debate." *American Libraries* 1, no. 8 (September 1970): 745.

Gareau, Frederick H. "International Institutions and the Gramscian Legacy." *Social Science Journal* 33, no. 2 (1996): 223–235.

Geller, Evelyn. "Think Session at High John." *Library Journal* 93, no. 15 (1 September 1968): 2963–2971.

Gordon, Ruth, and Jovanna Brown. "Chicago Boycott." *Library Journal* 94, no. 6 (15 March 1969): 1077–1078.

"Government Intimidation." *American Libraries* 2, no. 8 (September 1971): 804.

"A Great Show — In Two Parts and a Cast of Thousands." *ALA Bulletin* 63, no. 7 (July-August 1969): 915–964.

"Green Light on Intellectual Freedom Support Fund." *Wilson Library Bulletin* 44, no. 1 (September 1969): 6.

"Groton Censors Win: Trustees Back Down." *Library Journal* 96, no. 8 (15 April 1971): 1318.

"Growing Pains and Generation Gaps: Kansas City Conference." *ALA Bulletin* 62, no. 7 (July-August 1968): 817–864.

Hagist, Barbara. "Resistance and Reluctance." *Library Journal* 93, no. 3 (1 February 1968): 518–520.

Hall, Stewart. "Gramsci's Relevance for the Study of Race and Ethnicity." *Journal of Communication Enquiry* 10, no. 2 (Summer 1986): 5–27.

Harmeyer, Dave. "Potential Collection Development Bias: Some Evidence on a Controversial Topic in California." *College and Research Libraries* 56, no. 2 (March 1995): 101–111.

Haro, Robert P. "Chicago — No Happy Medium." *Library Journal* 93, no. 18 (15 October 1968): 3723–3724.

_____. "Creative Restlessness." *Library Journal* 93, no. 15 (1 September 1968): 2941.

Harris, Michael H. "No Love Lost: Library Women vs. Women Who Use Libraries." *Progressive Librarian* 5 (Summer 1992): 1–18.

_____. "Portrait in Paradox: Commitment and Ambivalence in American Librarianship, 1876–1976. *Libri* 26, no. 4 (1976): 281–301.

_____. "State, Class and Cultural Reproduction: Toward a Theory of Library Service in the United States." *Advances in Librarianship*. 14 (1986): 211–252.

"Headin' for the Last Roundup." *American Libraries* 2, no. 3 (March 1971): 243–273.

"A Hearing for Doiron." *Library Journal* 96, no. 21 (1 December 1971): 3931.

Heinzkill, Richard. "Literary Canon Building." *Collection Management* 13, nos. 1/2 (1990): 51–64.

"High John." *Library Journal* 93, no. 2 (15 January 1968): 147–155.

Hildenbrand, Suzanne. "Ambiguous Authority and Aborted Ambition: Gender, Professionalism and the Rise and Fall of the Welfare State." *Library Trends* 34, no. 2 (Fall 1985): 185–198.

"Historically Neglected Materials." *Wilson Library Bulletin* 45, no. 8 (April 1971): 733.

Hopkins, Dianne McAfee. "The Library Bill of Rights and School Library Media Programs. *Library Trends* 45, no. 1 (Summer 1996): 61–74.

Hubbard, Katherine. "Protest Indecency." *American Libraries* 2, no. 10 (November 1971): 1039.

Hunt, Alan. "Rights and Social Movements: Counter-Hegemonic Strategies." *Journal of Law and Society* 17, no. 3 (Autumn 1990): 309–328.

Hupp, Stephen L. "The Left and the Right: A Preliminary Study of Bias in Collection Development in Ohio Libraries." *Collection Management* 14, nos. 1/2 (1991): 139–154.

"In Search of Soul." *Library Journal* 95, no. 14 (August 1970): 2632–2634.

"Intellectual Freedom and the Jurisdictional Jungle." *Library Journal* 96, no. 6 (15 March 1971): 925–929.

"Intellectual Freedom at Dallas." *Library Journal* 96, no. 14 (August 1971): 2447–2449.

"Introduction." *Workforce* 34 (March-April 1973): 5.

Jansen, Sue Curry. "Gender and the Information Society: A Socially Structured Silence." *Journal of Communication* 39, no. 3 (Summer 1989): 196–215.

Kaser, D. "Advances in American Library History." *Advances in Librarianship* 8 (1978): 181–99.

Katz, Bill. "Liberated Librarian Newsletter." *Library Journal* 97, no. 16 (15 September 1972): 2823.

_____. "Statistical Wailing Wall: A Nationwide Survey." *Library Journal* 93, no. 11 (1 June 1968): 2203–2208.

Kister, Kenneth. "Educating Librarians in Intellectual Freedom." *Library Trends* 19, no. 1 (July 1970): 159–168.

"Know Your ALA: Services to Members and Aids to Collections." *ALA Bulletin* 63, no. 1 (January 1969): 47–58.

Kraus, Joe W. "The Progressive Librarians' Council." *Library Journal* 97, no. 13 (July 1972): 2351–2354.

Krug, Judith F. "Intellectual Freedom." *American Libraries* 1, no. 4 (April 1970): 336–338.

Kurtz, Donald V. "Hegemony and Anthropology: Gramsci, Exegeses, Reinterpretations." *Critique of Anthropology* 16, no. 2 (1996): 103–135.

Lacy, Dan. "Suppression and Intellectual Freedom." *American Libraries* 3, no. 7 (July-August 1972): 807–810.

Lears, T.J. Jackson. "The Concept of Cultural Hegemony: Problems and Possibilities." *American Historical Review* 90, no. 3 (1985): 567–593.

Lehman, James O. "*Choice* as a Selection Tool." *Wilson Library Bulletin* 44, no. 9 (May 1970): 957–961.

Leon, S. J. "Book Selection in Philadelphia." *Library Journal* 98, no. 7 (1 April 1973): 1081–1089.

Leontidou, Lila. "Alternatives to Modernism in (Southern) Urban Theory: Exploring In-between Spaces." *International Journal of Urban and Regional Research* 20, no. 2 (1996): 178–195.

Lewis, Roger. "The American Underground Press." *The Assistant Librarian* 63, no. 8 (August 1970): 122–124.

"Liberated Librarians." *Workforce* 34 (March-April 1973): 24–29.

"Librarians for 321.8." *SRRT Newsletter* 2 (1 September 1969): 5.

Lincove, David A. "Propaganda and the American Public Library from the 1930's to the Eve of World War II." *RQ* 33, no. 4 (Summer 1994): 510–523.

Lindsay, John V. "Censorship Feeds on Complacency." *Library Journal* 89, no. 18 (15 October 1964): 3909–3923.

Luttrell, Jeffrey R. Review of *Prejudices and Antipathies: A Tract on the LC Subject Heads Concerning People,* by Sanford Berman. In *The Journal of Academic Librarianship* 19, no. 4 (September 1993): 246.

Manoff, Marlene. "Academic Libraries and the Culture Wars: The Politics of Collection Development." *Collection Management* 16, no. 4 (1992): 1–17.

Marston, Betsy. "Libraries and Democracy: Information for All." *Wilson Library Bulletin* 65, no. 7 (March 1991): 47–50.

McClarren, Robert. "Tax-Exempt Status." *American Libraries* 1, no. 6 (June 1970): 607.

McConachie, Bruce A. "Using the Concept of Cultural Hegemony to Write Theatre History." In *Interpreting the Theatrical Past: Essays in the Historiography of Performance,* ed. Thomas Postlewait and Bruce A. McConachie, 37–58. Iowa City: University of Iowa Press, 1989.

McKenney, Mary. "Alternative Press Index." *Library Journal* 96, no. 1 (1 January 1971): 55.

_____. "Neutrality Is Partisan." *Library Journal* 96, no. 6 (15 March 1971): 902.

McReynolds, Rosalee. "Trouble in Big Sky's Ivory Tower: The Montana Tenure Dispute of 1937–1939." *Libraries & Culture* 32, no. 2 (Spring 1997): 163– 190.

McShean, Gordon. "SRRT-IF Task Force Report." *American Libraries* 2, no. 4 (April 1971): 342.

Metz, Paul. "A Social History of Madness — or, Who's Buying This Round: Anticipating Avoiding Gaps in Collection Development." *College and Research Libraries* 51, no. 1 (1990): 33–39.

"Midwinter Night's Summer Dream." *American Libraries* 2, no. 1 (January 1971): 23.

"The Month in Review." *Wilson Library Bulletin* 44, no. 7 (March 1970): 687–704.

"The Month in Review." *Wilson Library Bulletin* 44, no. 9 (May 1970): 901–923.

Moon, Eric. "Association Agonies: Life with ALA." *American Libraries* 3, no. 4 (April 1972): 395–400.

_____. "Caucus and Round Table." *Library Journal* 93, no. 17 (1 October 1968): 3487.

_____. "A Clear Choice." *Library Journal* 89, no. 18 (15 October 1964): 3927.

_____. "The Generation Gap." *Library Journal* 93, no. 14 (August 1968): 2775.

_____. "Hungry and Not Very Scrupulous." *Ohio Library Association Bulletin* 37, no. 5 (January 1967): 6–14.

_____. "Voices on Vietnam." *Library Journal* 92, no. 18 (15 October 1967): 3577.

"Mrs. Bodger Resigns." *Wilson Library Bulletin* 44, no. 3 (November 1969): 275.

Mulligan, Georgia. Review of *Revolting Librarians,* eds. Celeste West and Elizabeth Katz. In *College & Research Libraries* 34, no. 2 (March 1973): 165–166.

Nelson, Bonnie R. "The Chimera of Professionalism," *Library Journal* 105, no. 17 (1 October 1980): 2029–2033.

Nelson, James B. "ALA's Relevancy Gap." *Library Journal* 93, no. 17 (1 October 1968): 3483.

_____. "The Chimera of Professionalism." *Library Journal* 105, no. 17: 2029–2033.

_____. "Telling of Congress for Change." *Library Journal* 94, no. 14 (August 1969): 2759.

"New Directions." *American Libraries* 1, no. 8 (September 1970): 745–747.

"New Directions." *American Libraries* 1, no. 9 (October 1970): 841–842.

"A New Management Mood." *Library Journal* 98, no. 6 (15 March 1973): 827–833.

Newberry, Joan L. "Social or Political." *American Libraries* 2, no. 8 (September 1971): 791.

"News Report: 1968." *Library Journal* 94, no. 1 (1 January 1969): 29–36.

Marshall, Joan K. "Bawl & Howl." *Booklegger Magazine* 5 (July/August 1974): 22–25.

Nord, David Paul. "The Nature of Historical Research." In *Research Methods in Mass Communication*, ed. Guido H. Stempel III and Bruce H. Westley, 290–315. New York: Prentice Hall, 1989.

Nyren, Karl. "The Gathering Storm." *Library Journal* 93, no. 16 (15 September 1968): 3063.

Oboler, Eli M. "Congress as Censor." *Library Trends* 19, no. 1 (July 1970): 64–73.

Oltman, Ruth M. "Women in the Professional Caucuses." In *Women in the Professions: What's All the Fuss About?*, eds. Linda S. Fiddell and John DeLamater, 123–144. Beverly Hills: Sage Publications, 1971.

Pearce, Frank, and Steve Tombs. "Hegemony, Risk and Governance: 'Social Regulation' and the American Chemical Industry." *Economy and Society* 25, no. 3 (1996): 424–454.

Peattie, Noel. "The Fortunes of *Synergy*." *Sipapu* 4, no. 2 (July 1973): 8–10.

_____. "Intellectual Freedom Activism in the Sixties: Defense of a Professional Standard." In *Activism in American Librarianship, 1962–1973*, ed. Mary Lee Bundy, and Frederick J. Stielow, 43–58. New York: Greenwood Press, 1987.

_____. "On My Mind: Reflections on the *Sipapu* Years." *American Libraries* 27, no. 5 (May 1996): 39–40.

Pendergrast, Mark. "Sandy Berman: A Man for All Subjects." *Wilson Library Bulletin* 63, no. 7 (March 1989): 50–53.

"Peter Doiron Seeks Appeal." *Wilson Library Bulletin* 46, no. 2 (October 1971): 124.

Pierson, Ruth Roach. "Experience, Difference, Dominance and Voice in the Writing of Canadian Women's History." In *Writing Women's History: International Perspectives*, eds. Karen Offen, Ruth Roach Pierson, and Jane Rendall, 79–106. Bloomington: University of Indiana Press, 1991.

Plotnik, Art. "The Berman File." *Wilson Library Bulletin* 47, no. 10 (June 1973): 856–861.

Price, Sylvia. "Books for the Counter-Culture." *Library Journal* 94, no. 11 (1 June 1969): 2193–2202.

Radford, Gary P. "Positivism, Foucault, and the Fantasia of the Library: Conceptions of Knowledge and the Modern Library Experience." *Library Quarterly* 62, no. 4 (1992): 408–424.

Raymond, Boris. "ACONDA and ANACONDA Revisited: A Retrospective Glance at the Sounds of Fury of the Sixties," *Journal of Library History* 14, no. 3 (Summer 1979): 349–362.

"Rise Up So Early in the Morn." *Sipapu* 7, no. 2 (July 1976): 2.

Robbins, Louise S. "Champions of a Cause: American Librarians and the Library Bill of Rights in the 1950s." *Library Trends* 45, no. 1 (Summer 1996): 28–49.

_____. "Racism and Censorship in Cold War Oklahoma: The Case of Ruth W. Brown and the Bartlesville Public Library." *Southwestern Historical Quarterly* 100, no. 1 (1996): 19–46.

Samek, Toni. "Intellectual Freedom Flux: A Selected Guide to Resources." *Feliciter* 45, no. 1 (1999): 34–36.

_____. "Library and Information Studies Press and Freedom of Expression." *Proceedings of the 27th Annual Conference of the Canadian Association for Information Science*, 267–301.

_____. "The Library Bill of Rights in the 1960s: One Profession, One Ethic." *Library Trends* 45, no. 1 (Summer 1996): 50–60.

"San Francisco '67." *Library Journal* 92, no. 14 (August 1967): 2707–2712.

Schaub, Uta Liebmann. "Foucault, Alternative Presses, and Alternative Ideology in West Germany: A Report." *German Studies Review* 12, no. 1 (February 1989): 139–153.

Schell, Bernadette, and Lionel Bonin. "Factors Affecting Censorship in Canadian Libraries." *Journal of Psychology* 123, no. 44 (July 1989): 357–388.

Schladweiller, Chris. "The Library Bill of Rights and Intellectual Freedom: A Selective Bibliography." *Library Trends* 45, no. 1 (Summer 1996): 97–125.

Schrader, Alvin M. "Censorship Iceberg: Results of an Alberta Public Library Survey." *Canadian Library Journal* 43, no. 2 (April 1986): 91–95.

Schuman, Patricia Glass. "Perception Gap." *Library Journal* 95, no. 10 (15 May 1970): 1781–1782.

_____. "Social Responsibility: A Progress Report." *Library Journal* 94, no. 10 (15 May 1969): 1950–1952.

Schwartz, Charles. "Research Significance: Behavioral Patterns and Outcome Characteristics." *Library Quarterly* 62, no. 2 (April 1992): 123–149.

"A Season for Change." *Library Journal* 93, no. 14 (August 1968): 2811–2821.

"Selection of Library Materials." *American Libraries* 2, no. 5 (May 1971): 452.

Serebnick, Judith. "An Analysis of Publishers of Books Reviewed in Key Library Journals." *Library and Information Science Research* 6, no. 3 (1984). 289–303.

_____. "Book Reviews and the Selection of Potentially Controversial Books in Public Libraries." *Library Quarterly* 51, no. 4 (1981): 390–409.

_____. "Selection and Holdings of Small Publishers' Books in OCLC Libraries: A Study of the Influence of Reviews, Publishers and Vendors." *Library Quarterly* 62, no. 3 (July 1992): 259–294.

_____. "Self-censorship by Librarians: An Analysis of Checklist-Based Research." *Drexel Library Quarterly* 18, no. 1 (1982): 35–56.

"Shadows of the Future." *Library Journal* 96, no. 14 (August 1971): 2431–2446.

Shera, Jesse H. "On the Value of Library History." *Library Quarterly* 22 (July 1952): 240–51.

_____. "The Playgirl of the Western World." *Wilson Library Bulletin* 52, no. 5 (January 1968): 529.

_____. "Plus ça Change." *Library Journal* 95, no. 6 (15 March 1970): 979–986.

Sheridan, Robert. "A Membership Dilemma." *American Libraries* 1, no. 1 (January 1970): 52–55.

Shiflett, Orvin Lee. "Clio's Claim: The Role of Historical Research in Library and Information Science." *Library Trends* 32, no. 4 (Spring 1984): 385–406.

Sipapu 5, no. 1 (January 1974): 16.

Sipapu 7, no. 6 (July 1976).

Smart, Barry. "The Politics of Truth and the Problem of Hegemony." In *Foucault: A Critical Reader,* ed. David Couzens Hoy, 157–173. Oxford: Blackwell, 1986.

Smith, Eldred. "Kansas City Stirring." *Library Journal* 93, no. 17 (1 October 1968): 3483.

"Social Responsibilities Discussed at ALA." *Library Journal* 94, no. 1 (1 January 1969): 18.

"Social Responsibility Group Meets in Philadelphia." *Library Journal* 93, no. 15 (15 October 1968): 3729.

"Social Responsibility Plugged in New York." *Library Journal* 93, no. 21 (1 December 1968): 4469.

"Social Responsibility: The Neighborhood Alternative." *Library Journal* 96, no. 6 (15 March 1971): 929–930.

Spahn, Theodore Jurgen. "Recent Publications." *College and Research Libraries* 32, no. 1 (January 1971): 51–53.

"SRRT $200 for Angela Davis Approved by ALA Executive Board." *Library Journal* 96, no. 1 (1 July 1971): 1913.

"SRRT Blues." *Wilson Library Bulletin* 45, no. 8 (April 1971): 737.

SRRT Newsletter 1, Rev. (22 June 1969).

SRRT Newsletter 5 (1 June 1970).

SRRT Newsletter 12 (February 1971): 1–10.

SRRT Newsletter 15 (1 August 1971): 4.

SRRT Newsletter 20 (June 1972): 2.

SRRT Newsletter 24 (February 1973): 1.

SRRT Newsletter 25 (April 1973): 2.

SRRT Newsletter 27 (August 1973): 2–3.

SRRT Newsletter 29 (January 1974): 6.

Stevens, Debra. "Social Responsibility and Librarianship: A Dilemma of Professionalism." *Canadian Library Journal* 46, no. 1 (February 1989): 17–22.

Stielow, Frederick J. "Censorship in the Early Professionalization of American Libraries, 1876–1929." *Journal of Library History* 18, no. 1 (Winter 1983): 37–54.

"Support for Zoia Horn: Issue Splitting ALA." *Library Journal* 97, no. 9 (15 May 1972): 1760–1761.

"Supreme Court Refuses to Hear Hodgin Case." *Wilson Library Bulletin* 47, no. 1 (September 1972): 8.

Swan, John C. "Librarianship IS Censorship." *Library Journal* 104, no. 17 (1 October 1979): 2040–2043.

_____. "Minimum Qualifications and Intellectual Freedom." *Library Journal* 106, no. 15 (1 September 1981): 1595–99.

Swanson, Edward. "*Synergy* Protest." *American Libraries* 7, no. 4 (July/August 1973): 408.

"*Synergy* Editor Resigns." *American Libraries* 7, no. 4 (July/August 1973): 412.

Taylor, Harold. "Society and Revolution." *Library Journal* 93, no. 3 (1 February 1968): 509–512.

"Through a Crystal Ball — Dimly: The Coming ALA Annual Convention." *Library Journal* 97, no. 11 (1 June 1972): 2051–2053.

"Underground Press Freedom Plugged by DC Librarians." *Library Journal* 94, no. 20 (15 November 1969): 4083.

"Vietnam Moratorium Honored by ALA." *Library Journal* 94, no. 20 (15 November 1969): 4081.

"Vietnam Moratorium Support Asked of ALA Board." *Library Journal* 94, no. 20 (15 November 1969): 4081.

"Viewpoint: Oral History." *Library Journal* 98, no. 20 (15 November 1973): 3355.

"Wait 'Til Atlantic City." *Library Journal* 94, no. 6 (15 March 1969): 1104–1108.

Watson, Paula D. "Founding Mothers: The Contributions of Women's Organizations to Public Library Development in the United States." *Library Quarterly* 64, no. 3 (July 1994): 233–269.

Wedgeworth, Robert, et al. "Social Responsibility and the Library Bill of Rights: The Berninghausen Debate." *Library Journal* 98, no. 1 (1 January 1973): 25–41.

Weis, Robert. "The Military Underground Press." In *The Magic Writing Machine*, ed. Everett E. Dennis, 60–61. Eugene: School of Journalism, University of Oregon, 1971.

West, Celeste. "The Body Politic." *Synergy* 29 (October 1970): 1–7.

_____. "Congloms: Stalking the Literary-Industrial Complex." *American Libraries* 13, no. 5 (1982): 298–301.

_____. "Stop! The Print Is Killing Me." *Synergy* 33 (1971): 2–5.

Whitmore, Harry E. "Confrontation: The Library and THOSE Magazines." *RQ* 10, no. 4 (Summer 1971): 313–317.

Wiegand, Shirley A. "Reality Bites: The Collision of Rhetoric, Rights, and Reality and the Library Bill of Rights." *Library Trends* 45, no. 1 (Summer 1996): 75–86.

Wiegand, Wayne A. "The Development of Librarianship in the United States." *Libraries & Culture* 24, no. 1 (1989): 99–109._____.

_____. "Popular Culture; A New Frontier for Academic Libraries." *Journal of Academic Librarianship* 5, no. 4 (1979): 200–204.

_____. "The Role of the Library in American History." In *The Bowker Annual of Library and Book Trade Information*, comp. and ed. Filomena Simora, 69–76. New York: R.R. Bowker, 1988.

_____. "The Socialization of Library and Information Science Students: Reflections on a Centruy of Formal Education for Librarianship," *Library Trends* 34, no.3 (Winter 1986): 383–399.

Wilkinson, Billy R. "Columbia Recap: The School of Library Service During and After the Spring of 1968: A Personal Account." *Library Journal* 94, no. 13 (July 1969): 2567–2570.

Wolkoff, Kathleen Nietzke. "The Problem of Holocaust Denial Literature in Libraries." *Library Trends* 45, no. 1 (Summer 1996): 87–96.

"Women: Preconference Hassles, But Otherwise Good Vibes." *SRRT Newsletter* 28 (November 1973): 4.

Workforce (March-April 1973): 20–23.

"Zoia Horn Released on Bail During Berrigan Trial." *Library Journal* 97, no. 8 (15 April 1972): 1367–68.

Index